GUINNESS WORLD RECORDS

GUINNESS WORLD RECORDS™

GAMER'S EDITION 2008

FACTS

British Library Cataloguing-in-Publication Data: a catalogue record for this book is available from the British Library

ISBN:
978-1-904994-20-6

Check the official GWR video game website **www.guinnessworldrecords.com/gamers** regularly for record-breaking gaming news as it happens, plus exclusive interviews and competitions.

Sustainability
Guinness World Records: Gamer's Edition is printed on paper certified in accordance with the guidelines of the Forest Stewardship Council for responsible forestry management. SGS-COC-1425 (valid until 22 June 2008).

FSC
Mixed Sources
Product group from well-managed forests and other controlled sources

Cert no. SGS-COC-1425
www.fsc.org
© 1996 Forest Stewardship Council

Owing to the innovative use of a combined gas and steam turbine power plant, our printer, Mohn Media, emits 52% less CO_2 in comparison to the average energy mix in Germany.

HiT entertainment

© 2008 Guinness World Records Ltd, a HIT Entertainment Ltd company

EDITOR-IN-CHIEF
Craig Glenday

GAMER'S EDITOR
Keith Pullin

SENIOR EDITORS
Matthew Boulton
Ben Way

EDITORIAL TEAM
Robert Cave
Rob Dimery
Mike Richardson
Matthew White

CONSULTANT EDITORS
Games: Ellie Gibson, Barry Hitchings
Records: Stuart Claxton, Kim Lacey

VP, PUBLISHING
Patricia Magill

PRODUCTION EXECUTIVE
Jane Boatfield

PRINTING & BINDING
Mohn Media Mohndruck GmbH, Gütersloh, Germany

PRODUCTION CONSULTANTS
Roger Hawkins, Simon Thompson

COLOUR ORIGINATION
Resmiye Kahraman at Colour Systems, London, UK

COVER
Designed by Itonic Design; holographic origination and embossing by API Group

PICTURE EDITOR
Michael Whitty

DEPUTY PICTURE EDITOR
Laura Jackson

PICTURE RESEARCH
Noni Stacey

ORIGINAL PHOTOGRAPHY
Paul Michael Hughes

DESIGN CONCEPT/CREATION
Keren Turner and Lisa Garner at Itonic Design Ltd, Brighton, UK (www.itonicdesign.com)

INDEX
Chris Bernstein

VIDEO GAME CONSULTANTS
Action-adventure games: Dan Whitehead
Fighting games: Mike Flynn
Platform games: Oli Welsh
MMORPGs: David Hawksett
Music games: Ellie Gibson
Puzzle & maze games: Martyn Carroll
Racing games: Duncan Harris
Role-playing games: Jon Hamblin
Shooting games: David McCarthy
Simulation games: Adam Phillips
Sports games: Martin Korda
Strategy games: Dan Griliopoulos

DIRECTOR OF RECORDS MANAGEMENT
Marco Frigatti

RECORDS MANAGEMENT TEAM
Andrea Bánfi
Laura Hughes
Kaoru Ishikawa
Carlos Martinez
Lucia Singaglies
Amanda Sprague
Kristian Teufel
Sophie Whiting
Wu Xiaohong

ACCREDITATION
Guinness World Records Limited has a very thorough accreditation system for records verification. However, while every effort is made to ensure accuracy, Guinness World Records Limited cannot be held responsible for any errors contained in this work. Feedback from our readers on any point of accuracy is always welcomed.

ABBREVIATIONS & MEASUREMENTS
Guinness World Records Limited uses both metric and imperial measurements. The sole exceptions are for some scientific data where metric measurements only are universally accepted, and for some sports data. Where a specific date is given, the exchange rate is calculated according to the currency values that were in operation at the time. Where only a year date is given, the exchange rate is calculated from December of that year. "One billion" is taken to mean one thousand million. "GDR" (the German Democratic Republic) refers to the East German state, which was unified with West Germany in 1990. The abbreviation is used for sports records broken before 1990. The USSR (Union of Soviet Socialist Republics) split into a number of parts in 1991, the largest of these being Russia. The CIS (Commonwealth of Independent States) replaced it and the abbreviation is used mainly for sporting records broken at the 1992 Olympic Games. Guinness World Records Limited does not claim to own any right, title or interest in the trademarks of others reproduced in this book.

GENERAL WARNING
Attempting to break records or set new records can be dangerous. Appropriate advice should be taken first and all record attempts are undertaken at the participant's risk. In no circumstances will Guinness World Records Limited have any liability for death or injury suffered in any record attempt. Guinness World Records Limited has complete discretion over whether or not to include any particular records in the book. Being a Guinness World Record holder does not guarantee you a place in the book.

GUINNESS WORLD RECORDS

GUINNESS
WORLD RECORDS

GAMER'S
EDITION
2008

CONTENTS

Expert writers from within the gaming community share their years of expertise

Timelines explain the fascinating history of video gaming

Full, detailed specifications given for the major gaming consoles and handhelds

PLATFORM GAMES

PLAYSTATION 3

20 million - The number of copies of 1990's Super Mario World sold for the SNES. 2006's New Super Mario Bros. on the DS has sold 10 million

PS3 SPECS

Major gamers and creators profiled and interviewed

RECORDS

Text in **bold type** refers to an official Guinness World Record.

The high scores and fastest times listed throughout the book come from various sources; only those marked with the Twin Galaxies logo are considered by Guinness World Records to be official world record scores/ times. The tables on pp. 238–251 contain *only* scores and times ratified by Twin Galaxies.

If you wish to submit a record, visit p.7 for details, or log on to www. guinnessworldrecords. com/gamers for full instructions.

4,401,169 - the highest single-player score for Gauntlet, achieved by Charles Nagle of the USA on 28 March 2003

GAMES: 20 & 6

THE YEAR IN GAMING

200 million

20 RIDGE RACER

16 DIG DUG

12 TEMPEST

9 OUT RUN

8 GAUNTLET

7 KALAGA

15 MISSILE COMMAND

11 ROBOTRON: 2084

JANUARY

FEBRUARY

MARCH

STARCRAFT

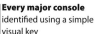

Tables and charts reveal record-worthy facts at a glance

Full colour photos throughout from screengrabs, packaging, artwork and posters

Facts and figures from the video gaming world on every page

Every major console identified using a simple visual key

Video game trivia across every subject arms you with fascinating snippets about your favourite games

Official high scores and fastest times as ratified by video-game judges Twin Galaxies – organized in easy-to-read reference charts

ACCURACY

Every effort has been made to bring to you the most accurate and up to date records. If, however, you believe that you know of a more impressive achievement or higher score, please let us know. We rely on your help to keep our books as fresh and as accurate as possible. Visit www.guinnessworldrecords.com/gamers to find out more...

ABOUT THIS BOOK

TELL US...

Like its more famous big brother, *Guinness World Records*, the *Gamer's Edition* relies on feedback from its readers. Presently, we receive around 1,000 claims every week for the records book. While most claimants fail to make the grade, the small percentage that succeed ensures that only the world's most amazing superlatives make it into print.

WELCOME TO THE FIRST EVER EDITION OF THE GUINNESS WORLD RECORDS GAMER'S EDITION. THIS IS THE FIRST OF AN ANNUAL CELEBRATION OF SUPERLATIVES FROM THE DYNAMIC WORLD OF VIDEO GAMING.

The book you're now holding is the result of a year of research by a team of video game experts from around the world. It's not Guinness World Records' first foray into gaming – each year, our famous annual records book features a selection of superlatives from the video gaming community – but it is certainly our most audacious.

Even though we've been collecting video games records for 12 months, we're aware that we've just scraped the surface of this incredibly diverse subject area. That's where we need you! Are you a gamer with an achievement you want recognized? Perhaps you're in the games industry and you've worked on a game that you think is a record-breaker? Or are you part of a gaming clan that deserves a mention? If so, you must get in touch with our records team.

Gaming lends itself perfectly to the realm of record-keeping. Indeed, the words "high score" have been synonymous with video games from their earliest days. But we're not simply focused on collecting scores – this job has been left to the experts in scores and times, Twin Galaxies. For 20 years, Twin Galaxies and its founder Walter Day (the **longest-serving professional video game judge**) have been amassing an unrivalled archive of gaming achievements, and we're indebted to them for supplying the majority of stats in this book.

*" The Gamer's Edition offers you the **unique chance** to have your gaming achievements **recognized by the world authority** in record-breaking "*

Craig Glenday,
Editor-in-Chief, *Guinness World Records*

LARGEST UPRIGHT ARCADE MACHINE

An arcade machine measuring 4.11 m (13 ft 6 in) tall, 2.84 m (9 ft 4 in) deep and 1.72 m (5 ft 8 in) wide ① was created by G4's *Attack of the Show!* and Cinnabar and unveiled in Los Angeles, California, USA, on 9 November 2007. It weighs 680 kg (1,500 lb) and can play 150 different games on a screen measuring 1.82 m (6 ft).

While TG have supplied the scores, we've amassed a team of video games experts to focus on all the other record-breaking aspects of gaming that may not be quite so obvious. Sales figures, of course, can be tracked – you'll find many stats on **best-** and **fastest-sellers** – but then there are the technical achievements, such as the **fastest gaming engine** and the **most polygons used in a video game character**; and in-game records, such as the **largest playing environment** and the **largest celebrity cast in a game**.

More incredible facts and feats come from the gamers themselves – you'll meet the **highest earners**, the **youngest** and **oldest players** and various gaming league champions. Also helping us

round off this record book are the industry insiders: the programmers, developers, composers, artists and designers who create the games.

We've also been out and about at various gaming events throughout the year, such as the Games Convention in Leipzig, Germany, where we acknowledged the **largest collection of playable gaming systems** 6 and the unveiling of the **world's largest arcade game** 1 on *Attack of the Show* (G4) in the USA. We also held some record attempts at the launch of games such as *Unreal Tournament 3* in the Omega Sektor gaming centre in Birmingham, UK, and *Guitar Hero III* in London, UK, as well as our very own *Wii Tennis* tournament 4, which took

place on the Champs-Élysées in Paris, France.

Not only that… we got so immersed in the world of video games that we decided to make our own! We teamed up with TT Games to put together a fantastic *Guinness World Records Game* 5, so that you can break real records on your console or mobile phone.

So thanks to everyone who invited us to their events, and to those who took part in the record attempts. And thanks to everyone who, inspired by this book, sends in claims for next year! Good luck!

LARGEST COLLECTION OF PLAYABLE GAMING SYSTEMS

German-born journalist René Meyer 6, centre, has a collection of 274 playable gaming systems – the largest collection of its kind. The collection, which was exhibited at Telespiele 1972-2007 during the GC Art section of the Games Convention, in Leipzig, Germany, on 23 August 2007, includes consoles, hand-helds, home computers, LCD games and educational computers.

INTRODUCTION
TWIN GALAXIES

TWIN GALAXIES IS THE WORLD AUTHORITY ON GAMING STATISTICS, AND HAS BEEN ADJUDICATING VIDEO GAME HIGH SCORES FOR GUINNESS WORLD RECORDS SINCE THE MID-1980S

Twin Galaxies is the electronic gaming industry's premiere statistician, dedicated to preserving the history of video gaming in a huge database that documents gaming milestones.

Founded in 1981, Twin Galaxies grew from modest origins as an arcade chain to gain recognition as the "official scorekeeper for the world of video game and pinball playing," invested with the authority to verify "official" world record high scores and crown new world champions.

Founder Walter Day  was working as a travelling salesman in the early 1980s, which allowed him to pursue his interest in arcade gaming.

Covering the length and breadth of the US for his work, Walter took time out to visit as many video game arcades as possible to record the high scores he found on each game.

On 9 February 1982, Walter's growing database of high score statistics was made available to the public as the Twin Galaxies National Scoreboard. The release received immediate recognition from the major game manufacturers of the day – Atari, Midway, Williams Electronics, Universal, Stern, Nintendo and Exidy – in addition to support from *RePlay* and *Playmeter* magazines, the two premier coin-op publications of the era.

Twin Galaxies' role as scorekeeper grew in importance as "player rankings"

became a major focus of the media. As the pioneer in ranking top players, Twin Galaxies was called upon to bring the superstar players together for many well-publicized contests and media events. On 8 November 1982, for example, *LIFE* magazine visited Twin Galaxies to capture 16 of North America's best players in a group photograph. Two months later, on 9 January 1983, ABC-TV's *That's Incredible* came to Ottumwa, Iowa, to film 19 of the world's best players competing in the first-ever video game world championship.

Following this exposure the first US video game team was formed, made up of the very best talent. With Walter as the founding captain, the US National Video Game Team issued international video game challenges to Japan, Italy and the UK, even hand-delivering proclamations to their respective

No one Can Tell Me To Stop Playing Video Games.

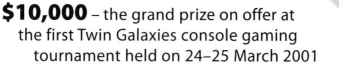

OLDEST COMPETITIVE FEMALE GAMER

Doris Self 1 (seen here with *Donkey Kong* king Billy Mitchell) was one of Walter Day's most-admired gamers. Doris set a record score of 1,112,300 on Q*Bert on 1 July 1984 at the age of 58. She was still competing for the world title until the date of her death in November 2006 at the age of 79, making her the world's oldest competitive female gamer.

FACT

Thousands of classic arcade games can be played on a PC using emulator software available on the internet. The Multiple Arcade Machine Emulator (MAME) project has one of the biggest game archives available for download at www.mamedev.org.

embassies in Washington, DC! Eventually, the team toured America, Europe and Asia during the 1980s.

By 1985, Twin Galaxies had enjoyed major media coverage in *LIFE* magazine, Marvel Comics, the *Wall Street Journal*, *USA Today*, Stern, the *Washington Post* and nearly 100 TV appearances, including ABC-TV's Entertainment Tonight and NBC Nightly News. As fame spread further, Walter was designated an assistant editor in charge of video game scores for Guinness World Records.

Under his direction, Twin Galaxies wrote the first official rulebook for video game playing and established the rules and standardized settings for each game.

Today, Twin Galaxies continues to be recognized as the world's premiere electronic games referee, having judged contests 3 and high scores submitted by console gamers, arcades and PC gamers worldwide. Currently in its 27th year, Twin Galaxies still creates the contests, enforces the rules, maintains the records and crowns the champions on home consoles, PC-based releases and arcade games.

❝ The first three months of Twin Galaxies were like living in a dream. *I loved playing the games and the arcade was busting with business.* ❞

Walter Day, founder of Twin Galaxies

OUR THANKS

Guinness World Records is indebted to Walter Day and his team for their help in creating this book. Our thanks go to: Mike Arsenault, Tim Balderramos, Martin Bedard, Shawn Cram, Tom Duncan, Greg Erway, Kelly R. Flewin, Brien King, Blaine Locklair, Rodrigo Lopes, Jeffrey D. Lowe, Nik Meeks, Wolff Morrow, Robert Mruczek, David Nelson, Terence O'Neill, Jean-Claude Padilla, Perry Rodgers, Todd Rogers, Gregory Sakundiak, Timothy Stodden, Ryan Sullivan, Tom Votava, Troy Whelan, William Willemstyn, and Adam Wood. Special thanks to Pete Bouvier and Ben Gold.

THE YEAR IN GAMING

PS3 LAUNCH

➲ PlayStation 3 was the last of the next-gen consoles to arrive in Europe, launching on 23 March 2007.

➲ Special events were held to mark the launch across the continent. In the UK, fans were invited to camp out the night before in London's Virgin Megastore. The **first person to buy a PS3** was 17-year-old Ritatsu Thomas **3**, who waited more than 36 hours in the queue!

➲ Microsoft marked the occasion by handing out free "360 branded" stools to those queueing at the London launch. And, as the PS3 went on sale in Paris, an Xbox 360-branded barge sailed down the river Seine.

➲ One week later, more than 600,000 PS3 consoles had been sold across Europe.

JANUARY

Electronic Arts scored the **first UK games chart No.1 of 2007** with *FIFA '07* ➲ Nintendo announced record profits, revealing that 3.19 million Wii units had been sold since the console launched ➲ Microsoft revealed the **most played Xbox 360 game of 2006** was *Gears of War* **1**, of which 3 million copies had been sold ➲ Microsoft also announced that the **most purchased Xbox Live arcade game of 2006** was *Uno* ➲ Sony announced that 1 million PlayStation 3 units had been shipped across North America in the six weeks following its launch. This broke the record previously set by PlayStation 2 ➲ Blizzard announced the total number of people playing *World of Warcraft* had topped 8 million.

FEBRUARY

HMV's London, UK, store hosted the European launch of Final Fantasy XII. Executive producer Akitoshi Kawazu and game director Hiroshi Minagawa were there to greet the hundreds of fans who attended, many in costume **2** ➲ Sony reported the **highest ever January sales figures for the PlayStation brand**, as total revenues for PS2, PS3 and PSP reached a record $550 million in North America.

MARCH

Microsoft announced more than 6 million people had now signed up for Xbox Live. It was also revealed that live users sent more than 2 million voice and text messages each day ➲ At the Game Developers conference in San Francisco, California, USA, Sony unveiled a new online service for the PlayStation 3. Titled PlayStation Home, it was designed to let players customise their own virtual living space and interact with other gamers ➲ Police in Mexico City began offering Xbox consoles as a reward for turning in handguns. Those handing over high-calibre weapons, such as machine guns, received PCs.

200 million – combined worldwide sales of the PlayStation and PlayStation 2 announced in April 2007

APRIL

Ken Kutaragi, known as the "Father of PlayStation", announced his retirement. Kutaragi, who joined the company in 1994, invented the PlayStation and PlayStation 2. He was replaced by SCEI president and CEO Kazuo Hirai ➲ *Pokémon Ranger* for the Nintendo DS **4** became the sixth title in the series to go straight into the UK chart at No.1 ➲ Sony hit the headlines after a headless goat was displayed at a party for the launch of *God of War 2*.

MAY

The *Halo 3* beta test began on 16 May. It ran for just under a month, during which 820,000 players tried out the game, racking up 12 million hours of game time – equivalent to one person playing for 1400 years straight! ➲ Police in Fort Bend, Texas, USA, arrested a student for designing a Counter-Strike map based on his high school. He was later released without charge ➲ Microsoft began banning Xbox 360 **5** owners who modify their consoles (by changing the hardware to allow the play of copied games) from using Xbox Live, in a bid to clamp down on piracy.

FACT

On 16 January 2007, Blizzard launched *World of Warcraft: The Burning Crusade* – the first ever *WoW* expansion pack. Over 5,000 stores around the world opened at midnight for the launch. In the first 24 hours after the game went on sale, *WoW* fans snapped up 2.4 million copies. This made it **the fastest-selling PC game** ever in Europe and North America.

JUNE

The British Board of Film Classification banned *Manhunt 2* **6** from sale in the UK, claiming the level of violence in the game was too high ➲ PAC-Man got the first set of new mazes crafted by PAC-Man creator Toru Iwatani in more than 25 years with the release of *PAC-Man Championship Edition* on Xbox Live Arcade ➲ Lara Croft **7** returned in *Tomb Raider: Anniversary*, a remake of the 1996 original ➲ The Church of England demanded that Sony withdraw PS3 title *Resistance: Fall of Man*, complaining permission had not been given for the depiction of Manchester Cathedral.

THE YEAR IN GAMING

E3 RENAMED

For many years the Electronic Entertainment Expo, or E3 for short, was the biggest event in the gaming calendar. More than 60,000 people descended on the Los Angeles Convention Centre each May to do business and see the latest games and consoles.

But everything changed in 2007. The event was renamed the E3 Media and Business Summit and entry was by invitation only, reducing the number of visitors to just 5,000.

There were still plenty of exciting announcements, however. Microsoft unveiled a *Halo 3*-themed Xbox 360 **2**, while Sony showed off a redesigned PSP. The highlight of Nintendo's conference was *Wii Fit*, a new game with a balance board peripheral designed to improve players' levels of fitness.

JULY

The video games industry **gathered in Santa Monica, California, USA, for the E3 Media and Business Summit**. ➲ *Pokémon Diamond/Pearl* went straight to the top of the UK charts on release, becoming the **fastest-selling DS game of all time**. ➲ **Microsoft admitted the number of Xbox 360s breaking down was "unacceptable"**. ➲ Sony reported that **US PlayStation 3 sales doubled** after the price of the console was cut by $100. ➲ Peter Moore **1** resigned as head of Xbox to join Electronic Arts.

AUGUST

MTV **announced plans to spend $500 million on developing video games** over the next two years. ➲ The **Wii became the UK's fastest-selling home console in history** when sales topped the 1 million mark after 38 weeks on sale. ➲ More than 185,000 people attended the **Leipzig Games Convention**. The star of the show was Tony Hawk **3**, who performed tricks for the crowd. *Pro Evolution Soccer 08* picked up **Best in Show awards** in the PS2 and PS3 categories, while *BioShock* won in the Xbox 360 category.

SEPTEMBER

Rally driver Colin McRae died in a helicopter crash. McRae was known to millions of gamers as the face of the rally game series he helped create. ➲ Sony Computer Entertainment president Kaz Hirai unveiled **the Dual Shock 3 4, a new PS3 controller with rumble feature** at the Tokyo Game Show. ➲ An Emmy award was presented to the creators of South Park for the episode *Make Love, Not Warcraft* **5**, in which Cartman and co. become addicted to *WoW*. ➲ British Prime Minister Gordon Brown announced the launch of a review looking at the issue of violence in video games.

15.56 million – worldwide sales of the Wii, as of 1 December 2007, representing 42.7% of global console sales

OCTOBER

In the UK, *Halo 3* was confirmed as the **second fastest-selling game of all time** (after *Grand Theft Auto: San Andreas*) when more than 466,000 copies were sold in four days. ➲ Actor **David Hayter** 6, the voice of Solid Snake, **confirmed he would be reprising his role for a special appearance in *Super Smash Bros. Brawl**. ➲ *BioShock* won the award for **Best Game at the video game BAFTAs**. *Wii Sports* walked away with the most trophies, winning six awards. *Sims* creator **Will Wright received a Lifetime Achievement award**.

NOVEMBER

Super Mario Galaxy 8 stormed straight to the **top of the Japanese charts with 251,000 copies sold in the first week** – over three times as many as the next best-selling game, *Ace Combat 6*. ➲ PS3 application folding@home was recognized by *Guinness World Records* as the **world's most powerful distributed computing network**. ➲ UK retailer HMV reported deliveries of the **Wii console selling out just 34 minutes after going on shelves**. ➲ Sierra announced plans to release a *Ghostbusters* 7 game starring all four of the original movie leads.

HALO 3...

On 25 September 2007, *Halo 3* enjoyed what Microsoft described as "the **largest entertainment launch in history**". Sales of the game topped $170 million within 24 hours in the US alone. *Halo 3* also broke records for pre-orders, with 1.7 million fans reserving copies in advance.

DECEMBER

Nintendo released *Pokémon Battle Revolution* 9, the **first Wii game to allow players to compete online**. It was also the **first game to link the Wii and Nintendo DS**. ➲ Activision and Vivendi announced plans to merge and become the world's **largest independent video games publisher** in a deal worth **$18.9 billion**. ➲ PlayStation 3 owners got the chance to test their vocal skills with the launch of *SingStar PS3* 10, the **first game in the series to let players download songs**.

...HALO 3

➲ For the European launch of *Halo 3*, Microsoft organized a celebrity tournament on Xbox Live. Pharrell Williams was at the London IMAX, UK, while Carmen Electra was in Paris and LL Cool J in Amsterdam.

➲ A special bundle including an Xbox 360 console signed by Bill Gates was sold in a charity online auction for $8,400.

FIGURES

$300 million – first week sales of *Halo 3*, as reported by Reuters.

$125 million – first day sales for *Halo 2*, launched in 2004.

14.8 million – number of copies of *Halo* and *Halo 2* sold prior to the release of *Halo 3*.

4 – number of playable characters available in *Halo 3*'s co-operative campaign mode.

HOT TIP

Aside from new weapons and vehicles, *Halo 3* also contains some other new toys that can greatly aid gameplay. The bubble shield can protect the player from gunfire for short periods, while the portable grav lift is a great way of setting traps for pursuing enemies and the trip mine is perfect for booby-trapping vehicles or objectives.

HALO 3

1

Developer: Bungie
Publisher: Microsoft
Format: Xbox 360
Released: 25 September 07

Halo: Combat Evolved revolutionised the design of shooting games. The follow-up, *Halo 2*, was just as breathtaking,

pushing the boundaries back even further. So how could *Halo 3* live up to its forebears and justify the hype? By taking a sweeping narrative of epic proportions and peppering it with improved AI, new vehicles, new weapons and new equipment, and wrapping it up with a vastly improved set of multiplayer options that make it just as brilliant as, if not better than, its two predecessors.

The story picks up where *Halo 2* left off: with Master Chief hurtling to Earth in the middle of a galaxy-spanning conflict between humanity and alien Covenant forces. By the end of the game, he'll have fought alongside his previous arch-enemy, the Arbiter, against Covenant Brutes and a resurgent

(and evolved) Flood. It's a story that's full of shifting alliances and extraordinary plot twists and, most importantly, an abundance of action.

All this is displayed with cutting-edge, high-definition panache, using a graphics engine that supports all sorts of fancy features from enhanced lighting effects to parallax mapped textures. And it sounds amazing too, thanks to over 50,000 separate pieces of audio.

Of course, it looks and sounds incredible in its multiplayer modes as well; from the co-operative campaign mode to various matchmaking modes that allow competition over Xbox Live. It is these multiplayer options where the game's new 'equipment', such as forcefields, gravity lifts, trip mines and power drains, comes into their own.

That's why the game lives on long after Master Chief has made his mark and why *Halo 3* is one of the best games ever.

SUPER MARIO GALAXY

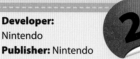

2

Developer: Nintendo
Publisher: Nintendo
Format: Wii
Released: 1 November 07

Games like *Super Mario Galaxy* barely come along once a decade, never mind once a year. Games that turn your world upside down and your brain inside out, that make you laugh with glee and gasp with surprise every time you pick them up. Games that delight in doing the impossible and making it look easy.

That's what Super Mario games were always about, and the reason it's one of the best-selling, most-loved and most highly-regarded game series of all time. But they haven't hit those highs for 11 long years, since the mighty *Mario 64* redefined gaming in 3D. Make no mistake, though, *Super Mario Galaxy* is a return to form for the plucky plumber, and then some. It's been years since we played a game that had so many ideas crammed into it; every new galaxy offers something new; you never know what to expect. It can even surprise you several times within a single level, as the star gates send Mario soaring and whooping through space between planets, and you hold your breath with him, wondering what could possibly come next.

It's also the best-looking game on the Wii by a long way; its graphics are solid, sparkling and soaked in stunning colours. The sound is just as good, with Nintendo using a full orchestra for the first time to record a sweeping soundtrack worthy of a big-budget movie. And then there's the remote pointer, letting you – and a friend – reach in and touch the worlds on the screen.

But our favourite thing about *Galaxy* is that it's pure nonsense. It's innocent and inventive, gloriously stupid and stark raving mad. They don't make 'em like this any more. Except at Nintendo, where they do.

FIGURES

60 – number of stars that Mario must collect before he is given the opportunity to pursue Bowser and rescue Princess Peach.

100 – number of coins Mario needs to collect in the purple coin levels.

FACT

Super Mario Galaxy is split into 40 galaxy-themed levels, each containing between one and six stars. Obtaining these stars allows the player to unlock more features in each galaxy.

FACTS

➲ Aperture Science Inc., the fictional research corporation featured in the *Half-Life* series, also features heavily in *Portal*. Both created by Valve, these games are available together in *The Orange Box*.

➲ *The Legend of Zelda: Phantom Hourglass* is the first game in the series for the Nintendo DS and was specially designed to make use of all of the platform's hardware, with players able to control Link using the touch screen interface alone.

HOT TIP

Ammunition is scarce in *Bioshock*, so the best advice is to keep your trusty wrench handy. The wrench can even be powered up with specific tonics that make it hit harder and faster. Stealth-related tonics are also useful in enabling you to sneak up on enemies before wrenching them to death.

3 BIOSHOCK

Developer: Irrational Games
Publisher: 2K Games
Format: Xbox 360
Released: 21 August 07

Inspired by the writings of American philosopher Ayn Rand, *Bioshock* is one of the most critically acclaimed video games of all time.

It's easy to see why. The sense of atmosphere is unparalleled. The game's creators have constructed a wholly believable game world in Rapture, a 1950s underwater utopia fractured by human greed. As players piece together what happened from old notebooks and diaries, to the distinctive strains of an authentic period soundtrack, they're confronted with unsettling questions about the nature of free-will and morality.

PROJECT GOTHAM RACING 4

Developer: Bizarre Creations
Publisher: Microsoft
4
Format: Xbox 360
Released: 2 October 07

If you judged each *Project Gotham Racing* game by its own Kudos scoring system, by which players are judged for style as well as speed, only *PGR4* would achieve something close to perfection.

PGR4 inherits all that was great about *PGR3*, and regains much that was lost after the second instalment in the series: the colourful mix of cities, the quick-start Arcade mode, the greater variety of road widths and elevations, the slower street cars, the moody weather… with motorbikes thrown in.

Contrary to expectations, this wasn't a careful, gradual improvement, a spot of polish on the existing chassis. It was a *PGR* that finally lived by its own rules: it took risks, made changes and, for once, didn't make mistakes. Its real-life roads felt less detached from their surroundings. And in ways you never imagined before, the package became complete.

FINAL FANTASY XII

Developer: Square Enix
Publisher: Square Enix
Format: PS2
Released: 23 February 07 (International)
5

Easily one of the most epic adventures ever to grace PlayStation 2, *Final Fantasy XII* was a bold experiment which paid off handsomely. The game plays like a single-player version of

World of Warcraft as you explore a huge world and fight monsters in real-time. The new Gambit system allows you to pre-program your characters with simple rules, which frees you from the potion-related micro-management that often occurs in RPGs, and gives you more time to devise detailed combat strategies. The places you visit on your travels are fantastically beautiful, the story is exceptionally well told and it's a hard-hearted gamer who doesn't shed a tear at the finale. Is it the best RPG on the PS2? Definitely.

6 POKÉMON DIAMOND/PEARL

Developer: Game Freak
Publisher: Nintendo
Format: Nintendo DS
Released: 27 July 07

We were expecting the latest instalment in the *Pokémon* franchise to be good, but the sheer amount of content on display here is staggering.

In addition to the usual "become the best *Pokémon* trainer in the world" campaign, the wi-fi capabilities of the DS mean that close physical proximity is no longer necessary when fighting and trading with friends.

The basic gameplay is as compelling as ever, but there's so much more on offer, including gardening, cooking and 'best in show' talent contests for your lovingly groomed creatures. Even if you haven't taken to previous *Pokémon* titles, you owe it to yourself to take a Pikachu at this one.

THE ORANGE BOX

7

Developer: Valve
Publisher: Electronic Arts
Formats: Xbox 360, PC, PS3
Released: 10 October 07

This brilliant compilation is a collection of some of the most memorable first-person shooter games in recent years. The revolutionary *Half-Life*, and its two-part sequel, *Half-Life 2*, episodes one and two, follow scientist Gordon Freeman from the Black Mesa research complex to the Orwellian environs of City 17, where he's faced with the nefarious evil of an alien entity called the Combine. All three

games are immensely playable and are probably worth the price of entry on their own; however, *The Orange Box* has more treats.

Portal, also included in *The Orange Box*, allows gamers to open up rifts in the space-time continuum to solve mind-bending puzzles. The collection also includes *Team Fortress 2*, which offers all the tactical multiplayer shooting action anyone could ever want.

8 THE LEGEND OF ZELDA: PHANTOM HOURGLASS

Developer: Nintendo
Publisher: Nintendo
Format: Nintendo DS
Released: 23 June 07

The first *Zelda* title for the Nintendo DS manages to be both instantly familiar and thrillingly new at the same time.

A direct sequel to the GameCube outing, *The Wind Waker*, it takes the cartoon-style graphics of that game and flips them into a charming top-down view familiar from the classic *Zelda* games of old. It's short by *Zelda* standards, with just six dungeons and one enormous Sea King castle that you return to throughout, but it's what the game does with the DS stylus that shakes things up.

Tapping away on the bottom screen allows you to fire arrows and throw bombs with pinpoint accuracy, and even the map gets an overhaul, allowing you to scribble your own notes and markers as you go along. A Classic.

FIGURES

2.38 million – copies of *Final Fantasy XII* sold in Japan in 2006, according to Square Enix's financial results.

96 – score out of 100 awarded to the five games in *The Orange Box* by games review aggregator website metacritic.com.

MASS EFFECT

Developer: BioWare
Publisher: Microsoft
Formats: Xbox 360,
Released: 23 November 07

Despite taking advantage of the Xbox 360 hardware in ways other games can only dream about, the true brilliance of Mass Effect lies in the scaleability of its gameplay. This epic space saga bends over backwards to make itself appealing to all types of player; and it succeeds.

You want an arcadey combat game with a galaxy spanning storyline thrown in? You've got it. You'd rather have a statistic-heavy experience that lets you tweak characters' attributes to within an inch of their lives? Sure, it's here!

Every planet you land on is packed with things to do, thanks to the huge number of additional side-quests and mini-games that compliment and enhance the main storyline. Quite simply, if you want the ultimate RPG experience on Xbox 360, forget going large - go massive.

FIGURES

250 – planets that can be explored in *Mass Effect*, although some of these are nothing more than barren wastelands.

900,000 – copies of *Crackdown* sold worldwide in the first two months on sale.

1,600 – copies of *The Burning Crusade* arrived in Romania at launch. A country with over **10,000** subscribers.

CRACKDOWN

Developer: Realtime Worlds
Publisher: Microsoft
Formats: Xbox 360
Released: 2 February 07

Impressive ascent, agent! Whether flinging yourself from rooftop to rooftop, booting a truck down the road with one kick or teaming up with a friend online to storm a ganglord's fortified headquarters, few games offer the sort of immediate adrenalin rush as Real Time Worlds' free-roaming, crime-busting caper.

Cast as an experimental supercop in a city that's rapidly sinking into chaos, the genius of *Crackdown* is that you have the freedom to do what you like, when you like, and to make sure that whatever you choose is insanely fun.

Nowhere is this playground of excess better demonstrated than in the challenge of climbing the Agency Tower. Manage to scale this monolithic building and you get to survey the city spread out below you… Before taking a running jump off the edge!

If you ever wondered what it'd be like to play *Grand Theft Auto* as a ruthless super-cop, here's your answer.

RATCHET & CLANK FUTURE: TOOLS OF DESTRUCTION

Developer: Insomniac Games
Publisher: Sony
Formats: PS3
Released: 9 November 07

Thankfully, after the disappointment of *Ratchet: Gladiator* things were back as they should be for this latest Ratchet & Clank outing. The storyline delves into Ratchet's background, explaining where he comes from and why he's the last of his kind. His faithful mechanical sidekick, Clank, is on hand to provide the sarcasm.

The core gameplay still involves blasting cartoony enemies with your expanding range of weaponry while smashing up crates to collect the nuts and bolts necessary for progress. However, the variety of missions more than compensates.

Most of all, this is a game worth playing for the sheer loveliness of the presentation. Blurring the line between video games and cinema animation, roaming around Ratchet & Clank's next-generation world is the closest you'll come to stepping through the screen into a Pixar movie.

MARIO & SONIC AT THE OLYMPIC GAMES

12

Developer: SEGA / Nintendo
Publisher: SEGA
Formats: Nintendo DS, Wii
Released: 23 November

None of us ever thought we'd see the day when Nintendo and SEGA's mascots starred side by side in the same game. Until now! In *Mario & Sonic at the Olympic Games*, everyone's favourite plumber and hedgehog go head-to-head in a series of exciting events to determine who will walk away with the gold.

Competing in a wide variety of events such as athletics, gymnastics, table tennis and archery, you and up to three friends can go head to head to see who is the greatest Olympian of them all. What's more, some excellent unlockable stages ensure longevity and variety.

Packed with humour and endless hours of fun, *Mario & Sonic at the Olympic Games* is a triumphant collaboration from two of the world's most loved and recognised gaming characters. So invite your friends over and get ready for a gold medal-winning gaming experience.

WORLD OF WARCRAFT: THE BURNING CRUSADE

13

Developer: Blizzard
Publisher: Blizzard
Formats: PC, Mac
Released: 16 January 07

Announced at the end of 2005, this first first expansion pack for *World Of Warcraft* became the soul focus for millions of obsessed fans. On release it instantly became the fastest selling PC game, hitting over 2 million sales worldwide in the first 24 hours and over 3.5 million in the first month. Not bad for a mere expansion pack.

The Burning Crusade gives players two new races (Draenei and Blood Elf) to choose from, raises the character experience level limit 70 and adds new player abilities (including one new profession; jewelcrafting).

The pack also expands on the existing *Warcraft* universe offering new areas to explore, hundreds of dungeons to raid, new monsters to fight and items to find.

All of this, along with the new player Vs player team battles, ensures that the devout *Warcraft* fan need never leave their seat.

COLIN McRAE: DiRT

14

Developer: Codemasters
Publisher: Codemasters
Formats: PC, Xbox 360, PlayStation 3
Released: 15 June 07

A cruel irony of Colin McRae's death in 2007 was that *DiRT*, the sixth game, marked something of a rebirth. After nine years of tough time-trialling, the off-roader welcomed big rigs, buggies, supercars and 4x4s. Arcade powerslides replaced merciless simulation handling and violent dirt tracks joined the usual countryside. About the only things left unchanged were the class and ambition which had made the series' name. Codemasters' new Neon technology brought unparalleled realism to cars and tracks, with crash barriers buckling under impact, caution tape fluttering in the wind, and crashes deforming everything in sight. Not to mention the meticulous audio sampling vehicles down to their internal components.

Players bemoaned the lack of multiplayer options, but *DiRT* stayed true to the essence of rally, pitting you against the clock.

2007 CHART: 15-20

FIGURES

5,000 – suggestions received by EA for improvements to the *FIFA* series, through the *FIFA* website. Polls on the site, asking fans about directions *FIFA '08* should take, also generated over **200,000** votes.

210,547,465 – points scored by "ChadCasket" on the Xbox 360 version of *Guitar Hero III*. Chad was the top ranked Xbox player on the Guitarhero.com scoreboards as of 28 November 2007.

3,000 – individually licensed players featured in *Pro Evolution Soccer 2008*. There are over **250** teams featured in the 2008 edition.

$60,000 – won by Team Dignitas playing *World in Conflict* at the Cyber-athlete Pro League (CPL) tournament in 2007.

HOT TIP

To beat the boss battles in *Guitar Hero III*, time your attacks carefully. Watch your opponent and only attack either when they have a screen full of notes or, better yet, just as they are about to get "star power". This will stop them from attacking you.

WORLD IN CONFLICT — 15

Developer: Massive Entertainment
Publisher: Sierra
Formats: PC, Xbox 360
Released: 21 September 07
World in Conflict may not be ground-breaking, but it's the best strategy of the year.

The game is set in 1989 and the Soviet Union has started a worldwide war in a bid to stave

off economic collapse. You follow three officers striving to defeat the enemy. The story may sound a bit suspect, but strong voice acting and great cutscenes make the plot entirely believable.

Not only does it have a passable storyline, it has a good strategy mechanics and looks wonderful. Artillery barrages, nukes and carpet-bombing damage buildings realistically and look grotesquely believeable. Finally, the unique multiplayer mode allows players to drop in and drop out as they wish and emphasises co-ordination of attacks above all, as players have to work together to win.

Wish you were here!

WORLD IN CONFLICT

GUITAR HERO III

Developer: Neversoft
Publisher: RedOctane
Formats: PlayStation 2, Wii, Xbox 360, PlayStation 3
— 16 Released: 23 November 07
After the huge success of the first two *Guitar Hero* titles, the heat was on to see if new developers Neversoft could match the high standard set by series creators Harmonix.

Happily *Guitar Hero III* is just as good as its predecessors, if not better. It certainly has the best tracklist, with more songs by the original artists than ever before. The Sex Pistols even recorded a new version of "Anarchy in the UK" especially for the game. Other tracks include "School's Out" by Alice Cooper and The Rolling Stones' "Paint it Black".

Guitar Hero III also features new online, career co-op and boss battle modes and is the first game in the series to be bundled with a wireless guitar.

Neversoft sensibly opted not to fiddle with the gameplay fundamentals, and as a result *GHIII* is just as addictive. Maybe it doesn't represent a great leap forward for the series, but it is still a great game.

PRO EVOLUTION SOCCER 2008/ FIFA 08 — 17

Developer: *Pro Evo* - Konami, *FIFA 08* - Electronic Arts
Publisher: *Pro Evo* - Konami, *FIFA 08* - Electronic Arts
Formats: *Pro Evo* – PC, PS2, PS3, PSP, DS, Xbox 360. *FIFA 08* – PC, PS2, PS3, PSP, DS, Xbox 360, Wii
Released: *Pro Evo* – 26 October 07. *FIFA 08* – 27 September 07
There's nothing to separate the latest editions of these giants of the football genre. If you're looking for realism over pick-up-and-play entertainment, then your best bet is *FIFA 08*. It's a game that superbly recreates the slower, more tactical side of the game while never skimping on the thrill factor, plus the sheer number of licensed leagues and some excellent player likenesses are highly impressive.

If all-out action is your thing, you're probably better off picking Konami's *Pro Evolution Soccer 2008*. Considerably quicker than FIFA without ever straying into the realms of arcade action, this is a thrilling footballing experience that sees you gliding past defenders with silky skills, scoring scorching goals and competing against the greatest teams in the world in a variety of cups and leagues.

802,678 – the highest Expert-level score on "Through the Fire and Flames" on *Guitar Hero III*, achieved on the Xbox 360 by "ParadigmShift89"

18 PEGGLE

Developer: PopCap Games
Publisher: PopCap Games
Format: PC
First released: 28 February 07
The problem with puzzle games is they're all so similar. When

you're not arranging shapes or matching colours you're arranging colours or matching shapes. *Peggle* feels much fresher, although it's basically a mix of Capcom's *Bust-a-Move* and good old-fashioned pinball.

You play by firing a ball at pegs that act like bumpers on a pinball table. The aim is to hit 25 orange pegs with 10 balls. There are other coloured pegs which increase your score or affect the gameplay in different ways.

As you remove pegs from the playing field, you slowly begin to see how you can strategically aim the ball to hit multiple orange pegs, amass huge scores and earn bonus balls.

And that's the key to *Peggle*'s success – anyone can play and progress with ease, yet it's deep enough to draw you back, time and time again.

19 VIRTUA FIGHTER 5

Developer: Sega-AM2
Publisher: Sega
Formats: PlayStation 3, Xbox 360
Released 8 February 07
Forget about *Mortal Kombat*, *Tekken* or *Dead or Alive*, if you're serious about your fighting games, you'll be playing either *Street Fighter* or this.

Renowned for its technical gameplay, *Virtua Fighter* has always been considered the true test of any professional fighter. The fast reaction times and sheer depth of skill required to win a bout puts this leagues above any other 3D fighting series, which is why this franchise also has such a large tournament following.

The latest addition, *Virtua Fighter 5*, continues that heritage with great style, boasting high-resolution visuals, silky smooth animations and fluid combat. Unsurprisingly, it has become a big hit with fans of the series.

As well as adding new characters and moves, *Virtua Fighter 5* also allows players to fight against each other online for the first time, although this feature is only available on the Xbox 360 version.

THE SIMPSONS 20

Developer: EA
Publisher: EA
Formats: PlayStation 2, PSP, DS, PlayStation 3, Wii, Xbox 360
Released: 30 October 07
As a platformer, *The Simpsons Game* is good, but not great. As a *Simpsons* game, however, it's perfect, capturing the crazy satirical spirit of the TV show in its crisp cartoon graphics, hilarious cutscenes and never-ending flow of gags.

Instead of cooking up some absurd plot to explain away the action,

The Simpsons Game cleverly sends itself up by trapping your favourite dysfunctional family in a video game. No genre is safe, from RPGs to Nintendogs, and lazy licensed platformers get short shrift too – you get points for collecting clichés like crates and invisible walls.

The Simpsons Game is mostly simple, fun platforming, puzzles and combat, with occasional moments of inspired genius. But, with many of the team from the TV show involved, the laughs are what makes this game stand out, and they come thick and fast.

FIGURES

55 – hand-painted levels in the main "Adventure" mode of *Peggle*. The Challenge mode features an additional **75** levels.

88 – items of clothing and accessories that can be used to customise Akira in *Virtua Fighter 5*. Each one of the **18** fighters can be modified to suit your own tastes. There are over **1,000** items in total to be found.

8,000 – lines of dialogue in *The Simpsons Game*. The story is broken down into **16** original episodes, written by the same people who write the TV show. The game also features the original voice cast from the show, with over **100** familiar *Simpsons* characters making an appearance.

HARDWARE

CONTENTS

Last sixth generation console

The sixth generation of home consoles began in November 1998 with the release of the Sega Dreamcast, joined by the Sony PlayStation 2 in March 2000. The Nintendo GameCube was released in September 2001 and Microsoft finally entered the console market in November 2001 with its first ever home console, the massively popular Xbox.

HARDWARE HISTORY I

FIGURES

12 million – number of copies of the PAC-Man cartridge Atari published for its Atari 2600 console in 1982.

10 million – number of Atari 2600 consoles sold by 1982.

7 million – estimated number of copies of PAC-Man for the Atari 2600 sold.

FACTS

↪Released in 1975, the Magnavox Odyssey 100 **1** could only boast a choice of two games; *Tennis* and *Hockey*. It also lacked onscreen digital scoring. Players had to use plastic sliders built into the console.

↪Atari manufactured its first home console version of the tennis game *Pong* in 1975. An instant success, Atari produced over 150,000 units for the 1975 Christmas season.

EACH MAJOR DEVELOPMENT IN GAME CONSOLE TECHNOLOGY IS DEFINED AS A "GENERATION". HERE WE JOURNEY THROUGH THE HISTORY OF GAMING HARDWARE FROM THE FIRST GENERATION TO THE PRESENT DAY.

First Generation

The first generation of games consoles is considered to begin in 1972, with the release of the Magnavox Odyssey. It was a simple beast that worked through a television set and was powered by batteries. It was the **world's first console** and, despite selling poorly, it started the computer and video game revolution. By 1975, it was being distributed in Japan by Nintendo. One of the key players in this era was Nolan Bushnell, who quickly realised the commercial potential for gaming after he saw *Spacewar!*, an early computer game, in 1970. The result was *Computer Space*, which became the **first coin-operated game sold commercially**. It was released six months before the Odyssey and was a commercial failure but

Bushnell, who went on to found Atari, then developed an arcade machine that played a game inspired by the Odyssey. The legendary tennis game *Pong* was released in 1972. By 1975, *Pong* had found its way into the home on simple consoles, inspiring many copycat machines.

Second Generation

In August 1976, Fairchild Semiconductor released the Fairchild VES **2**. It was the **first console with a CPU**, allowing owners to access new games rather than just those hardwired into the console – as had been the case for the original Magnavox. This spurred Atari on to release their second generation console, the Atari VCS, or 2600. Launched in 1977, it quickly outsold the Fairchild. The early cartridge games for the Atari 2600 were 2K in size.

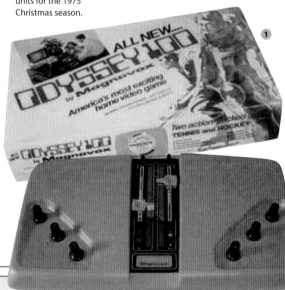

$26 million – the price Warner Communications (now Time Warner) reportedly paid when they bought Atari in 1976

In 1979, a group of former Atari employees created the now global games company Activision, the **first third party games developers**, paving the way for a multitude of other people to do the same.

The first real threat to Atari's dominance came from Mattel, who had already created the **first hand-held electronic game** in 1976. In 1980, they released their Intellivision console ❸, which had 4K cartridge games. The memory size of cartridge games continued to increase, reaching 32K by the time the console and game market crashed in America in 1983, bringing the second generation era to an end.

Third Generation

Beginning after the great crash of 1983, people started referring to consoles by their processor power. The 8-bit consoles dominated the third generation. Many manufacturers and game-makers had gone bust during the crash, but the companies that survived came out stronger. The Famicon console was released in Japan in 1983 and became the Nintendo Entertainment System, or NES, in the USA. This era saw the launch

> **"** *I crushed [the competition].* **We had an 85 percent market share three years later.** **"**
>
> Atari founder, Nolan Bushnell

of *Super Mario Bros.* for the NES in 1985, which revolutionised how computer games were played. An early side-scrolling game, it went on to sell more than 40 million copies worldwide, making it the **best-selling console game in history**. The biggest competitor to the NES was the Sega Master System, launched in 1986. It failed to knock Nintendo off the top spot in the USA and Japan but was more successful in other countries. **(continued over page)**

FIGURES

26 – number of game cartridges released for the Fairchild VES. The cartridges were numbered in the hope that people would collect the whole set.

200,000 – number of units in the initial production run of the Intellivision console.

FACT

Code-named MARIA, the Atari 7800 was first released in 1986. The console had its own games and improved hardware, but retained the ability to play Atari 2600 game cartridges.

ATARI VCS/2600

In the eyes of many people, the Atari VCS ❹, or 2600 as it was later known, was the console that heralded the birth of home video games. When it arrived on the market in 1977, the world suddenly discovered that playing games at home could be an exciting and dynamic experience; and realised that if you got tired of one game, you could simply go out and buy another. The Atari 2600 proved so popular that it is believed to have sold more than 40 million units worldwide in its lifespan.

HARDWARE HISTORY II

Fourth Generation

The fourth generation began in 1987 with the launch of the PC Engine in Japan – also known as the TurboGrafx. It was the **first console to have a 16-bit graphics chip, able to display 482 colours simultaneously**. This was also the **first console with an optional CD drive**. But this 16-bit era really belonged to Sega and Nintendo, whose bitter rivalry led many to refer to the period as the "Console Wars". This was the time when many game franchises, series of games based on the same story or characters, were first established, including *Final Fantasy* and *Mortal Kombat*.

In 1991, Sega released *Sonic the Hedgehog* as an attempt to offer gamers a cooler alternative mascot to Nintendo's Mario. The Sonic series went on to sell more than 45 million copies worldwide.

The fourth generation also saw the rise of the hand-held console, with the Nintendo Game Boy in 1989 – the **first globally successful hand-held console**. In 1991, Atari finally ceased producing the Atari 2600, which had been shipped since 1977, giving it the **longest production run for a console**.

Fifth Generation

From 1993, home PCs were finally becoming powerful enough to play fully 3D games and rival the consoles as a gaming platform. This 32/64-bit era saw the dominance of Sega and Nintendo threatened by a new kid on the block: Sony. The Sony PlayStation took the market by storm, trumping the Saturn ②, for which Sega and the gaming industry had anticipated big things. The Nintendo 64 still used cartridges, from which games loaded much more quickly but, by this time, most manufacturers were beginning to embrace the optical disc as the primary storage medium, with its much larger capacity. The Nintendo 64 was the last major console to use cartridges. The Atari Jaguar console was released in 1993 amidst controversial claims that it was the **first 64-bit console**, but the machine failed to find a large enough market and the Jaguar proved to be Atari's last console.

> *It was originally intended as **a machine to teach computing**… the games market was… secondary.*
>
> Sir Clive Sinclair, ZX Spectrum inventor

A GAMING INSPIRATION

The rubber-keyed Sinclair ZX Spectrum, created by British inventor Sir Clive Sinclair ①, was released in the United Kingdom in April 1982. By March 1983, over 200,000 units had been sold. A major factor in the Spectrum's popularity was the ease with which it could be programmed: users could type in programs listed in magazines and have games up and running in minutes.

The computer remains an icon of British design and some industry professionals believe the humble Spectrum's fostering of talent is one of the reasons why the UK remains a hotbed of games development today.

CARTRIDGE-BASED MEDIA

Game cartridges were the first external media used with home consoles, arriving in the earliest days of the gaming scene in the 1970s with the Fairchild and Atari platforms. They carried not only the software required for the game itself, but also, as technology improved, extra RAM and components to improve the console's functionality.

Cartridges remained the most common form of storage media until the mid-1990s, when they gave way to CD-ROMs and then DVDs, which offered improved performance, greater storage and lower manufacturing costs.

Sixth Generation

The sixth generation was kicked off by Sega's Dreamcast ③, in 1998. But despite being the world's **first 128-bit console** and offering online gaming capabilities, it failed to kill off the PlayStation. In 2000, the PlayStation 2, or PS2, was launched with huge success. Sega discontinued the Dreamcast the following year. In 2001, the world's biggest software-maker entered the global console war with the Xbox – the **first console by Microsoft**. It had an impressive array of launch titles, including *Halo: Combat Evolved*, which was seen as the "killer app" for the console. Despite being a 32-bit machine in a 64-bit era, the Xbox impressed users with its graphics and the console's performance was aided by its 733 MHz CPU, making it the **fastest sixth generation console**. Also in 2001, Nintendo released its long-awaited GameCube as a successor to the Nintendo 64. Although not as successful as the PS2 or Xbox, the GameCube was powerful, compact and contained innovations that allowed users to connect their Game Boy Advances and use them as a controller, using the hand-held's screen to display extra information about the game being played.

Seventh Generation

The Nintendo DS initiated the seventh generation when it launched in November 2004, and was followed by the PSP the next March. But, so far, the current generation has been dominated by the three major home consoles: the PlayStation 3, Xbox 360 and the Nintendo Wii. All three consoles use optical disc storage, the PS3 has adopted the new blu-ray technology using shorter wavelength blue lasers and higher density discs that can store more game data.

To date, the Wii seems to be winning, being slightly ahead of the Xbox 360 and way ahead of the PS3, making it the **best-selling seventh generation console** so far.

NINTENDO 64 & GAMECUBE

FIGURES

500,000 – N64s sold in the first four months in North America. In total, the console went on to sell over **32.9 million** units worldwide.

21.6 million – number of GameCube consoles that have been sold worldwide (from launch to Sept 2007), according to Nintendo.

6 – GameCube games released in 2007. No titles are currently due for release in 2008.

First rumble controller The Rumble Pak was launched in April 1997 to coincide with the release of the scrolling space shooter game *Star Fox 64*. It snapped into the hand controller's memory cartridge slot and gave feedback to the player – ie, it made the controller rumble at appropriate moments. This rumble feedback has since become an industry standard feature.

Largest games The largest cartridges available for the N64 were 512 megabits (64 MB) in size. The first N64 game to use one of these was *Resident Evil 2*. This was originally released on PlayStation, where it appeared on two discs.

Compressing this onto one N64 cartridge was hailed as a technical triumph.

First Nintendo console to use discs Matsushita's Nintendo GameCube discs were created especially for the Nintendo GameCube ①. Smaller than standard discs, these measured just 8 cm. They were chosen to make it harder for people to make illegal copies of games. This proved unpopular, as gamers were unable to play their DVDs or CDs.

First analog console controller stick Although the Vectrex was first to incorporate an analog stick onto its controller, the Nintendo 64 ② was the first major console to do so. An analog stick, as opposed to a tetradirectional four-button pad, greatly improves the options for character control in 3D.

First console built for four-player use *Mario Kart 64*, first released in December 1996 in Japan, was the sequel to the SNES *Super Mario Kart*. It allowed up to four players to simultaneously take part in races against each other.

First first-party RF wireless controller for a home console Nintendo led the way for controller innovation on the N64, so it should come as no surprise to learn that the Japanese company was also the first to release a radio frequency wireless controller; the GameCube's "WaveBird".

PAINTING BY NUMBERS

The GameCube has been released in a wide variety of colour variations. Colours have included indigo, platinum, black and red ③. There have also been country-specific editions, such as spice orange (Japan) and pearl white (Europe), and game specific releases like the *Resident Evil 4* platinum/black combo.

200 million – the number of GameCube games that have been sold worldwide since the launch of the console in 2001

*We aim to **entertain, excite and inspire**, whether by bringing a new dimension or delivering something people have never seen before.*

George Harrison, Nintendo

FACTS

➥ The launch games for the N64 were *Super Mario 64*, *Pilotwings 64*, and *Saikyou Habu Shogi* – all released on June 23, 1996.

➥ The last N64 game to be released was *Tony Hawk's Pro Skater 3* in 2002 in the US. Just 396 cartridges were made.

N64 SPEC

CPU
• 64-Bit MIPS CPU
• 94MHz clock speed
• 32KB L1 cache
• Bandwidth: 250MB per second

GPU
• 64-Bit RISC (custom)

• 62 MHz clock speed
• Bandwidth: 1GB per second

Memory
• 4MB D-RAM (+4MB with expansion)
• Bandwidth: 500MB per second

Sound
• Stereo
• 64 audio channels (PCM)

Overall performance
• Up to 100,000 polygons per second

Supported media
Game: N64 Cartridge (64MB), Nintendo 64DD (only released in Japan)

Storage
• 256KB-1MB removable "Controller Pak"
• Some game cartridges also featured onboard storage for game saves

Connections
• 4x Controllers
• 1x Memory expansion slot

GAMECUBE SPEC

CPU
• 485MHz PowerPC "Gekko" (IBM)
• 32KB L1 cache / 256KB L2 cache
• Bandwidth: 1.3GB per second

GPU
• 162MHz LSI "Flipper" (NEC/ArtX)
• 16MB Video RAM
• Bandwidth: 2.6GB per second

Memory
• 24MB 1T-RAM (2.6GB per second)
• 16MB DRAM (81MB per second)

Overall performance
• Up to 12 million polygons per second

Sound
• Stereo, Dolby Pro Logic II
• Dolby 5.1 (Panasonic Q model only)
• 64 audio channels (ADPCM)

Supported media
Basic model: Matsushita Mini-DVD (1.5GB)
Panasonic Q: DVD, CD, CD-R

AV output
• 480i, 480p (with component cable)

Storage
• 4-64MB memory card

Connections
• 4x controller ports
• 2x memory slots
• Broadband adapter (sold separately)

NINTENDO Wii

Smallest Nintendo home entertainment system

Measuring just 44 x 157 x 215 mm, the Wii is much less bulky than any of its other Nintendo predecessors. It is roughly the same width as three DVD boxes stacked together. Also, with a mass of just 1.2 kg, the Wii is lighter than either the PS3 or the Xbox 360.

Best-selling seventh generation console

According to the Financial Times, as of August 2007, Nintendo had sold over 9 million Wii worldwide. The Xbox 360 had sold 8.9 million units and the PlayStation 3 just 3.7 million.

Greenest seventh generation console

At peak capacity, the Wii uses 18.4 Watts of power, compared to 186.5 for the Xbox 360 and 199.7 for the PlayStation 3. This is equivalent to less than 10% of the power required by the average PC.

First console to function in standby

WiiConnect24 is an online service allowing game updates, emails and Internet channel content to stream while in standby. Nintendo President Satoru Iwata describes the service as "the system that never sleeps".

Largest number of game downloads

Using the "Virtual Console" store, Wii users are able to download a wide variety of classic games. Although similar services exist on other consoles, the Wii has far more to offer. As of November 2007 there were 235 full games available for download.

Fastest-selling UK console

The Wii launched in the UK on 6 December 2006. In just 38 weeks, it hit 1 million sales, becoming the fastest console to hit this target in the UK. This was 11 weeks faster than the PlayStation 2 and 22 weeks faster than the Xbox 360.

FIRST VIRTUAL LIGHTSABRE

Lego Star Wars: The Complete Saga for the Wii is the first video game that allows players to wield a virtual lightsabre. The game utilises the motion sensing capabilities of the Wii Remote ④, allowing players to control their lightsabre by swinging the controller. *Star Wars: The Force Unleashed*, due for release in spring 2008, will also include a similar virtual lightsabre control via the Wii Remote.

Wii SPECS

CPU
• 729MHz PowerPC Custom "Broadway" Processor
• Bandwidth: 1.9GB per second
• 32KB L1 cache
• 3x L2 cache (up to 128-Byte)

GPU
• 243MHz "Hollywood" Processor (ATI)
• 3MB eDRAM and 24MB RAM on board (running at 486MHz)
• Bandwidth: 3.9GB per second

Memory
• 88MB RAM
• 64Mb GDDR3 RAM
• Bandwidth: 3.9GB per second

Sound
• Stereo, Dolby Pro-Logic II

Overall performance
• Up to 500 million polygons per second

Supported media
Game: Wii DVD-ROM (8.5GB), GameCube Matsushita Mini-DVD (1.5GB)
DVD: DVD-ROM, DVD-R, DVD+R, DVD-RW
CD: CD, CD-ROM, CD-R, CD-RW

AV output
• 480i, 480p

Storage
• 512MB Internal flash memory
• 1-2GB removable memory SD card

Connections
• All models: 4x Wii Remote, 1x Wii Sensor Bar, 4x GameCube Controller, 2x SD memory card, 1x AV

*" Wii will break down the wall that separates video game players from everybody else, because it's not really about you or me. **It's about Wii**. "*

Nintendo mission statement

HOT TIP
To get the most out of your Wii you need to be making use of the "Wii Channels". These offer everything from internet browsing and news feed checking to Wii community interaction and video game downloads.

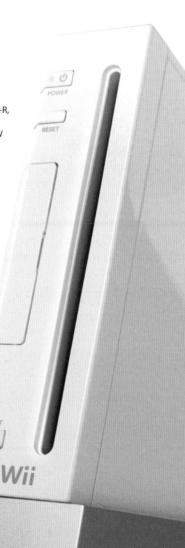

GAME BOY/GBA/DS

Most number of players on a single Game Boy multiplayer session *Faceball 2000*, released in 1991, was the only Game Boy title to allow 16 players to play together, via cables and link ports. *Faceball 2000* was also the first (and only) Game Boy black and white game played from the first person perspective.

Most advanced hand-held screen The display for the Game Boy Micro is a two-inch backlit colour LCD TFT screen with a resolution of 240 x 160 pixels. Capable of displaying 32,000 colours, it received critical acclaim after launch. It has adjustable brightness and is noted for being far sharper and more colourful than the (considerably larger) screen on its predecessor, the Game Boy Advance SP.

FACTS

➲ More Game Boy Advance units were sold within the first two years of release than the original Game Boy sold after eight years on sale, the **best-selling hand-held** has also outsold the PlayStation 2 in the US.

➲ To celebrate the 20th anniversary of the Game Boy, Nintendo released a special edition Game Boy Micro modelled on the original Game & Watch.

Best-selling hand-held games console As of September 2007, Nintendo had sold some 80.4 million Game Boy Advance (GBA) consoles worldwide. All the generations of Game Boys together have sold more than 199 million units worldwide, making it not just the best-selling hand-held, but one of the world's most popular gaming platforms in history.

First games console to sell over 1 million units in just ten days Not only the best-selling hand-held, the Game Boy Advance is also the first – and so far only – console (hand-held or otherwise) to sell 1 million units in one territory in the space of just ten days. This was achieved in 2002 over the extended Thanksgiving holiday weekend, traditionally the busiest shopping period of the year in the United States of America.

Largest hand-held console party On 12 October 2007, 381 people gathered together at a mall in Parramatta, Sydney, Australia… each one brandishing their own Nintendo DS! Switching on and powering up their favourite games, they set the record for the largest hand-held console party, featuring most DS players gathered together in one location at the same time.

HOT TIP

If you're playing an original Game Boy game on the Game Boy Color you can change the colour palette used for the display. When the "Game Boy" logo displays after switching on, try different "A", "B" and directional button combinations.

GUNPEI YOKOI

Game Boy creator Gunpei Yokoi (1941-1997) began working at Nintendo in 1965, but it was in 1970 that his ability was recognised by a passing Nintendo executive who spotted a toy he had made in his spare time. The toy, the Ultra Hand, went on to become a huge success. So, when Nintendo started branching out into video games, it turned to Yokoi for ideas. In 1980 the Game & Watch series was born and, nine years later, the first Game Boy hit the shelves. Without Yokoi we might not have the hand-held consoles we know and love today. At the Game Developers Choice Awards in 2003, Yokoi posthumously received the "Lifetime Achievement Award".

TIMELINE

1980	1983	1989	1995
1980: First Game & Watch, "Silver" released	1983: Donkey Kong Game & Watch (multi-screen)	1989: The original Game Boy is released in Japan, bundled with the addictive Russian puzzler *Tetris*	1995: Game Boy relaunched in a range of new colours
1981: "Gold" Game & Watch introduced	1983: Mario makes his Game & Watch hand-held debut		1996: The slightly smaller Game Boy Pocket released
1982: Donkey Kong arrives on hand-held			

420 million – the number of hardware units sold by Nintendo across its entire hand-held and home console range by October 2007

*❚❚ The success of the Game Boy Advance has been **nothing short of phenomenal**. The console has revolutionised hand-held gaming. ❚❚*

Andy Williams, Nintendo

FIGURES

24% – female Game Boy Advance SP owners, according to a Nintendo press release that accompanied the release of the pink Advance SP.

80 – the weight, in paperclips, of the Game Boy Micro, which weighs just 2.8 ounces.

30 days – time taken for the Game Boy Advance to reach one million sales in the US. By 90 days that figure had doubled.

5 million – users connected to the Nintendo DS wireless network, as of May 2007. By this point over **200 million** game sessions had been logged by Nintendo.

First backward compatible hand-held

The Game Boy Color, launched in October 1998, introduced backward compatibility for the first time to a hand-held video game device, meaning gamers could play games from the original Game Boy and Game Boy Pocket on the new system. Since then, Game Boy models as well as most Nintendo home consoles have included this feature as standard. This idea of backward compatibility also became a big selling point for Sony with the PlayStation 2.

Smallest hand-held games console

Of all the descendants of the original Game Boy, the Game Boy Micro is the smallest. Released in Japan in September 2005, it measures just 50 x 101 x 17 mm.

By March 2007, over 2.4 million Game Boy Micro units had been sold worldwide.

Most profitable week in Nintendo gaming history

The Nintendo DS is largely responsible for the most profitable week in Nintendo history. During the Thanksgiving holiday weekend of 2007, the company sold 653,000 Nintendo DS and 350,000 Wii consoles. These figures only represent US sales.

1997

1997: Game Boy Light introduced, Nintendo's first backlit hand-held

1998: Game Boy Color features Nintendo's first colour screen

2001

2001: New-look Game Boy Advance introduced

2003: The "clam-shell" Game Boy Advance SP (frontlit) released

2004

2004: Nintendo launches the Nintendo DS, the company's first touch-screen hand-held

2005: Advance SP updated to include new backlit screen

2005

2005: The Game Boy Micro released, similar in style to the original Game & Watch. This is one of the smallest hand-held gaming systems

PLAYSTATION

graphics set a new benchmark for console games. The whole game took up a total of five CDs for the PlayStation.

First PlayStation game to sell one million copies Legendary fighting game *Tekken*, released as an arcade game in 1994, was ported to the PlayStation the following year. It pits the player against opponents in the finals of an international martial arts tournament. Players could choose from one of eight starter characters with a further 10 unlockable as gameplay progressed.

First commercially released development kit In 1997, Sony released the "Net Yaroze" PlayStation package. This included a special edition development version of the console along with software allowing players to create their own games. This was the first time any console manufacturer had allowed access under the hood.

First video game console to ship 100 million units

In May 2004, Sony announced that the PlayStation ② had sold 100 million units worldwide – the first console in history to do so. The figure includes sales for the PSOne, the smaller version launched in 2000 (pictured left), but does not include figures for the PlayStation 2, which was also launched in 2000.

First dual analog controller

The PlayStation "Dual Analog Controller" (SCPH-1150) ③ was the first controller for any console to feature dual analog sticks. Pre-Dualshock, this was first released in Japan in April 1997. The dual-stick set-up allowed precise control in 3D environments.

Largest PlayStation game

Riven, released for the PlayStation in November 1997, was the sequel to the hugely popular *Myst* and took four years to develop. Its extremely high quality and high-detail

FIRST CONSOLE TO GO MOBILE

When the PSOne was first released in Japan in 2000, Sony released a cable allowing users to connect specific models of mobile phone for data exchange and download ④. Although this completely failed to take off, it was one of the first examples of online networking and data exchange using a standard home video game console.

958,000,000 – the total number of
PlayStation video games sold worldwide, up to the
end of 2004, according to Sony

PLAYSTATION SPECS

CPU/GPU
- 33.9MHz RISC
- 4KB L1 cache
- 1KB Data cache
- Bandwidth: 132MB per second

Memory
- 2MB RAM
- Bandwidth: 132MB per second

Sound
- 512KB Sound RAM
- 16-bit stereo
- 24 audio channels

Overall performance
- 360,000 polygons per second

Supported media
Game: PlayStation Optical Disc
(700MB)
CD: CD, CD-DA, CD-ROM (CD-R
supported on later versions)

AV output
- 640x480

Storage
- 128KB removable
memory card

Connections
All models: 2x controller
ports, 1x AV

> **"** When the console was in
> its infancy we had a dream to
> elevate the quality of graphics
> from 2D to a **rich, realistic,
> 3D experience**. **"**
>
> Ken Kutaragi, Sony

PLAYSTATION 2

First PlayStation 2 game to support online play
Tony Hawk's Pro Skater 3, published by Activision, was released in 2001 and became the first PlayStation 2 game to allow online play. Unlike later online titles, this could be achieved without the need for an adaptor, by using a standard USB connector and a dial-up connection.

Fastest console to ship 100 million units
On 29 November 2005, five years and nine months after launch, Sony announced it had shipped 100 million PlayStation 2 units worldwide. This was over three years faster than the original PlayStation – the first console to reach 100 million sales.

First console in a nuclear weapons conspiracy
In December 2000, it was reported that the FBI and US Customs were investigating the shipment of up to 4,000 PlayStation 2 consoles to Iraq. As they were designated video game systems, rather than hardware, it was rumoured that this allowed Saddam Hussein to avoid UN sanctions prohibiting the sale of computer hardware to Iraq. It was speculated that the consoles could be adapted for use as guidance systems for long-range missiles.

Biggest PlayStation 2 shortage
In November 2004, a Russian-owned oil tanker, The Tulip Brilliant, reportedly became stuck in the Suez Canal, blocking 100 other ships. This included one vessel from China carrying thousands of PlayStation 2 units bound for the UK. As a result of the shortage, sales in the UK went from 70,000 to just 6,000 per week in December 2004.

*"Never before has a home entertainment system experienced **worldwide success** on such a scale."*

Jack Tretton, President, Sony

Best-selling gaming platform
On 26 October 2007, seven years after the PlayStation 2 had been released in America, Sony confirmed that it was indeed the best-selling gaming platform, with over 120 million units sold worldwide. This figure is expected to grow as more PlayStation 2 games are released in 2008.

MULTI-TALENTED

As well as being backward compatible with most original PlayStation games, the PlayStation 2 drive also allows users to watch DVD movies, a world first for games consoles. Subsequent versions of the PlayStation 2, such as the one pictured here ④, also support DVD-9 (8.5GB Dual-Layer) and DVD-RW formats.

PS2 SPECS

CPU
• 300Mhz 128-bit Emotion Engine
• 24KB cache

GPU
• 150MHz graphics synthesiser
• 4MB RAM (additional 32MB VRAM also
available)
• Bandwidth: 38GB per second

Memory
• 32MB RAMBUS DRAM (400MHz)
• Bandwidth: 3.2GB per second

Sound
• Stereo, Dolby Digital 5.1, DTS
• 48 audio channels

Overall performance
• Up to 75 million polygons per second

Supported media
Game: PlayStation 2 CD-ROM,
PlayStation CD-ROM
DVD: DVD-ROM, DVD-R,
DVD-RW
CD: CD, CD-R, CD-RW

Storage
• 1-8MB Sony
memory card

PLAYSTATION 3

Most powerful computing network
In March 2007, Stanford University and Sony announced that the PlayStation 3 was to join the Folding@Home project. This allows users to contribute the processing power of their machines to the scientific study of protein folding and associated diseases like Alzheimers. As of October 2007, more than 289,000 PlayStation 3 users have signed up, making this the largest and most powerful distributed computing project for a games console.

First console to support Blu-ray
Blu-ray uses a blue laser that has a shorter wavelength than conventional discs and readers, allowing more data to be stored. A single-layer Blu-ray can hold 25GB while a double-layer disk can hold 50GB. The PlayStation 3 is the first console to use this new technology.

First commercial use of the "Cell" processor
The much-hyped Cell Engine was first used in the PlayStation 3 ③. Described as a "breakthrough microprocessor", the Cell – designed by Sony, Toshiba and IBM – is aimed at applications requiring 3D graphics and video. In other words, perfect for gaming.

Biggest PlayStation 3 cluster
In March 2007, North Carolina State University announced that it had built a small "supercomputer" out of a cluster of eight PlayStation 3s ①. The team, led by Professor Frank Mueller, uses the cluster for research purposes.

First games console to win an EISA
The PlayStation 3 ② was the first video game console to win at the Eurpoean Image and Sound Awards. Sony scooped the award for Best Product of 2007.

> **❝** *The next generation doesn't start **until we say it does**.* **❞**
>
> Kaz Hirai, CEO, Sony

AWARD-WINNING CONTROL
In 2007, Sony picked up a "Technology and Engineering Emmy" for the PlayStation 3 SIXAXIS ④. The wireless controller features motion-sensing technology, allowing players to move beyond the standard "button-pushing" and get involved with the on-screen action.

PS3 SPECS

CPU
- 3.2GHz PowerPC Core
- 7 SPE (3.2GHz each)
- 512KB L2 cache

GPU
- 550MHz RSX (NVIDIA)
- 256MB GDDR 3 Video RAM (700MHz)
- Bandwidth: 22GB per second

Memory
- 256MB XDR RAM (3.2Ghz)
- Bandwidth: 25GB per second

Sound
- Stereo, Dolby Digital 5.1, Dolby Digital 7.1, DTS
- 320 audio channels (compressed)

Overall performance
- 2 Teraflops

Supported media
Game: PlayStation 3 BD-ROM (54GB), PlayStation 2 CD-ROM, PlayStation CD-ROM
Blu-Ray: BD-ROM, BD-R, BD-RE
DVD: DVD-ROM, DVD+R, DVD-R, DVD+RW, DVD-RW
CD: CD, CD-DA, CD-R, CD-RW, SACD, SACD HD, VCD

AV output
- 480i, 480p, 720p, 1080i, 1080p

Storage
- 20-80GB hard drive
- USB, SD, MMC

Connections
- Basic model: 4x USB, 1x AV, 1x HDMI, 1x optical (digital audio), 1x ethernet
- Additional on the premium model: 1x Sony memory stick (Standard/Duo), 1x SD memory, 1x CF memory

FIGURES

33% – the amount lighter the newer PSP Lite is compared to the original PSP. Released in 2007, the svelte unit is also **19%** thinner.

7,000 – number of free T-Mobile "HotSpot" Wi-Fi locations that are available to PSP owners in America.

10 million – PSP consoles shipped worldwide within the first ten months of release, according to Sony. Also, by this point **19.6 million** games had been sold for the system, of the **183** available titles.

222MHz – the speed of the PSP CPU processor. The chip is more powerful, but surprisingly the speed has been deliberately capped by Sony.

HOT TIP

The PSP is capable of playing back movies from a memory stick. However, if you want to do this you need to make sure that the movie is either in MPEG-4 or AVC format as other file types will not be recognised.

First handheld games console to use an optical disc

The PlayStation Portable (PSP), first launched in Japan in December 2004, plays its games from an optical disc specially developed by Sony for the console. The Universal Media Disc (UMD) is a read-only disc measuring 65 mm across and is held inside a plastic casing that slots into the top of the PSP. The disc is capable of holding up to 900MB of data – 1.8GB for dual layer discs.

First GPS-enabled PSP game

The PSP GPS receiver was launched in Japan in December 2006 and has functionality with a number of games. *Minna no Golf Ba* was released in Japan at the same time as the GPS receiver and allows people to get details from the game on real golf courses while playing on them. It is due for release to the rest of the world in 2008, under the name *Go!Explore*.

Largest screen on a handheld games console

One of the most popular features of the PSP is its large TFT LCD screen. Measuring 110 mm diagonally, it has a widescreen 16:9 aspect ratio and 480 x 272 pixels capable of 16.77 million colours. Perfect for both games and movies, brightness is adjustable to four preset settings.

First console graffiti advertising campaign

In a first for game console marketing campaigns, Sony hired graffiti artists to spray paint PSP promotional material in seven US cities, including New York, Miama and San Francisco. The campaign, which features images of children playing with PSPs without including the words 'Sony' or 'PSP', was widely criticised, not just for encouraging vandalism, but also because graffiti artists felt that the adverts were cheapening their underground culture. The campaign was eventually stopped.

LIMITED EDITION

Unlike its rival, the Game Boy, there have been very few alternate colour options for the PSP. So far the handheld has been released in black, ceramic white, pink, blue, gold, silver and yellow. Sony also got together with LucasArts to create a "limited edition" version of the ceramic white PSP for the release of *Star Wars: Battlefront*. This PSP featured a screen print of Darth Vader on the back.

35 million – the maximum number of polygons that the PSP graphics engine can handle per second; in 2D this equates to 664 million pixels

" *Just as PlayStation revolutionised in-home entertainment, we aim to become **a new driving force in the portable entertainment arena**.* **"**

Ken Kutaragi, Sony

Largest PSP memory stick

As well as reading Universal Media Discs, the PSP can also read Sony Memory Stick PRO Duos. On 7 January 2007, at the Consumer Electronics Show in Las Vegas, Sony unveiled an eight Gigabyte version of the Memory Stick PRO Duo, enabling PSP users to store and play vast amounts of music and video on their consoles. The stick went on sale the next month, shortly followed by SanDisk versions.

FACTS

➲ The PSP is capable of joining an ad-hoc wireless network of up to 16 PSPs, with one PSP acting as a host for multiplayer gaming.

➲ Movies downloaded onto the PSP via the memory stick can be watched on a television screen by connecting the PSP via a PlayStation 3 or Xbox 360 and streaming it over a USB cable.

First handheld console made by Sony
The PlayStation Portable is Sony's first foray into the handheld console market. It measures 170 x 74 x 23 mm and weighs 280 g. A smaller and lighter version, the aptly named "PSP Slim and Lite", was first announced at E3 in Santa Monica in July 2007, and launched first in Europe on 5 September 2007. According to Sony, as of March 2007, more than 25 million PSP units (both standard and Slim) have shipped worldwide.

FIGURES

156 – developers who pledged their allegiance to the Xbox before the console launched. Of those, **25** also announced their support for – the then unfamiliar – Xbox Live.

500,000 – estimated number of sales of the Xbox console in Japan.

14.1 million – Xbox power cords recalled after worries of a fire hazard. Microsoft reassured users that **fewer than 1 in 10,000** were at risk.

947 – games released for the Xbox ①, up until the end of 2007. Microsoft has estimated an attach rate of **between 5 and 6** for the Xbox (average number of games bought per console).

4.5 million – hours of gameplay logged on Xbox Live on the original Xbox during the 2004 Christmas holidays. This is the equivalent of an impressive **500,000** hours per day.

*❝ We view Microsoft's entry into the console business as an **important and positive** event for the games industry. ❞*

Larry Probst, CEO, EA

First games console with an internal hard drive
The Xbox internal hard drive ②, similar to those in PCs, is a standard 3.5-inch drive with a speed of 5,400 RPM and memory size of 8GB. This means that a separate memory card for saving games is unnecessary. As well as saved games, the hard drive is used for content downloaded from Xbox Live, and as a disc cache for games, allowing faster loading times.

Best-selling Xbox game (first 24 hours)
Halo 2 launched on 9 November 2004, in the US and Canada, selling a massive 2.38 million copies in its first 24 hours. This was equivalent to more than $125 million in sales.

Largest console Measuring 320 x 100 x 260 mm, with a mass of 3.86 kg, the Xbox was heavier than the PlayStation 2, the Sega Dreamcast and the Nintendo GameCube. This was mainly due to the bulk of the internal hard drive and the large DVD-ROM drive. A section in the manual warned that a falling Xbox could cause injury!

First games console to feature built-in ethernet
The Xbox was the first console to provide an ethernet port (for online play) as standard. Although the Dreamcast and the PlayStation 2 supported online play, they both required additional hardware to connect to a modem or router.

The Xbox was the first console to popularise online gaming.

LEAST POPULAR CONSOLE IN JAPAN
With Nintendo and Sony well established in Japan, sales were going to be tough. Despite Bill Gates' ④ promise that Japan was going to play a "key role", the console was consistently outsold.

24 million – the total number of Xbox consoles sold worldwide by the end of 2005, just as its successor, the Xbox 360, went on sale

Biggest Xbox cluster

In August 2004, the XL-Cluster team finished linking together 12 of the Microsoft consoles to create the largest Xbox cluster.

First microsoft console to work with alternative operating systems

The addition of a hard drive meant that it was easy for hackers to install their own operating systems. Linux was available for the Xbox shortly after it was launched. Soon after this, Sony released a disc allowing users to run Linux on PlayStation 2.

CONTROL FREAK

The original controller released with the Xbox console was heavily criticised for its large size and weight, which made lengthy sessions uncomfortable for players. As a result, the smaller "Controller-S" was created. It was initially released with the console in Japan, before filtering through to shelves across the rest of the world. Despite the fact this was only intended as an optional alternative to the original controller, its popularity ensured that it went on to become the standard for both the Xbox and Xbox 360.

FACTS

➲ As with most other consoles, several limited edition versions have been released, often with matching controllers. These have included transparent green **3** and crystal white.

➲ The Microsoft "Play More" advertising campaign came under fire after one spot was aired showing a newly born baby speeding away from its mother and landing in a grave fully transformed into an old man. The advert was banned, but still received a gold award at Cannes Lion Festival.

XBOX SPECS

CPU

- 733MHz Intel PIII Custom Core
- 32KB L1 cache
- 128KB L2 cache
- Bandwidth: 6.4GB per second

GPU

- 250MHz Custom NV2X (nVidia)
- Bandwidth: 7.3GB per second

Memory

- 64MB RAM (running at 400MHz)
- Bandwidth: 6.4GB per second

Sound

- Stereo, Dolby Surround, Dolby Digital 5.1, DTS (DVD only)
- 64 audio channels (up to 256 channels in stereo mode)

Overall performance

- 116 million polygons per second

Supported Media

Game: Xbox DVD-ROM (8.5Gb)
DVD: DVD-ROM, DVD (DVD remote required)
CD: CD, CD-ROM, CD-R, CD-RW

AV Output

- 480i, 480p, 720p (with additional cable)

Storage

- 8GB internal hard drive
- 8MB removable memory unit

Connections

All models: 4x custom controller ports, 1x custom AV, 1x ethernet port (for online or network-based gaming)

XBOX 360

FIGURES

2.4 billion – dollars spent on Xbox 360 consoles, games and accessories since its launch in the US, up to November 2007, according to market research group NPD.

18 million – games sold for the Xbox 360 in America alone, up to November 2007. There are over **250** games available for the console.

37 – number of countries in which the Xbox 360 has officially been released for sale.

2.9 billion – hours spent on Xbox Live since the launch of the Xbox 360, up until November 2007. That's the same as **332,000** years of straight gaming!

13.4 million – consoles sold worldwide up to the end of September 2007, according to Microsoft.

> **1**

Best-selling Xbox 360 game

Halo 3 – the eagerly awaited and most pre-ordered game in Xbox history – was launched in the US on 25 September 2007. In its first 24 hours of release it had generated a massive $170 million, beating Hollywood blockbusters such as *Spider-Man 3*. Unsurprisingly it soon became the best-selling 360 title.

*Starting today with Xbox 360, our ambition is to **revolutionise** the way people think about fun.*

Robbie Bach, Microsoft

Largest console-based gaming network

Xbox Live **1** launched on the Xbox in November 2002. It started off as an online gaming service, but went on to include downloads, movie renting and more. By November 2007, more than 8 million users had signed up.

Most popular Xbox Live day

On the first day that *Halo 3* was available, the Xbox Live service saw over one million users connect online to try out the new action blockbuster.

Largest water balloon fight

A water fight might not be something you would readily associate with a piece of electrical equipment, but on 23 March 2006 Microsoft set the record for the largest water balloon

fight at the Xbox 360 launch in Australia. A total of 2,849 people gathered on Coogee Beach, forming the shape of the Xbox 360 logo and brandishing 51,400 water balloons.

Longest games console warranty

The infamous "Red Ring of Death" (otherwise known as total hardware failure) that plagued many Xbox 360 owners forced Microsoft to extend the warranty of the Xbox 360 to three years. This is longer than any other console.

> **2**

> **3**

LUCKY SEVEN

The Xbox 360, successor to the Xbox, was launched on 22 November 2005 **3** and became the first seventh-generation console, beating both the PlayStation 3 and Nintendo Wii to market by almost a year. An improved version of the console, the Elite **2**, arrived in 2007.

466 million – Xbox 360 Achievements unlocked since launch, making a global Gamerscore of over 11 billion points

XBOX 360 SPECS

CPU
• 3.2GHz IBM PowerPC Custom Core
• 3 Symmetrical Core
(running at 3.2GHz)
• 1MB L2 cache

GPU
• 500MHz Xenos with 10MB DRAM (ATI)
• 512MB GDDR 3 Video RAM
(running at 700MHz)
• 22GB per second bandwidth

Memory
• 512MB GDDR3 RAM
(running at 700MHz)
• 22GB per second bandwidth

Sound
• Dolby Pro-Logic II, Dolby
Digital 5.1, DTS
• 256 audio channels

Overall performance
• 1 Teraflop

Supported media
Game: Xbox 360 DVD-ROM (17Gb)
HD-DVD: With external drive only
DVD: Xbox DVD-ROM, DVD-ROM,
DVD-R, DVD+R, DVD-RW
CD: CD, CD-DA, CD-ROM,
CD-R, CD-RW

AV output
• 480i, 480p, 720p, 1080i, 1080p

Storage
• 20-120GB removable hard drive
• 64-512MB removable memory unit

Connections
All models: 4x USB, 2x memory card,
1x AV, 1x ethernet
Xbox 360 Elite: 1x HDMI

DESIGNER

The shape for the Xbox 360 console that you see here was created not by Microsoft, but by two design studios; San Francisco-based Astro Studios and Osaka-based Hers Experimental Design. Throughout the design process the console was described as a combination of **The Hulk and Bruce Lee**. The famous dual-concaved sides were actually added to give the feel of a powerful fighter breathing in, ready to deliver an explosive blow.

FACTS

➲ Microsoft regularly organises "Game With Fame" sessions over Xbox Live, where players get to face off against the stars. Contestants so far have included Jack Black, Jenny McCarthy, Andy Roddick and Rihanna.

➲ On 6 November 2006, Microsoft launched its video download service in America. This allows Xbox Live users to download HD movies and TV shows. Microsoft is also planning an IPTV service for 2008 that will allow people to stream and record TV using their Xbox 360.

PC GAMING

FIRST PC

The original PC dates back to 1981 and was known simply as the IBM Personal Computer (Model 5150). It had a maximum memory of just 256K and used a cassette drive as storage, with a floppy drive as an optional extra. It included the **first video card** – the Monochrome Display Adaptor, which could only display text.

previously believed that the size limit would be 65 nanometres (1 mm equals 1,000,000 nanometres). Known as the Penryn microprocessor, the chip will allow for higher performance PCs and was named one of the best inventions of 2007 by *Time Magazine*.

Most computer sales

Even with minimal upgrading, approximately 30 million Commodore 64 desktop computers were sold between its release date in 1982 and its commercial decline in 1993. In March 2007, Commodore announced a return to the PC market with the release of a high specification gaming machine that features a quad core intel processor and two NVIDIA 8800 GTX 768MB graphics cards.

FACTS

➲ Graphics card manufacture ATI and NVIDIA both have technology that allows two graphics cards to be installed in the same machine – significantly boosting graphical performance.

➲ Forcing a PC component to run faster than it was designed to is called overclocking and can cause critical failures, usually due to thermal damage. Experiments on the Pentium Duel Core chip have yielded performance improvements of up to 80%.

Largest LAN party The largest LAN (Local Area Network) party consisted of 8,531 unique computers and 9,184 participants at the DreamHack event in the Elmia Exhibition Centre, Jönköping, Sweden, from 30 November–2 December 2006.

> **"** *PC gaming is where you will see that really* **cutting edge, high-end type stuff happening.* **"**
>
> Bill Gates, Microsoft founder

First one terabyte hard drive

The hard drive, first invented in 1956, has become the standard way of storing large amounts of data on a PC, and is where computer game software is usually kept. The first standard 3.5-inch drive to reach one terabyte in capacity was the Hitachi Deskstar 7K1000, which has a spin rate of 7,200 revolutions per minute. It was launched in 2007.

Smallest transistors in a desktop processor

In January 2007, Intel revealed its first working chip built with transistors just 45 nanometres across. It was

FIRST GAMER-BRANDED PC COMPONENTS

US champion gamer Jonathan "Fatal1ty" Wendell first began selling mouse mats aimed at gamers. As of 2007, high-end gamers can now buy motherboards, graphics cards, sound cards and other items such as mice and gaming keyboards with the "Fatal1ty" brand on them, with design input from the champion himself.

MODDING

⮌ Case Modding is
the art of modifying
a PC chassis with
embellishments,
such as Mark Purney's
forced induction mod
6, Paul "Crimson Sky"
Capello's amazing
Doom-themed creation
7, the limited edition
graffiti make-over of
the new Commodore
PC **8** or G-gnome's
bizarre "Weapon of
Mass Destruction"
bomb modification **9**.
Many mods are
performed to increase
cooling efficiency and
thus performance, but
some simply strive for
an eye-popping
design.

FUTURE TECHNOLOGY

FACTS

➲ The Virtual Retinal Display was first created at the University of Washington in 1991. This technology could eventually kill the need for gamers to use a display screen at all. The idea is that low energy laser light can be projected directly into the human eye and onto the retina – your eye becoming the monitor.

➲ Since the first Internet games on dial-up modems became popular, the increase in bandwidth available due to broadband has been staggering. This will continue to increase, led by research groups such as the Internet2 Consortium. Eventually the only limiting factor will be the speed of light itself.

It's obvious to any gamer that a fantastic benefit of the relentless advance in computer technology is that games just keep getting better. But the ever-increasing power of computer chips is gradually leading to a major problem. That noise your PC makes is essentially the noise of the fans trying to keep the chips on the motherboard and graphics card cool by blasting air at them at point blank range. Intel's Chief Technology Officer Pat Gelsinger ② has famously predicted that, at the current rate of progress, PC chips at the end of the decade could well be as hot as the exhaust gases coming out of a rocket engine. Pretty soon after that, PC chips could be as hot as the surface of the Sun – so something needs to be done!

Thankfully, it is. As well as refining techniques to make silicon chips more efficient, as well as powerful, brand new ways of computing are beginning to emerge that will prevent future PCs from setting fire to your house. Quantum computing and biological computing are two of the infant technologies that we can expect to start gradually hearing more about in the news in the years ahead.

In the meantime we can expect our games to keep improving in various ways. For years we have been used to interacting with games via traditional devices such as joysticks, mice, keyboards and other gadgets like light guns. But motion sensing devices such as those inside the Nintendo Wii Controller are showing us what is to come. Within the next few years we may see much more interactive input into games using Hollywood-style full motion capture, similar to that used in recent blockbusters such as *Lord of the Rings* ⑧ and *Beowulf*, precisely imitating a

MOORE'S LAW

In 1965, Intel co-founder Gordon Moore ③ published a research paper containing a prediction that has since become known as "Moore's Law". He said that the number of transistors on a silicon chip would double every year for the next 10 years. He soon revised his estimate to double every two years and this has proven a very accurate prediction for the trend of improvement in computer performance.

TION

ARE WE REALLY HERE?

A few years ago Nick Bostrom ⑤, Director of the Future of Humanity Institute, Oxford University, published a research paper in which he claimed we are probably already living in a simulated world like *The Matrix* ④. An advanced human future civilisation would have the ability to create such worlds, inhabited by computer programs so complex that they think they are people. A practically infinite number of these could be run, with virtual people vastly outnumbering real ones. Statistically, we would have more chance of being virtual than real so, as far as the future of games go, we could be already living in it!

gamer's real movement into a game environment.

On games consoles, the number of polygons that a console could display per second has already increased roughly a hundred times every five years. Movie-like realistic environments are just around the corner. The current game *Armed Assault* ⑥, by Bohemia Interactive, illustrates how close we are. In a massive 400km² theatre of war, gamers can operate soliders, vehicles and aircraft in a lush terrain with towns and mountain ranges. Each blade of grass sways in the wind in an environment that includes realistic star constellations and lunar phases. The same development studio also makes professional versions of their classic soldier simulator for real militaries

> **"** *Computers in the future **may weigh no more than 1.5 tons.** **"**
>
> *Popular Mechanics*, 1949

and, in the coming years, the visual difference between a game for a home computer and a professional simulator version will decrease.

As far as monitors and televisions are concerned, while they will continue to improve in quality, approaching that of the human eye, other technologies such as projectors and virtual reality headsets will probably surpass them. Although VR headsets have been around for a while in areas such as military training ①, reduced component costs and advances in technology mean that we should finally see them making

the move into the gaming arena. One of the biggest problems that the gaming industry has always faced is that, occasionally, one must get up and leave the house. As portable computing becomes better this will no longer be an issue as the highest power machines will be small and will not need to be tethered to your TV.

FACT

Non-player characters can be as beautifully rendered as one likes, but the effect will be useless if they do not behave in a logical manner – taking cover when fired at, talking intelligently and reacting to players as if they were players themselves. The groundbreaking *Black and White* ⑦ (2001), by Lionhead Studios, featured a creature that learned from experience and developed personality traits based on the actions of the player.

BEST-SELLERS BY PLATFORM

CAST YOUR EYES ACROSS THE BEST OF THE BEST. BY PLATFORM, THE AWARD-WINNING, HIGH-SCORING, GENRE-DEFINING TITLES THAT HAVE OUTPERFORMED ALL TO BECOME THE BEST-SELLING VIDEO GAMES OF ALL TIME BY UNITS SOLD.

FACTS

➲ The surest way to reach the top spot on any chart is the "video game bundle". When a game is packaged with a console by default, every single person who owns the console also owns that game. This is why the original *Super Mario Bros.* became the best-selling game of all time with sales of over 40 million units.

➲ With one or two exceptions, every single game you see on these pages was released between September and November. This magic Christmas run-up period has always been important for the games industry and, as a result, has traditionally seen bigger launches.

NINTENDO 64

	GAME	PUBLISHER	SALES
1	Super Mario 64	Nintendo	11.8 million
2	Mario Kart 64	Nintendo	8.5 million
3	GoldenEye 007 ①	Nintendo	8.0 million
4	The Legend of Zelda: Ocarina of Time	Nintendo	7.6 million
5	Pokémon Stadium	Nintendo	5.8 million

GAME BOY/GBA

	GAME	PUBLISHER	SALES
1	Tetris	Nintendo	32.0 million
2	Pokémon: Red/ Blue/Green	Nintendo	29.7 million
3	Pokémon: Gold/Silver	Nintendo	21.2 million
4	Super Mario Land	Nintendo	18.4 million
5	Pokémon: Ruby/Sapphire	Nintendo	15.1 million

NINTENDO DS

	GAME	PUBLISHER	SALES
1	Nintendogs	Nintendo	15.0 million
2	Pokémon: Diamond/Pearl	Nintendo	12.1 million
3	New Super Mario Bros.	Nintendo	10.7 million
4	Brain Age	Nintendo	8.6 million
5	Animal Crossing: Wild World ③	Nintendo	8.1 million

GAMECUBE

	GAME	PUBLISHER	SALES
1	Mario Kart: Double Dash	Nintendo	6.6 million
2	Super Smash Bros. Melee	Nintendo	6.5 million
3	Super Mario Sunshine	Nintendo	5.9 million
4	The Legend of Zelda: The Wind Waker	Nintendo	4.3 million
5	Luigi's Mansion	Nintendo	3.3 million

Wii

	GAME	PUBLISHER	SALES
1	Wii Sports ②	Nintendo	11.4 million
2	Wii Play	Nintendo	6.5 million
3	The Legend of Zelda: Twilight Princess	Nintendo	3.8 million
4	Mario Party 8	Nintendo	2.8 million
5	Wario Ware: Smooth Moves	Nintendo	1.9 million

PLAYSTATION

	GAME	PUBLISHER	SALES
1	Gran Turismo	Sony	10.8 million
2	Final Fantasy VII	Sony	9.8 million
3	Gran Turismo 2	Sony	9.4 million
4	Final Fantasy VIII	Sony	7.8 million
5	Tekken 3	Namco	7.5 million

PLAYSTATION 2

	GAME	PUBLISHER	SALES
1	Grand Theft Auto: San Andreas	Rockstar	15.0 million
2	Gran Turismo 3: A-Spec	Sony	14.8 million
3	Grand Theft Auto: Vice City	Rockstar	14.2 million
4	Grand Theft Auto III	Rockstar	11.6 million
5	Gran Turismo 4	Sony	8.7 million

PLAYSTATION 3

	GAME	PUBLISHER	SALES
1	Resistance: Fall of Man	Sony	1.7 million
2	MotorStorm	Sony	1.4 million
3	Need for Speed: Carbon	EA	580,000
4	Call of Duty 3	Activision	500,000
5	Madden NFL 08	EA	490,000

PC

	GAME	PUBLISHER	SALES
1	The Sims	EA	16.0 million
2	Starcraft	Blizzard	9.5 million
3	World of Warcraft	Vivendi	9.1 million
4	Half-Life	Sierra	8.0 million
5	Myst	Brøderbund	7.7 million

> **"** Decades from now, cultural historians will look back at this time and say it is **when the definition of entertainment changed forever. "**

Doug Lowenstein, President, ESA

PSP

	GAME	PUBLISHER	SALES
1	Grand Theft Auto: Liberty City Stories	Rockstar	4.4 million
2	Grand Theft Auto: Vice City Stories	Rockstar	2.0 million
3	Need for Speed: Most Wanted	EA	1.6 million
4	Midnight Club 3: Dub Edition	Rockstar	1.6 million
5	Monster Hunter Freedom 2	Capcom	1.5 million

XBOX

	GAME	PUBLISHER	SALES
1	Halo 2	Microsoft	8.3 million
2	Halo: Combat Evolved	Microsoft	5.7 million
3	Tom Clancy's Splinter Cell	Ubisoft	2.9 million
4	Fable	Microsoft	2.6 million
5	Project Gotham Racing	Microsoft	2.1 million

XBOX 360

	GAME	PUBLISHER	SALES
1	Halo 3	Microsoft	5.7 million
2	Gears of War	Microsoft	4.8 million
3	The Elder Scrolls IV: Oblivion	2K Games	2.1 million
4	Ghost Recon Advanced Warfighter	Ubisoft	1.9 million
5	Call of Duty 2	Activision	1.9 million

SALES

There are many different arbiters of sales figures in the gaming industry, from games companies through to independent monitors. Inevitably, this means that opinions vary on who sold exactly what, but as with the rest of the sales figures in this book, we have strived to bring you the most accurate data available.

RECORD-BREAKING GAMES

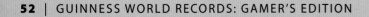

CONTENTS

Greatest "draw distance"
The "draw distance" is the area in a 3D scene between the player's point of view and the horizon; beyond this point, nothing is rendered (drawn). The greater the draw distance, the more power is needed to render all the objects on screen. *Halo 3*, the final instalment of Bungie Studios' trilogy, boasts a rendering engine with record draw distance of 22 km (14 miles).

ACTION-ADVENTURE GAMES

OUTLINE

Action-adventure is such a diverse genre that it is difficult to define. Action-adventure games are usually characterised by investigation, exploration and puzzle-solving, and focus on story, as well as testing gamers' button-pounding skills.

WITH STRONG STORIES AND FIENDISH PUZZLES SPREAD AROUND VAST GAME ENVIRONMENTS, ACTION-ADVENTURE GAMES CHALLENGE PLAYERS TO THINK AND FIGHT TO SOLVE THEIR PROBLEMS.

As the name suggests, action-adventure is a genre that includes a diverse range of games of vastly differing styles and gameplay. Originally, adventure games were text-only. It wasn't until graphics advanced that adventure games that also required action and movement became possible. Quicksilver's *Ant Attack*, released in 1983, is widely believed to be the **first action-adventure game**. In it, players explored an isometric city overrun by giant ants. The next big step came in 1986 when *The Legend of Zelda* launched on the NES. *The Legend of Zelda* was the **first game to allow players to explore an open world**. Instead of taking a linear

path, players were free to explore a massive and colourful fantasy world through the game's bird's-eye scrolling view. *Zelda* set many standards for action-adventure games for the next few years.

The Amiga 500, a powerful machine capable of impressive 3D polygon graphics, was launched in 1987, and

TIMELINE

1976

1976: *Colossal Cave Adventure*, arguably the first text-adventure game, is created on the PDP-10 computer

1987

1980: *Mystery House* **1**, the first text game with graphics, released for the Apple II

1983: *Ant Attack* comes out on the ZX Spectrum

1984: *Knight Lore* **2** released

1986: *The Legend of Zelda* released

1987: *Maniac Mansion* comes to the PC

1989

1989: *Midwinter* **7** makes its debut

1992: *Alone in the Dark* scares PC owners everywhere

1996

1996: Capcom releases *Resident Evil*

1997: first game in the *Grand Theft Auto* franchise is unleashed

TRIVIA

➲ A 1987 text adventure based on *Jack the Ripper* ③ was the first game to be rated 18 in the UK because of its images of murder victims.

➲ The classic point-and-click adventure game *Secret of Monkey Island* was partly inspired by the Pirates of the Caribbean ride at Disney World.

➲ In 2007, the British Intelligence agency, GCHQ, took the bold step of placing recruitment adverts in UK versions of the spy action-adventure game *Tom Clancy's Splinter Cell* ⑥.

FIGURE

500,000 – estimated number of copies of *The Hobbit*, a real-time text adventure released in 1982, sold for the ZX Spectrum.

Midwinter, released in 1989, was the **first free-roaming 3D adventure** to take full advantage of its powers. By the time the Sony PlayStation arrived on the scene in 1995, console hardware was capable of producing even richer gaming environments. Several developers exploited the improved technology by pushing the definition of action-adventure games further, establishing many new sub-genres.

Resident Evil popularised the sub-genre of survival horror upon its release in 1996, while Tomb Raider, released in the same year, melded gameplay elements drawn from 2D platform games with 3D exploration and shooting.

In 2001, *Grand Theft Auto III* became the **first full 'sandbox' action-adventure**. The key

❝ *With our games, we produce everything in real time. **By simply changing the camera angles** and letting the characters move on a real time basis, **we achieve a game with the feel of a movie.**❞*

Shigeru Miyamoto, creator of the *Zelda* series of games

characteristic of 'sandbox' games are an open-ended and non-linear style of gameplay.

Today, action-adventure games account for almost all of the most popular game franchises, and with innovative new titles such as Realtime Worlds' award-winning *Crackdown* ⑤, the genre looks set to continue growing in popularity.

CARTOON LINK

Link, star of the *Legend of Zelda* series, also starred in his own 13-episode cartoon series in the USA as part of *The Super Mario Bros. Super Show!* from 1989 to 1990.

1999	2002	2005	2007
1999: 989 Studios releases *Syphon Filter*	2002: *Ratchet and Clank* hits the PlayStation 2	2005: Quantic Dream's *Fahrenheit*, also known as *Indigo Prophecy* in the United States and Canada, is released	2007: Realtime Worlds' *Crackdown* comes to the Xbox 360
2002: *Ubisoft's Tom Clancy's Splinter Cell* ⑥ is released for the Xbox	2003: Ubisoft releases *Beyond Good and Evil* ④		

THE LEGEND OF ZELDA

PLATFORMS

PC · XBOX 360 · XBOX · DS · 3 · GAME BOY ADVANCE · Wii

SPEC

Developer:
Nintendo
Publisher:
Nintendo
Initial release:
The Legend of Zelda (1986), NES

GAMEPLAY

Epic action-adventure series, following the young hero Link **6** *in the fantasy world of Hyrule. Players embark on a series of challenges that combine action, puzzle-solving, adventure, racing and even elements of platforming. The series is renowned for being brilliantly crafted, featuring beautiful settings, interesting characters and original music.*

Highest-rated game of all time
Ocarina of Time **5**, the fifth game in the *Zelda* series, is the highest-rated video game of all time. The website GameRankings.com gives it a combined score of 97.7%, while on the similar website Metacritic.com it has a near-perfect 99%. Both *Ocarina of Time* and *The Wind Waker* **2** earned 40/40 from Japanese gaming magazine *Famitsu*, making Zelda the only series to achieve two perfect scores.

First game with a battery-powered save feature
Published outside of Japan on the NES, 1986's *The Legend of Zelda* **3** was the first game to have a battery as part of the game cartridge, which enabled players to save progress.

Longest-running action-adventure series
The Legend of Zelda is the longest-running action-adventure series in gaming history, running from the 1986 release of *The Legend of Zelda* to the 2007 release *Phantom Hourglass* **4** .

Best video game of all time (*Edge*)
Multi-format video game magazine *Edge* (UK) voted *The Legend of Zelda: Ocarina of Time* **5** the best game of all time.

Best-selling *Zelda* game
The best-selling game in the *Zelda* series is 1998's *The Legend of Zelda: Ocarina of Time*, which has sold 7.6 million copies. *The Legend of Zelda* is one of the most successful video game series, with over 47 million copies sold.

> ❝Ocarina of Time's position at the **top slot** in Edge's 100 Best Video Games shows that **great game design does not age.** ❞
>
> Tony Mott, Editor-in-Chief, *Edge*

7.6 million – copies
sold of *Ocarina of Time*, the
biggest-selling Zelda game

5

1999 GAME OF THE YEAR

THE LEGEND OF
ZELDA
OCARINA OF TIME

PLAYERS CHOICE
MILLION SELLER

E

FACTS

➲ With pre-orders of around 500,000, *The Wind Waker* (2002) was, at the time, the most pre-ordered game ever.

➲ Zelda mastermind Shigeru Miyamoto was inspired to create his fantasy series after watching the 1985 Tom Cruise movie *Legend*.

➲ The only Zelda games given a T (teen only) rating by the American Entertainment Software Rating Board are *Twilight Princess* and *Link's Crossbow Training*. The others are rated E for everyone.

6

TRIVIA

➲ Despite the title, the character of Princess Zelda is not often seen on-screen during the series. In most games she is imprisoned or trapped and is only encountered at certain points of the adventure. She does not feature at all in *Link's Awakening* (1993).

➲ *The Adventure of Link* (1987) was the only game in the series to use a side-on viewpoint. Previous and subsequent games displayed the gameworld from a birds-eye view, until *Ocarina of Time* (1998) marked the first Zelda game in full 3D.

➲ The release of *Twilight Princess* ① was delayed so that the game could be rewritten to launch on the Wii. This marked the first time that Nintendo had launched a new console with a Zelda game.

THE LEGEND OF ZELDA SERIES: FASTEST COMPLETION TIMES

GAME	PLATFORM	PLAYER	TIME	DATE
The Legend of Zelda	NES	Rodrigo Lopes	31 min 37 sec	12 Jun 2006
Zelda II: The Adventure of Link (with warping)	NES	Rodrigo Lopes	1 hr 01 min 19 sec	12 Oct 2004
A Link to the Past	NES	Rodrigo Lopes	1 hr 36 min 43 sec	5 Jun 2003
Link's Awakening	Game Boy	Rodrigo Lopes	1 hr 22 min 57 sec	12 Jun 2006
Ocarina of Time	Nintendo 64	Mike Damiani	5 hr 00 min 40 sec	17 Jul 2005
Four Swords Adventures	GameCube	Rodrigo Lopes	3 hr 04 min 49 sec	24 Jun 2007
The Minish Cap	Game Boy Advance	Mike Damiani	2 hr 46 min 32 sec	2 May 2005
The Wind Waker	GameCube	Ryan Williamson	9 hr 36 min 13 sec	27 May 2004

TOMB RAIDER

PLATFORMS

PC
XBOX 360
XBOX
PS2
DS
3
Wii
PSP

SPEC

Developer:
Core Design/Crystal Dynamics
Publisher:
Eidos
Initial release:
Tomb Raider,
(1996),
PlayStation

GAMEPLAY

Players help thrill-seeking treasure hunter Lara Croft leap, run and climb through 3D environments in search of mythical objects.

Fastest-selling *Tomb Raider* game *Tomb Raider: Legend*, released in 2006, is the fastest-selling game in the series. In the first five weeks on sale, the game sold over 2.5 million copies worldwide and reached the top of numerous games charts around the world.

Highest-rated *Tomb Raider* game The most critically acclaimed *Tomb Raider* game is the first ⑤, released for the Sony PlayStation in 1996. It received an average score of 91% from the gaming press at the time of its release.

Most official real-life stand-ins Having been officially portrayed by nine different models since 1996, Lara Croft ① is the video game character with the most real life stand-ins. Actress Rhona Mitra and TV presenter Nell McAndrew ② are among the stars who became famous as the official face (and body) of Lara Croft. The current "real-life" Lara is UK actress/model Karima Adebibe.

Largest *Tomb Raider* enemy The largest foe that Lara has faced on her adventures is a giant sea serpent from *Tomb Raider: Legend* ③. It appears in front of what may be King Arthur's tomb, and can only be defeated by stunning it with sound before dropping metal cages on its head.

Highest-grossing video-game movie The first *Tomb Raider* (USA, 2001) movie ④ grossed $274,703,340 at cinemas worldwide, making it the most successful film based on a video game. The 2003 sequel was less successful, grossing $156,505,388.

32 million – worldwide sales of the *Tomb Raider* series, dwarfing the 5 million total sales of the first *Tomb Raider* movie on video and DVD

TOMB RAIDER FASTEST COMPLETIONS

GAME	PLATFORM	TIME	PLAYER	DATE
Tomb Raider	PlayStation	2 hr 39 min 30 sec	Stacy Corron	29 Mar 05
Tomb Raider II	PlayStation	2 hr 44 min 02 sec	Shaun Friend	27 Sep 05
Tomb Raider III	PlayStation	2 hr 28 min 20 sec	Shaun Friend	16 Nov 05
Tomb Raider: Angel of Darkness	PC	1 hr 57 min 55 sec	Aleš Horák	17 Nov 06

> **❝** *It's a big responsibility. Those fans are expecting that they are going to see a character they know so well, this character they love. So you have a lot to live up to, and there's always the anxiety of not being able to pull that off.* **❞**
>
> Angelina Jolie, discussing her role as Lara Croft

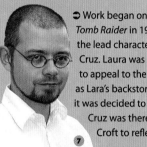

MOST RECOGNISABLE FEMALE VIDEO-GAME CHARACTER

Lara Croft remains the most famous female video-game character in the world. As well as two blockbuster movies, she has appeared in TV advertisements for Lucozade and SEAT cars, on the front cover of style magazine *The Face* and on stage with rock band U2.

TRIVIA

➲ Lara's legendary bust size **6** was apparently the result of a design error. Graphic artist Toby Gard **7** was fiddling with the character's dimensions and accidently increased her breasts by 150%. As he was resizing her dimensions back to normal other members of the creative team saw what he had done and argued that her outlandish proportions should be kept.

➲ Work began on *Tomb Raider* in 1993, and at that time the lead character was known as Laura Cruz. Laura was later changed to Lara to appeal to the US audience, and – as Lara's backstory began to evolve – it was decided to make her British. Cruz was therefore changed to Croft to reflect these changes.

HOT TIP

There is a secret treasure room in Lara's mansion in *Tomb Raider II*. To find it, solve the garden maze (always go left unless there is no left path) and drop into the hole at the end. Press the button there and return through the maze. Run into the house and the door to the treasure room is open.

To unlock Lara's Union Jack costume in *Legend*, you must find all the silver rewards in the Bolivia level.

GRAND THEFT AUTO

PLATFORMS

PC | XBOX 360
PS1 | XBOX
PS2 | DS
3 |
PSP | Wii

SPEC

Developer:
Rockstar North
Publisher:
Rockstar
Initial release:
Grand Theft Auto (1997),
PlayStation

GAMEPLAY

*Notoriously violent
free-roaming urban
adventure series in
which you undertake
missions of a criminal
nature while trying to
avoid the police.*

❝ *The most important
personality in any* Grand
Theft Auto *game is the
city, not the lead character,
because* **the city that
you explore is the most
memorable thing.❞**

Dan Houser, Vice-President of Creative,
Rockstar Games

Best-selling PlayStation 2 video game

Grand Theft Auto: Vice City sold an unprecedented 15 million copies on the PS2. *GTA: San Andreas* is the third biggest selling, with 14.2 million, and *GTA III* fourth with 11.6 million. This string of successes also makes *Grand Theft Auto* the **most successful video game series on the PS2.**

Biggest-selling game of 2001

GTA III, the first game in the series to feature a third-person view, was the most successful video game of 2001, selling over 6 million copies by mid-2002. It won "Game of the Year" and "Excellence in Game Design" at the annual Game Developers Choice Awards. The **biggest-selling game of 2002** was *GTA: Vice City*, with *GTA III* taking second place!

First game to win an ELSPA Diamond Million-Seller award

GTA III was the first game to be recognised by the Entertainment & Leisure Software Publishers Association (ELSPA) for selling over 1 million copies in the UK. Notably, it is also the **first British game to make the ELSPA Award Million-Seller list**.

Fastest-selling video game in the UK

Grand Theft Auto: San Andreas sold one million copies in its first nine days on sale in Britain, making it the UK's fastest-selling video game ever.

Largest in-game soundtrack

Grand Theft Auto: San Andreas features 11 radio stations and 11 DJs playing a commercial soundtrack of 156 licensed tracks, covering genres such as rap, house, country and rock. Because of the vast number of tracks – accessible in the game via the cars' stereos – the soundtrack had to be issued as an eight-CD box-set (featuring 85 tracks) when it was released to the public in 2004.

MOST CONTROVERSIAL VIDEO GAME SERIES

Grand Theft Auto has been the most consistently controversial video game series in history. It has been accused of racism, sexism and of glorifying violence, and was publicly criticised by Mayor Michael Bloomberg of New York City and Senator Hillary Clinton **❶**. American lawyer Jack Thompson has tried, unsuccessfully, to connect the games to real life murders, and in September 2006 filed a "wrongful death" lawsuit against Take Two Entertainment, Rockstar's parent company, following a shooting spree by a 16-year-old.

GRAND THEFT AUTO SPEED RUNS (PS2)

GAME	TIME	NAME	DATE
GTA III (US version)	1 hr 43 min 44 sec	Mike Morrow	21 Dec 03
GTA: Vice City (US)	3 hr 20 min 58 sec	Shane Aukerman	28 May 06
GTA: San Andreas (US)	7 hr 46 min	Andy Nelson	13 May 06

TRIVIA

➲ *GTA: Vice City* was heavily influenced by the Al Pacino gangster movie *Scarface*, and even follows the same plot lines (including a dramatic climax in a mansion house). Other gangster movies referenced in the series include *Carlito's Way*, *The Godfather* and *Goodfellas*.

➲ In May 2007, Rockstar Games announced that limited pre-orders were being taken for a *GTA IV Special Edition*. A steal at just $89.99 (£69.99 in the UK), you get yourself a metal safe-deposit box filled with a keyring, a duffel bag, artwork from the game, a *GTA IV* soundtrack CD and a copy of the game for PlayStation 3 or Xbox 360.

FIGURES

7 weeks – time it took for *GTA: Vice City* to sell 1 million copies.
9 days – time it took for *San Andreas* to sell 1 million in the UK.

Largest *Grand Theft Auto* environment

The *Grand Theft Auto* game with the largest playing area is *San Andreas*, which takes place over an area (or, because of its open-ended style, a "sandbox") of roughly 44 km² (17 miles²). Up to four times larger than other *GTA* titles, it contains three cities, 12 towns and many miles of virtual countryside.

Largest voice cast in a video game

Grand Theft Auto: San Andreas has a credited cast of 339 voice actors, more than any other video game. More than fifty of these portray important gameplay characters, some of whom are voiced by a stellar cast of famous actors and musicians, including Ice T, Axl Rose, Danny Dyer and James Woods. *See box below for more.*

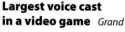

MOST GUEST STARS IN A VIDEO GAME SERIES

The *Grand Theft Auto* franchise boasts the largest cast of celebrity voice actors in a video game series. Among those featured are Joe Pantoliano, Michael Madsen, Kyle MacLachlan, Ray Liotta, Chris Penn, Ice T, Axl Rose, Dennis Hopper, Robert Loggia and Burt Reynolds.

Samuel L. Jackson **2**, who voiced Officer Tenpenny in *GTA: San Andreas*, even won an award for his role: he is pictured here accepting his trophy for Best Performance by a Human Male at the 2004 Spike TV Video Game Awards.

RESIDENT EVIL

resident evil

" September 28th, daylight. The monsters have overtaken the city. Somehow, I'm still alive… "

Jill Valentine,
Resident Evil 3: Nemesis

PLATFORMS

PC	XBOX360
PS1	XBOX
PS2	DS
3	GAMEBOY ADVANCE
	Wii

SPEC

Developer:
Capcom
Publisher:
Capcom
Initial release:
Biohazard (1996),
PlayStation

GAMEPLAY

Tense horror series centred on the nefarious Umbrella Corporation and the zombies and monsters created by its dangerous experiments.

Most live-action movie sequels
Resident Evil is the first video game series to inspire a movie and two sequels. Starting in 2002, the trilogy of movies have all starred Ukrainian supermodel Milla Jovovich ➊. Resident Evil: Extinction opened in September 2007.

Most successful live-action transfer
The first two Resident Evil films, Resident Evil, released in 2002, and Resident Evil: Apocalypse grossed in excess of £100 million in 2004, making the game the most successful live-action game to film transfer of all time. The third film in the series, Resident Evil: Extinction, looks set to increase this figure even further.

Action-adventure game with the most novelizations
Resident Evil has spawned more novelisations than any other computer game in its genre. Biohazard: The Beginning, released as part of a pre-order bundle in 1997, was the first, with a further 12 being published to date. The film series has also inspired four further novelisations (see the box below to find out more).

MIGHTIER THAN THE SWORD: THE *RESIDENT EVIL* NOVELS

Surprisingly, there have been far more Resident Evil novels than games. The first novel, titled Biohazard: The Beginning and written by Japan's Hiroyuki Ariga, was published in 1997. Since then, famed American sci-fi author S. D. Perry has written novelisations of five of the Resident Evil games ➌, with an extra couple of novels produced between games. Japanese author Kyu Asakura published a trio of Biohazard novels in 1998, and an additional couple of novels, available in Japanese and German, were published in 2002 by fellow Japanese writer Tadashi Aizawa. There have also been four novelisations of the first three films by various authors.

31 million – total worldwide sales of all the games that make up the *Resident Evil* series since the release of the first game in 1996

Worst game dialogue ever

In 2002, the line "Here's a lockpick. It might be handy if you, the master of unlocking, take it with you" was voted the worst game dialogue ever by US games magazine *Electronic Gaming Monthly*. It appears near the start of the first *Resident Evil* game.

Best-selling *Resident Evil* game on the PlayStation

Resident Evil 2  is the most popular of the series on the PS2, with worldwide sales of 4,960,000 copies as of 2007. *Resident Evil 3* is the second most popular, with global PS2 sales of 3,500,000.

Most violent *Resident Evil* game

Having been designed with more weapons and monsters for a faster-paced experience, *Resident Evil 4*  is the most violent game in the series. An average play-through requires gamers to kill over 900 enemies.

Longest development period for a *Resident Evil* game

Resident Evil 4 began development in 1998 and went through at least three different variations before release in 2005.

TRIVIA

➲ George A. Romero, the famous zombie movie director, shot a live-action 30-second Japanese TV commercial for *Resident Evil 2*, and was the original choice to write and direct the first *Resident Evil* film, but Paul W. S. Anderson eventually took these roles.

➲ Shinji Mikami, the Japanese creator of *Resident Evil*, was inspired by cult horror movie *Zombie*  (Italy, 1979), directed by Lucio Fulci. He claimed to be unhappy with some of the action scenes and vowed to create a better zombie movie. Instead, he created the now infamous video game, and designed it to give the player the feeling that he's the main character in a horror movie.

➲ If you beat six scenarios in *Resident Evil 2* with an "A" rating, you unlock a special mode in which you replay the game controlling a giant lump of tofu! Tofu starts out with a knife for protection, but can take much more damage than the human characters.

HOT TIP

As spare bullets are scarce in *Resident Evil* games, ammunition can be conserved by killing zombies with a knife rather than a gun.

METROID

PLATFORMS

PC XBOX 360
PLAYSTATION XBOX
PS2 DS
GBA GAME BOY
Wii

SPEC

Developer:
Nintendo
Publisher:
Nintendo
Initial release:
Metroid (1986), Famicom

GAMEPLAY

Free-roaming futuristic action-adventure in which bounty hunter Samus Aran seeks out additional weapons and abilities in order to reach new areas. Its revolutionary left and right scrolling changed forever how action-adventure games would be played.

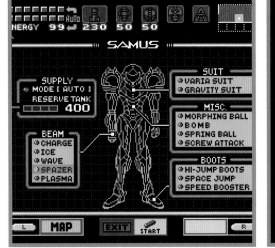

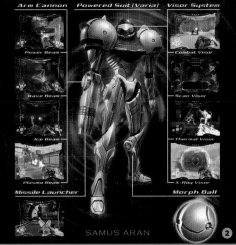

SAMUS ARAN

Fastest-selling *Metroid* game

Metroid Prime, released in the US in November 2002, sold 250,000 copies in its first week on sale, making it the fastest-selling game of the series.

First human female video game star When players completed the first *Metroid* within a certain time it was revealed that Samus Aran, the armoured hero they had been playing, was actually a woman. At the time of release it was extremely unusual to feature a woman in a lead video game role. Prior to the release of *Metroid,* the most high profile female game character was Ms PAC-Man.

Most popular *Metroid* game

Metroid Prime (GameCube) – the first 3D game in the series – is the highest-rated game of the franchise, receiving average review scores of 97%. However, the 1994 installment *Super Metroid* (SNES) is often cited as the best game of the series: in 2002 it was voted the best game of all time by 12 editors from *Electronic Gaming Monthly* magazine.

> **❝** *Whether you're a **tech-junkie** who gets off on the latest leaps in technology, or a **hardened old schooler, with thumbs like marbles**, you will find something to love about this game.* **❞**
>
> Garrett Elder, *Digital Press*

LONGEST GAP BETWEEN *METROID* GAMES

The longest break in the series was eight years, between *Super Metroid* ❶ in 1994 and *Metroid Prime* ❷ in 2002. This gap meant that *Metroid* was the only leading Nintendo series to not appear on the Nintendo 64 console.

1.49 million – sales of *Metroid Prime* in the US alone, following release in November 2002. *Metroid Prime 3: Corruption* looks set to smash this record

TRIVIA

➲ Legendary action director John Woo ④ is trying to adapt the *Metroid* series into a movie. Although he bought the rights to the game in 2004, the film has yet to start production.

➲ The Metroids ⑤ are biologically engineered creatures which were designed by the alien Chozo race to combat a disease called Parasite X. When the disease was contained, the Metroids themselves became a deadly menace.

➲ The *Castlevania* ⑥ games share similarities with the Metroid series, in particular the free-roaming design in which new abilities allow access to different areas. Because of this, fans often refer to such games as "Metroidvania" in style.

➲ Samus Aran and Metroid have also appeared, or been referenced, in 18 other Nintendo games. Samus is also playable in the *Super Smash Bros.* fighting game series.

JENNIFER HALE

Jennifer Hale ③ , the voice of Samus Aran since 2002, is also the voice of Disney's Cinderella. She has played lead characters in games such as *Metal Gear Solid*, *Knights of the Old Republic* and *Syphon Filter*.

METROID FASTEST SPEEDRUN

GAME	PLATFORM	DIFFICULTY	TIME	PLAYER	DATE
Metroid	NES	Fastest minimalist (one life, mini-bosses not necessary)	17 mins 22 secs	Christopher Knight	30 Oct 2005
Metroid II: Return of Samus	Game Boy	Fastest 100% Completion	1 hr 15 mins 11 secs	Jonathan Fields	11 May 2004
Super Metroid	SNES	Fastest 100% Completion (one life, no saves)	1 hr 22 mins 00 secs	Lee A. Garasich	21 Feb 2006
Metroid Prime	GameCube	Fastest 100% Completion	2 hr 19 mins 00 secs	Henru Wang	10 May 2003

FACT

The original US release of *Metroid* was the first major Western game to use a password system to save progress.

CASTLEVANIA

PLATFORMS

PC | XBOX 360
PS1 | XBOX
PS2 | DS
PS3 | GBA
PSP | Wii

SPEC

Developer:
Konami
Publisher:
Konami
Initial release:
Akumajō Dracula
(1986), Famicom

GAMEPLAY

The Belmont family
and other heroes battle
through the ages
against the infamous
Dracula plus sundry
demonic foes. The game
advances by exploring
elaborate maze-like
castles via a mixture
of platform-leaping,
candle-whipping and
RPG-like stat-building.

Most games in an action-adventure series With 23 distinct and commercially released games, not including remakes or boxed compilations, there have been more titles released in the Castlevania series than any other action-adventure franchise.

Largest number of platforms for one series The Castlevania name has appeared on 19 platforms since 1986, which is more than any other action-adventure series so far. In 2008, the series makes its PSP debut, bringing the total number of platforms up to 20.

First Castlevania game to use voice actors Akumajō Dracula X Chi no Rondo, released in Europe on the SNES as Castlevania: Vampire's Kiss in 1995, was the first in the series to use recorded dialogue. Originally published for the PC Engine, this also used the console's CD format to include full-length music tracks.

> **❝ What is a man? A miserable little pile of secrets.** But enough talk… have at you! ❞
>
> Dracula, Castlevania

Longest Castlevania title
The Castlevania game with the longest original title is the 1999 release Castlevania: Legacy of Darkness ①. The full Japanese title, Akumajō Dracula Mokushiroku Gaiden: Legend of Cornell ③, is 47 characters long. It translates as the less-than-catchy "Demon Castle Dracula Apocalypse Supplemental Story: Legend of Cornell".

First Castlevania in 3D The first game in the series to be produced in full 3D was the 1999 N64 release, simply entitled Castlevania. Despite the modern look, the reception from the fans was not good. One website (ScrewAttack.com) voted it as the worst 2D to 3D conversion of all time.

Largest Castlevania play area The Castlevania with the largest play area is Castlevania: Portrait of Ruin ④, released for the Nintendo DS in 2006. Expanding on the gameplay of Castlevania: Dawn of Sorrow ②, this allows players to visit external locations by travelling through paintings, expanding on the playable area.

Most valuable Castlevania
The Castlevania game considered most valuable by collectors is Akumajō Dracula

SYLVAIN WHITE

A Castlevania movie is currently in production, due for release in 2009. Director Sylvain White ⑤ previously worked on the horror I'll Always Know What You Did Last Summer (USA, 2006). The script has been co-written by Paul W.S. Anderson, who wrote the Resident Evil movies.

1,890 – estimated number of rooms that are waiting to be found in the critically-acclaimed *Castlevania: Symphony of the Night*

X Chi no Rondo, which was released in limited numbers for the Japanese PC Engine console in 1993. Good quality original copies sell at online auction websites for several hundred dollars.

TRIVIA

➲ The music for the original 1986 *Castlevania* was composed by Kinuyo Yamashita. However, fictional English names were used in the credits when the game was released outside Japan, so Kinuyo was credited as James Banana.

➲ Additional *Castlevania* games were developed for both the Sega 32X in 1996 and the Sega Dreamcast in 2001. Unfortunately, both of these were cancelled before release.

➲ *Castlevania* characters can be found in several other Konami titles. Simon Belmont is a playable character in the 1988 Japanese platformer *Wai Wai World*, while the 2001 *Konami Krazy Racers* features Dracula as one of the drivers.

METAL GEAR

PLATFORMS

PC XBOX 360
    XBOX
    DS
    3
    Wii

SPEC

Developer:
Konami
Publisher:
Konami
Initial release:
Metal Gear (1987),
MSX2 home computer

GAMEPLAY

Tactical espionage action, as covert agent Solid Snake uses guile and gadgets to infiltrate enemy strongholds. His target: enormous mechanised weapon platforms known as Metal Gears.

First ever stealth video game

Created by Japanese designer Hideo Kojima , *Metal Gear* was the first video game to fully utilise stealth as part of the gameplay. Although earlier adventure games had used elements of stealth, such as hiding and disguises, *Metal Gear* was the first game to concentrate solely on these elements, effectively creating the "stealth game" sub-genre.

First collective AI in a stealth game *Metal Gear Solid 2* was the first stealth game to feature guards who could operate as

a team and even communicate with other guards off-screen to organise a counter-attack. Disabling them before they could call for help was a major part of the gameplay, and this level of Artificial Intelligence has since become integral to the stealth sub-genre as a whole.

Longest single *Metal Gear* cutscene The *Metal Gear* series is famous for its lengthy animated story sequences, or cutscenes. The longest single cutscene in the series lasts for 15 mins 17 secs and comes at the end of *Metal Gear Solid*, as Snake destroys Metal Gear Rex.

Most innovative use of a video game controller During *Metal Gear Solid*, the character Psycho Mantis addresses the player directly, commenting on the games saved on their memory card and telling them to drop the controller, which then "rumbles" violently. To defeat Psycho Mantis in battle, the player must break his "psychic connection" by unplugging the controller and reconnecting it to the second socket on the console.

METAL GEAR
FASTEST COMPLETIONS

GAME	RULES	TIME	PLAYER	DATE
Metal Gear Solid	One life, no saves	1 hr 55 min 31 sec	Rodrigo Lopes	30 Jun 00
Metal Gear Solid: VR Missions	Level 1, sneak mode	3.51 sec	Shin Sato	31 Mar 03
Metal Gear Solid: VR Missions	Level 2, sneak mode	5.29 sec	Shin Sato	31 Mar 03

7,000,000 – worldwide unit sales of *Metal Gear Solid 2: Sons of Liberty* since its release on the PS2 in 2001

PlayStation 2

METAL GEAR SOLID 2
SONS OF LIBERTY

BEST-SELLING STEALTH GAME

Until the release of *Grand Theft Auto* games *Vice City* and *San Andreas*, MGS2: *Sons of Liberty* was the **fastest-selling game on the PS2 in the UK**, having sold over 200,000 units in its first weekend. It remains the biggest seller in the stealth sub-genre, and the sixth best-selling game ever on the PlayStation2.

*❝ I originally wanted to make movies and novels, but I just couldn't do it… **I was really hyped up about making** Metal Gear, since it was going to be a game about war. ❞*

Hideo Kojima, creator and director of the *Metal Gear* series

First interactive digital graphic novel for the PSP

Released on 13 June 2006 in North America, *Metal Gear Solid: Digital Graphic Novel* is the first interactive graphic novel for the PSP. Made by Kojima Productions, the graphic novel features character backstories, Manga-style art and original music.

TRIVIA

➲ Since *Metal Gear Solid 2*, the music for the series has been composed by Hollywood composer Harry Gregson Williams. His famous movie soundtracks include *Shrek*, *The Rock* and *The Chronicles of Narnia*.

➲ The English language voice of Solid Snake is provided by David Hayter. As well as acting in movies such as *Guyver: Dark Hero*, Hayter has written many blockbuster scripts, including contributions to *Hulk* and *X-Men 2*.

➲ The *Metal Gear* series is referenced in Hideo Kojima's other games, most notably the adventure game *Policenauts*. There is a bar in the game called Solid Snake, and the character Meryl Silverburgh appears in both *Policenauts* and *Metal Gear Solid*.

Most "ghosts" hidden in a game In video game terms, a "ghost" is an image – usually of one of the games' production team – hidden in the game and very difficult to find. In *Metal Gear Solid*, there are 43 ghosts of the producers. To view the ghosts, you need to use the camera and take photos at certain spots in the game, such as at Sniper Wolf's dead body and while the guard is using the bathroom!

MOVIE NEWS

Rumours of a live action Metal Gear movie began at a Konami press conference in May 2006. After much speculation, game creator Hideo Kojima confirmed the rumours. "A movie project is underway", he stated, "I have finalized a Class-A contract with a party in Hollywood."

In February 2007, Sony Pictures Entertainment vice chairman Yair Landau announced that his studio would take on the challenge of turning Solid Snake into a movie star. "It's a very cinematic game, it really lends itself to movie-telling," Landau said, adding that his studio was also considering an EverQuest movie.

METAL GEAR
© KONAMI 1987 TM
MSX 2

ALONE IN THE DARK

PLATFORMS

PC
XBOX 360
XBOX
PS2
DS
PS3
Wii

SPEC

Developer:
Infogrames
Publisher:
Atari
Initial release:
Alone in the Dark (1992), PC

GAMEPLAY

Private detective Edward Carnby, sometimes assisted by others, investigates cases involving spooks, spirits, demons and monsters. Originally the games emphasised exploration and problem-solving, but later sequels have become more action-based.

> " *Luckily, **devil worship makes me smile**, so this is my idea of a paid vacation.* "
>
> Edward Carnby,
> *Alone in the Dark*

First-ever 3D survival horror Survival horror is usually defined as a game in which the player must fend off supernatural attacks. Although the term was coined in 1996 for *Resident Evil*, the original *Alone in the Dark* ②, released in 1992 for the PC, is widely considered to be the first 3D survival horror game.

Lowest-grossing game-based movie The 2005 *Alone in the Dark* movie, directed by Uwe Boll ⑥, is the lowest grossing internationally released film based on a game. Although it cost around $20 million to make, the film, which starred Christian Slater, earned just $5,178,569 during its US theatrical run.

MAN OF MYSTERY

Series protagonist Edward Carnby has changed radically in appearance and age between games. Atari has promised that the latest adventure will feature the original hero, despite an 85-year gap in storylines.

Shortest action adventure
The shortest officially released action adventure is *Jack in the Dark* ①, a spin-off created to promote the release of *Alone in the Dark 2*. The game, which involves haunted toys, can be completed in just thirteen steps.

Most powerful weapon in the *Alone in the Dark* franchise
The most powerful weapon in the series is the Lightning Gun, found in the fourth title, *Alone in the Dark:*

ALONE IN THE DARK
A Virtual Adventure Game Inspired by the Work of H.P. Lovecraft

The New Nightmare **3**. The weapon, which is only made available at the end of the game, shoots bolts of electricity that can damage multiple enemies at the same time.

Most unlikely weapon in the *Alone in the Dark* franchise

The strangest weapon in the series is a frying pan, which can be found in *Alone in the Dark 2*. The pan can be used to bash enemies over the head, should you run out of ammunition.

First game to feature television-style previews and recaps

A key innovation of the latest *Alone in the Dark* game is its use of television-style recaps and previews to improve the playing experience. Each time a player starts playing with a saved game, they will see a video summary of the previous section. Every section closes with a nail-biting cliff-hanger and, if the player is leaving the game, a video teaser of the next section to keep them wanting more.

TRIVIA

➲ The first *Alone in the Dark* game drew heavily on the work of famous horror author H.P. Lovecraft **7**. He wrote many short stories about the "Old Ones", terrible demon gods who wait in another dimension to reclaim the Earth from humankind.

➲ The first *Alone in the Dark* game is set in the 1920s and, along with its two sequels, forms a self-contained trilogy. The fourth game, released in 2001, is set in the present day, restarting the story from scratch. This time the character of Edward Carnby is a demon hunter.

➲ Some of the more unusual enemies to have appeared in the series include an undead voodoo pirate captain called Ezejial Pregzt, zombie cyborg cowboys and strange reptilian creatures from the centre of the Earth.

INTERVIEW WITH... NOUR POLLONI

Nour Polloni, Producer at Eden Studios on *Alone in the Dark* 4 , tells the story behind this latest installment in the series…

New York's Central Park is hiding a secret, and over the course of one night trapped in the park, our hero Edward Carnby needs to work out what he's doing there and what's going on.

How does the game take advantage of new console technology?
We've implemented an unprecedented level of environmental interaction based on real world rules where everything behaves exactly as you would expect it to, from the destructibility of environments, to full real-time manipulation of objects, including combining items in a way that's never been seen before to make really cool new weapons.

How have you made the game even more scary?
Music is an extremely powerful factor, and we have a unique and haunting score featuring a Bulgarian choir, heightening the tension and keeping the player glued to every nail-biting twist and turn. During gameplay, we've concentrated on the suggestion of fear, which is key to making things really scary – wondering what's behind a closed door or lurking in a dark corner!

HOT TIPS

Most of the time in *Alone in the Dark: A New Nightmare*, engaging the enemy is just a matter of working out whether you should fight or run. Monsters usually respawn when you leave and return to a room, so killing them can be a waste of time and ammunition. If you are just attempting to reach another room, it is best to avoid fighting altogether by running straight past the monster. This method allows you to conserve ammunition and, if you're lucky, the creature may have moved on by the time you return.

ACTION-ADVENTURE ROUND-UP

FACT

Psychic Killer Taromaru **1**, released for the Sega Saturn in 1996, is the rarest and most valuable console action-adventure. It was never published outside Japan, and only 7,500 copies were ever released. Buying a working copy today can cost over £100.

When playing the Japanese horror adventure series *Fatal Frame*, players must defeat supernatural enemies by taking their photograph rather than attacking them. The fourth game in the series is currently being developed for the Nintendo Wii.

Most playable characters in an action-adventure game

Game title: *Lego Star Wars II: The Original Trilogy*
Publisher: LucasArts
Lego Star Wars II: The Original Trilogy **2** features 50 characters unique to the game, with a further 46 available if a saved game from the original *Lego Star Wars* is loaded. The game also allows players to mix and match body parts to create over one million customised characters.

Most destructible action environment

Game title: *Mercenaries: Playground of Destruction*
Publisher: LucasArts
Mercenaries: Playground of Destruction **4**, the 2005 action-adventure released for the Xbox and PlayStation 2, features a large play area, based in Korea, within which every building can be totally obliterated by the player via either weapon fire or air strikes. The sequel, *Mercenaries 2: World in Flames*, will follow in 2008.

LEAST VIOLENT ADVENTURE GAME

Game title: *Myst* **Publisher:** Brøderbund
The least violent adventure game is *Myst* **3**, released on the Apple Macintosh in 1993. The game features almost no dialogue, no enemies, no time limit and no way of dying.

First video game treasure hunt

Game title: *Pimania*
Publisher: Automata
The first video game to involve a real life treasure hunt was the adventure *Pimania* ⑨, published in 1982. Players who reached the end of the game received a clue to the location of a golden sundial worth £6,000. The sundial could only be found on one day each year – 22 July – at Hindover Hill, East Sussex. The prize was finally claimed in 1985 by Sue Cooper and Lizi Newman.

Only action-adventure to be banned in the UK

Game title: *Manhunt 2*
Publisher: Take 2
Manhunt 2 ⑤ was refused a rating certificate by the British Board of Film Classification in June 2007, making it illegal for the game to be sold in the UK. It was found to feature an "unrelenting focus on brutal slaying". Although revised in October 2007, it was still considered too violent for a certificate.

First black action-adventure hero

Game title: *Akuji the Heartless*
Publisher: Eidos
The first action-adventure to revolve around a black lead character was *Akuji the Heartless* ⑥, released in 1998 for the Sony PlayStation. The titular hero was a voodoo priest who had to fight his way out of hell.

Largest action-adventure environment

Game title: *Just Cause*
Publisher: Eidos
The largest playable environment in an action-adventure

game can be found in *Just Cause* ⑦, published in 2006 for the Xbox 360. The game, set in South America, gives players freedom to explore over 250,000 virtual acres by land, sea and air.

First freeform 3D action-adventure

Game title: *Mercenary*
Publisher: Novagen
The first action-adventure game to offer players an open-ended 3D gameworld was *Mercenary*, published in 1986. The aim of the game is to escape from the planet Targ, and the player is allowed to choose the best way to achieve this goal.

Most popular Xbox Live demo

Game title: *Bioshock*
Publisher: 2K Games
The demo version of the acclaimed action-adventure *Bioshock* ⑧ is the most popular download on the Xbox Live online service. Within one month of the demo being made available, it had been downloaded more than one million times.

FACTS

➲ The 1990 PC adventure game *The Secret of Monkey Island*, by LucasArts, featured a sword-fighting system based on insulting your opponent. Choosing the wittiest riposte to your enemy's jibes would ensure that the hero, Guybrush Threepwood, won the fight.

➲ The 1983 action-adventure arcade game *Dragon's Lair* ⑩ was made up of cartoon sequences by former Disney animator Don Bluth. Gameplay involved simply pressing the correct direction at the right time during the animated sequence to make the hero, Dirk, avoid pre-scripted hazards.

FIGURES

1.5 million – sales of *Bioshock* since its August 2007 release

96% – average review score for *Bioshock* on metacritic.com

FIGHTING GAMES

WITH TITLES GEARED TOWARDS FRANTIC BUTTON-PUSHING, FIGHTING GAMES SHOW US THAT NO MATTER HOW CIVILISED WE PRETEND TO BE, WE STILL LOVE A GOOD PUNCH-UP...

OUR EXPERT

Mike Flynn is a freelance games designer and martial artist. A former curator at the Science Museum, he has published widely in the fields of mathematics, science and history. None of this compares, however, to the thrill of sparring with the world martial arts champion – an experience he likens to sticking his own face in a fan.

OUTLINE

A true fighting game involves bouts of face-to-face combat, usually between one or more pairs of opponents, each of whom is blessed with roughly equal skill and strength. Although Western fighting systems, such as boxing and wrestling, feature prominently in this genre, most favour the far more dramatic Eastern martial arts, such as Karate or Kung Fu.

The history of fighting games starts with *Warrior*, published by a company called Vectorbeam in 1979. Its 2D characters, modelled using black and white vector graphics, fought hard, but not to the death, against a simple backdrop. Unfortunately, the limited graphics of *Warrior* failed to grip the public's imagination. It was to be over a decade before fighting became a firmly established genre.

In 1987, the now familiar *Street Fighter* appeared in arcades for the first time. In a series of bouts spanning five countries in three continents, a lone Karate expert fought all competition – with a little user-help. Unfortunately, its overly complex and fragile controls meant that the game proved unpopular with gamers and arcade owners alike. But all this changed with the release of *Street Fighter II* in 1991.

Offering an inspiring choice of fighters, capable of over 30 moves each, plus a range of deadly foes and some simple controls, the game was an instant hit. It also rescued the otherwise flagging arcade games market, becoming the **biggest-selling coin-operated fighting game of all time.** Inevitably, every other game publisher wanted a piece of Capcom's kick-ass action.

Many titles followed, but few could rival the impact of Midway's *Mortal Kombat*, released in 1992. Gratuitously violent and bloody, gamers couldn't get

TIMELINE

1979
1979: Arcade game *Warrior*, believed to be the first true fighting game, is released to very little acclaim

1985
1985: *Way of the Exploding Fist* **3** , the first fighting game to feature realistic sound effects, goes on the market

1987
1987: *Street Fighter* first appears in arcades, but technical difficulties combined with a high level of complexity limit its appeal

1991
1991: A much improved *Street Fighter II* is released into arcades worldwide. Demand for this title establishes the fighting genre

1992
1992: *Mortal Kombat* is released. Offering blood, gore and fatalities, it proves to be a massive hit with gamers the world over

$23 million – the amount *Mortal Kombat*,
the film starring Christopher Lambert,
took in its opening weekend in the USA

enough of the carnage and *Mortal Kombat* took over a billion dollars in its first year, making it the **most successful launch of a fighting game ever**. Inevitably, the game provoked a backlash from concerned parents, and in 1994 the

Entertainment Software Rating Board (ESRB) came into existence.

But in a side-stepping move, worthy of a ninja assassin, the games industry continued to produce ever more impressive fighting games. Most prominent of these was *Virtua Fighter*, the **first 3D fighting game**. Released in 1993 as a rival to *Mortal Kombat*, the series really came into its own with the release of *Virtua Fighter 4* in 2001. The latest innovations revolve around controllers. *Dark Wind*, released in 2004, introduced wired boxing glove controllers using the GameTrak motion sensing device, while *Wii Sports Boxing* uses the motion sensing components in the Wii's nunchuk and wireless remote control.

TRIVIA

➲ On release, the Sega Mega Drive version of *Mortal Kombat* retained all of the guts and gore of the original arcade game while the SNES version did not. This may explain why the Sega version outsold the SNES by three to one. Certainly, when *Mortal Kombat II* was released intact onto the SNES it immediately out-sold Sega's version.

➲ *Vampire Chronicle*, released 2000 on the Dreamcast, is widely regarded as the first online fighting game. Just 5,000 copies of it were made and it was only available through Sega Direct in Japan.

➲ The arcade cabinet versions of *Dead or Alive ++* and *Street Fighter EX* share exactly the same hardware, the Sony-based "ZN" arcade board.

FIGURES

$33,423,521 – total takings of the *Street Fighter* movie at the US box office upon release in 1994.

$70,454,098 – total takings of the *Mortal Kombat* movie at the US box office upon release in 1995.

1994	1996	1999	2007
1992: *Art of Fighting* **4** , the first fighting game to feature taunting, is released	1996: *Dead or Alive* is released	1999: *Super Smash Bros.* **5** , a fighting game featuring some of Nintendo's most popular characters, is launched	2007: *Virtua Fighter 5* **1** , the latest addition to the Virtua Fighter franchise, is released on the Xbox 360
1994: The Entertainment Software Rating Board (ESRB) is established	1998: *Soul Calibur* premiers and wins the E3 Critics Award for "Best Fighting Game" of the year		
1993: *Virtua Fighter*, the world's first 3D fighting game, hits the market			
1994: *Tekken* **2** is unleashed			

STREET FIGHTER

PLATFORMS

PC · XBOX 360 · PS3 · XBOX · PS2 · DS · PS3 · Wii

SPEC

Developer:
Capcom
Publisher:
Capcom
Initial release:
*Street Fighter
(1987), Arcade*

GAMEPLAY

The player selects their character and battles the best fighters across the world in a series of best-two-of-three matches. Play advances through a variety of countries in sequence. The fights continue until the player is crowned world champion.

ARE YOU MAN ENOUGH TO FIGHT WITH ME?

First fighting game to use combos
Street Fighter II was the first-ever fighting game to introduce the concept of the combo. This term describes a series of deadly moves that can be triggered by a combination of button techniques, which can, if well executed, be relied upon to drop all but the most skilful (or lucky) opponent.

The arcade version set two more significant "firsts" in the history of fighting games. The cabinet was the one of the first to feature an eight-way joystick and six button controls, and it was the **first game to offer a choice of eight different playable characters**.

Fastest-selling downloadable fighting game
Released on 2 August 2006, *Street Fighter II: Hyper Fighting* is the fastest-selling downloadable fighting game on XBLA. Within 24 hours of release, hundreds of matches were being played every hour, either as single-player or head-to-head matches.

First game to be based on a movie… that was based on a game
Released in 1995, the game *Street Fighter: The Movie* is the first video game to be based on a movie that was based on a game. The title featured digitised graphics from the movie release, and was developed both for arcades and the home console market.

Most cloned fighting game
Although far from being the first fighting game ever released, *Street Fighter* became the most cloned fighting game after the success of *Street Fighter II* ensured its dominant presence in the market place. Original features of the game, such as combos, arenas and dedicated fighter profiles and characteristics, are now standard features in every other successful fighting game.

LEAST POPULAR FIGHTING GAME SPIN-OFF MOVIE
(INTERNATIONALLY RELEASED)
Street Fighter (1994), starring Kylie Minogue and Jean-Claude Van Damme ❹, is the least popular internationally released video game spin-off movie ever. It was torn to shreds by the critics, panned by fans and regularly features in the IMDB list of the worst movies of all time.

Most re-released fighting game

Since its initial release in 1987, *Street Fighter* ❶ has been re-released in a huge variety of updates and special editions. The current total stands at 74, excluding versions that have appeared in different guises or feature only a limited number of core characters.

❝ *Street Fighter has sold over 25 million console games and 500,000 arcade units, generating more than a billion dollars in revenue.* ❞

www.variety.com, 29 October 2006

TRIVIA

➲ *Street Fighter II* ❺ was followed by a plethora of updates, including *Super Street Fighter II: Turbo* ❸, which added the "SUPER" power bar, faster speeds and alternative endings for each character.

➲ The *Street Fighter* animated television series began with an episode called *The Adventure Begins* ❷; the second – and final – series ended with an episode called *Final Fight*. In total, 26 episodes aired in the US between 1995 and 1997.

➲ Twin Galaxies approved a record high score of 1,400,100 points for Brian Farris of Tacoma, Washington, USA, on *Street Fighter II: Hyper Fighting* – a favourite among many pro gamers, and one that Twin Galaxies judge Mike Morrow describes as "the perfect gaming engine".

➲ The Twin Galaxies champion on *Street Fighter III: New Generation* is Demetrius Stuwart, North Carolina, USA, who played on level 8 and scored 7,810,400 points.

FACT

An early test version of the arcade cabinet featured a punching pad (rather than buttons), which the player would hit to register one of three attack strengths. The interface was soon abandoned, owing to excessive damage to the pads!

BIGGEST-SELLING
COIN-OPERATED
FIGHTING GAME

When *Street Fighter II* was released into arcades in April 1989 ❻, it proved an instant hit. The series went on to generate sales of more than 500,000 coin-operated games, despite a declining market that had been hit hard by the development of the home console.

MORTAL KOMBAT

PLATFORMS

PC | XBOX 360
XBOX
PS3 | DS
3
PSP | Wii

SPEC

Developer:
Midway
Publisher:
Midway
Initial release:
*Mortal Kombat
(1992), Arcade*

GAMEPLAY

*Back in the
mists of time, the
annual Shaolin
Tournament
was won by
a human-
dragon hybrid
named Goro,
sent by the
evil Shang Tsung
to bring chaos to
Earth so that it might
be conquered by the
Outworld. Now the
Earth's finest warriors
must do battle with the
forces of darkness to
restore balance.*

**Most successful fighting
game franchise** Although a very
popular arcade game, when *Mortal
Kombat* ① was released for the
home market it took an incredible
$1 billion a year in the first few years
of release. Needless to say, the game
very quickly established itself as a
top choice among fighting gamers
the world over.

**Largest ever fighting game
promotional campaign**
According to CNN, in 1995 *Mortal
Kombat* staged the largest ever
promotional campaign for a video
game and its related products.
Leaving aside initial pre-release
promotion, the *Mortal Kombat*
movie opened on 2,000 screens in
the USA on 18 August of that year,
followed by a direct-to-video digital
animation special on 29 August,
a live-action *Mortal Kombat* tour
launched from Radio City Music Hall
in New York on 14 September, an
interactive CD-ROM on 1 October
and finally the release of *Mortal
Kombat 3* the video game on
15 October.

**Most successful
video game spin-off
soundtrack album**
Released on 15 August 1995,
the *Mortal Kombat* soundtrack
album, which accompanied
the $100 million movie, went
platinum within 10 days of
release. The album included
contributions from artists as
diverse as Orbital, Napalm
Death and Traci Lords.

**First video game poster to
be censored** On 22 April 2003,
Britain's Advertising Standard's
Authority (ASA) took the then
unprecedented step of condemning
the poster campaign promoting
Mortal Kombat: Deadly Alliance.
They claimed that the poster –
which showed a "hoodie" wiping his
bloodstained hand on a businessman
above the words "It's in us all" – was
"irresponsible" and "condoned
violence". The poster was promptly
taken out of circulation.

**First fighting
game to
trigger the
set-up
of a
software
ratings board** Established in
1994, the Entertainment Software
Rating Board (ESRB) is an industry
organisation set up in response
to the public reaction to *Mortal
Kombat*. In an effort to avoid
compulsory censorship, the ESRB
set about applying ratings to games
similar to those applied to movies.
The move came as a consequence
of pressure from US Congress.

First one-on-one fighting game to use digitised sprites

The 1992 launch of *Mortal Kombat* offered something that no other beat-'em-up had. In addition to ultraviolence and killing moves, it presented a brand new level of realism through the use of digitised sprites. Rather than using hand-drawn animation characters, the sprites used were based on graphics created using digitised footage of real actors.

Biggest fighting game series

Mortal Kombat has gone through more iterations than any other fighting game series. The eighth instalment is due in 2008. Although *Street Fighter* has been running far longer than *Mortal Kombat*, and has more variations available to buy, it has only reached the fourth change to its core gameplay. *Street Fighter IV* is also expected to arrive in 2008.

TRIVIA

➲ The impaled heads and body parts on display during the Pit stage of the game are based on the real-life features of the production company's employees, including game creators Ed Boon and John Tobias.

➲ The original version of *Mortal Kombat* was based on the Jean-Claude Van Damme movie *Bloodsport* (1988). Frank Dux ② – Van Damme's character in the movie – provided the inspiration for the infamous *Mortal Kombat* warrior Johnny Cage.

❝ *I'm in a hostile environment. I'm totally unprepared. And I'm **surrounded by a bunch of guys who probably want to kick my ass**… it's like being back in high school.* **❞**

Johnny Cage, *Mortal Kombat* (1995)

FACTS

➲ *Mortal Kombat* was the **first fighting game to feature a secret character**: Reptile.

➲ Series co-creator Ed Boon actually appears in the *Mortal Kombat* movie… as the voice of Scorpion.

TEKKEN

PLATFORMS

PC XBOX360
PS1 XBOX
PS2 DS
3 GBA
PSP Wii

SPEC

Developer:
Namco
Publisher:
Namco
Initial release:
Tekken (1994), Arcade

GAMEPLAY

A giant world martial arts championship nears its completion. Eight fighters must battle it out for the prize money and the title of "King of the Iron Fist". (Tekken literally means "Iron Fist".) The player selects a character and enters the ring prepared to fight to the death.

Most successful arcade games supplier

Namco, publishers of *Tekken*, are also the world's most successful arcade games supplier. Customers pay to play the arcade versions of their games nearly 800,000 times a day.

First PlayStation game to sell over one million units

Released for PlayStation in Japan in March 1995 – and the rest of the world in November of that year – Tekken went on to become the first PlayStation game to sell over one million units. *Tekken* remains one of the most successful fighting games of all time.

Most popular character (tournament level)

The fighter Jin Kazama is the most popular character with top-level *Tekken* players. First introduced in *Tekken 3* ①, Kazama became over-powered when changes to the software engine affected gameplay, favouring his high-speed jabs and punches over the more complex moves of other characters.

First fighting game to feature simulated 3D

Tekken was the first fighting game to simulate a 3D appearance. This feature did much to set it apart from existing fighting games such as *Street Fighter* and *Mortal Kombat*. Impressively,

this continued with the Game Boy Advance version released in 2001, *Tekken Advance* ②. Despite the limitations of the handheld device, this featured a pseudo-3D arena in which players were able to sidestep.

2.5 months – the amount of time it took to port *Tekken: Dark Resurrection* to the PS3, according to project director Haruki Suzaki

Best-selling fighting series for PlayStation consoles

The first five iterations of the *Tekken* series have managed to amass sales of over 20 million, making this the best-selling fighting game franchise on PlayStation consoles. This doesn't include the Game Boy Advance version, various spin-off titles (like *Tekken Card Challenge* and the action-adventure *Death By Degrees*) or the 2007 release *Tekken 6*. Add these and you've got one of the best-selling fighting game franchises of all time.

> **❝ We want to make a game that feels great to play, is fun to look at**... *We're putting everything we can into making a sequel that won't disappoint.* **❞**
>
> Katsuhiro Harada, game developer, discussing *Tekken 6*, August 2007

TRIVIA

➲ A comic book based on *Tekken* and called *Tekken Forever* ④ was published by Image Comics in 2001. It failed to live up to the promise of its title and folded after the first issue.

➲ The character of Marshall Law is thought to be based on Bruce Lee ⑤. He looks similar and fights using Master Lee's Jeet Kune Do style.

➲ Namco and Sega are currently looking at the possibilities of creating a crossover game based on *Tekken* and *Virtua Fighter*.

➲ *Tekken* is especially popular with game-playing martial artists, who appreciate the fact that many of the fighting styles are portrayed with relative accuracy.

➲ Ed Boon, creator of *Mortal Kombat*, is a huge fan of *Tekken*, which he describes as his favourite fighting game...

➲ ... but, the same cannot be said for Tomonobu Itagaki, creator of *Dead or Alive*, who claims that "Tekken sucks".

➲ The translator for the American version of the instruction manual for Tekken missed the pun on the character Marshall Law's "Marshall arts", rendering it as the rather less fun "martial arts".

"HOTTEST" FEMALE FIGHTING GAME CHARACTER

In an internet poll of serious martial artists who also happen to play fighting games, the character of Nina Williams ③, from *Tekken*, was voted the "hottest". The barely-clad blonde was admired for her fighting skills and fashion sense. Nina is the only female character to have appeared in every version of *Tekken*, and also starred in her own spin-off game, the 2005 PlayStation 2 title *Death by Degrees*.

FIGURES

4.3 m – copies of *Tekken 5* sold as of March 2007.

9.3/10 – score given to *Tekken 5* by game review website ign.com.

VIRTUA FIGHTER

PLATFORMS

PC
XBOX 360
PLAYSTATION
XBOX
PS2
3DS
PS3
Wii

SPEC

Developer:
Sega
Publisher:
Sega
Initial release:
November (1993),
Arcade

GAMEPLAY

Two fighters meet in a best-two-out-of-three contest, with an additional "instant-win" round in the case of a draw. If victorious, the gamer keeps playing until all other characters have been beaten and then enters a final against "The Boss".

First 3D arcade video game

Virtua Fighter wasn't Sega's first attempt at making a 3D fighting game. In 1983, the company released the first ever 3D arcade video game. *Subroc-3D* was a fighting game that switched between attacking underwater and air enemies and required the player to view the game through a special periscope, which delivered slightly shifted images to each eye in order the create a 3D effect. Sega went on to develop different approaches to 3D fighting.

First polygon-based fighting game

Released in 1993 and featuring hardware developed jointly with aerospace company Lockheed Martin, Sega's original *Virtua Fighter* 2 was the first-ever polygon-based fighting game. This version featured nine characters, each of whom had been rendered in full polygon glory.

First online *Virtua Fighter*

The Xbox 360 version of *Virtua Fighter 5* is the first game in the series to support online gaming through Xbox Live. The creators had initially been resistant to producing an online version of their prestigious fighter for fear that any lag would ruin the game experience.

First fighting game for a 32-bit console

Sega introduced the 32-bit Sega Saturn, pre-loaded with *Virtua Fighter*, in 1995. This was the first-ever console with 32-bit processing. Sega abandoned the platform in 1998 due to poor sales in all territories except for Sega's native Japan, where it outsold both PlayStation and Nintendo 64.

FIRST FEMALE HEAD OF A GAMES STUDIO

Mie Kumagai 1, Head of Research and Development at Sega's Amusement Software labs, is the first female head of a computer games design studio. She was responsible for the development of the *Crazy Taxi*, *Virtual On* and *Virtua Tennis* series, plus the racing game *Initial D Arcade Stage*.

1,500 – number of accessories, such as clothes or hairstyles, that can be used to customise characters in *Virtua Fighter 4: Evolution*

TRIVIA

➲ A "super-deformed" version of *Virtua Fighter 2*, called *Virtua Fighter Kids* **6**, was developed as part of the preparation for *Virtua Fighter 3*. The characters have larger than normal heads and allowed the designers to practice facial and eye movements.

➲ The system mechanics of *Virtua Fighter 4* were so complex that Taka-Arashi, a sumo character **4** who first appeared in *Virtua Fighter 3*, had to be dropped after developers found that they simply couldn't make him work properly.

➲ In *Virtua Quest* – which is yet another version of the game – Sonic the Hedgehog makes an appearance as a golden statue in the main hall.

➲ The introduction of a Quest Mode to *Virtua Fighter 4: Evolution* was inspired by Namco, the developers of the *Soulcalibur* series, who used the feature in *Soul Edge*.

" *I get a lot of inspiration outside of the game industry. I also get inspiration from dreams. Like Dali, the famous painter,* **I get a lot of my inspiration from dreams**. **"**

Yu Suzuki, *Virtua Fighter* producer

Sega's fastest-selling game to date
Virtua Fighter 4 **5**, released in 2001, sold almost 500,000 units during its first weekend on sale. This made it Sega's fastest-selling game ever, and one of the most successful fighting games of all time.

First 3D fighting game
The original *Virtua Fighter* **2** was the first ever 3D fighting game. Released in 1993, it featured 3D characters and arenas and a camera the roamed freely in 3D space. However, the fighters are forced to constantly face each other while they can move forward and back, they can't step out of their opponent's path.

First online fighting game
Sega released the first ever online fighting game in 1998. Called *Net Fighter* **3**, the game was a cross between *Street Fighter II*, *Mortal Kombat* and *Virtua Fighter*.

HOT TIP

To watch a classic victory pose, reach Level 2 Rank with a created fighter, then hold Punch + Kick + Guard after winning.

PROFILE: YU SUZUKI

Yu Suzuki **7** is a leading games designer and producer at Sega. He joined the company in 1983 as a computer programmer and was soon working on games of his own. His first arcade game was *Hang-On,* and he worked on *OutRun* and *After Burner II* before creating *Virtua Fighter* in 1993. In 2003, Suzuki was inducted into the Academy of Interactive Arts and Sciences' Hall of Fame and continues to work for Sega.

FIGHTING GAMES ROUND-UP

FACTS

➥ The *Art of Fighting* series is set in the 1970s and early 1980s, which can be figured out by anyone sharp-eyed enough to notice the birth dates given for the contenders. The series was a prequel to the *Fatal Fury* series.

➥ Anyone who enjoyed *The King of Fighters '94* game might be interested to know that there is a Japanese-only follow-up, which was released in 2004 for PlayStation 2 called *The King of Fighters '94 Re-bout*.

➥ A bug that remained undiscovered during the beta-testing stage of *X-Men vs. Street Fighter* (XSF) resulted in each character being able to perform at least one infinite combo. True fans of the game believe this to be a good thing.

> ❝ Once I decided to start developing games for the Xbox, I realised that there is no point to thinking of things that relate to only one country. **We are the transmitters, and the world is the receiver.** ❞
>
> Tomonobu Itagaki, creator of *Dead or Alive*

First 'create-a-fighter'

Game: *Super Fire Pro Wrestling X Premium*
Publisher: Human Entertainment
Released in 1996, *Super Fire Pro Wrestling X Premium* was the first fighting game that allowed the gamer to create his or her own fighting character. Players could select a set of moves and alter the appearance of their chosen fighter at will, a facility that proved highly popular in later fighting games.

First use of parrying

Game: *Street Fighter III*
Publisher: Capcom
Parrying, a subtle form of blocking designed to unbalance an opponent in order to draw him into a counter-strike, was first introduced to fighting games with the 1997 release of *Street Fighter III* ④. A key element of martial arts, parrying is distinguished from blocking by the way in which it can be adapted, mid-move, to form the basis for any number of retaliatory strikes or throws.

First use of air blocking

Game: *Darkstalkers*
Publisher: Capcom
Air blocking, in which a fighting character is able to block an offensive strike while in mid-air, first appeared in *Darkstalkers* ⑦, released in 1994. This was also the first fighting series to use Capcom's advanced animation engine, which allowed more animation frames per character than other fighting games of the time.

First use of taunting

Game: *Art of Fighting*
Publisher: SNK
The Art of Fighting ③ series, released in 1993, was the first fighting game to introduce taunting. Now a key component of gameplay across a host of similar releases, taunting involves one player "bad mouthing" another – often in a humorous way – and the extent to which it occurs varies from game to game.

FIRST TRIPLE TAG TEAM

Game: *Marvel vs. Capcom 2: New Age of Heroes*
Publisher: Capcom
New Age of Heroes ② was the last in the *Marvel vs. Capcom…* series, but the first to feature three-on-three tag-team fighting ⑤. Released in 2000, it was in every other respect a simplified version of the earlier games in the series and was designed to make fighting games more accessible to the casual player.

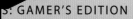

combat-action war game

TRIVIA

➲ Tomonobu Itagaki, lead programmer on the *Dead or Alive* series, came up with the name in response to the fact that the publishers, Tecmo, were in a "win or die" situation over the game's success or failure.

➲ Tecmo, publishers of *Dead or Alive* **8**, began life in 1967 as a supplier of cleaning equipment. In those days the company went by the name Tehkan (pronounced "Tekken"), but officially changed its name to Tecmo in 1986.

➲ 1985's *The Way of the Exploding Fist* **1**, developed by Beam Software, uses a digitised version of Bruce Lee's blood-curdling battle cry during the loading screen. The sound effect, taken from the classic movie *Enter the Dragon*, is one of the first examples of digital voice work in a video game.

8

First tag-team fighting game

Game: *X-Men vs. Street Fighter*
Publisher: Capcom
X-Men vs. Street Fighter **6** was the first tag-team fighting game. Released in 1996, it featured characters both from the *X-Men* and *Street Fighter* arcade games.

Most number of weapons in a fighting game

Game: *Soul Calibur II*
Publisher: Namco
Few fighting games give you the chance to use weapons. One of the most popular is the *Soul Calibur* series, which, unsurprisingly, also features more weapons than any other. *Soul Calibur II* alone contains 209 different weapons.

First co-operative fighter

Game: *Fatal Fury*
Publisher: SNK
Fatal Fury (1991) was the first fighting game to allow two players to join together to fight through each stage. This had been offered before in side-scrolling beat-'em-ups, but never in the classic "2D versus" fighter format.

9

FIRST 3-ON-3 ELIMINATION STYLE MATCH

Game: *The King of Fighters '94* **Publisher:** SNK
The King of Fighters '94 **9** saw the introduction of three-on-three elimination matches. Gamers chose three characters and the order in which they fought, before pitting them against their opponent's team with the aim of knocking out all of them.

FACT

Steve Rogers, aka Captain America, was one of the 50 playable characters in *Marvel vs. Capcom 2: New Age of Heroes*. Sadly, Marvel Comics killed the character off in *Captain America* Vol.5, No.25 (March 2007), after 60 years in print!

9

LIL POISON

FIGURE

LiL Poison's father is sure his son will be a **millionaire** by the time he's 18 – earning not only from tournaments, but also from licensing deals and his own clothing brand.

FACT

Game playing is just a small part of a typical LiL Poison day. His parents are very strict about keeping him in a routine and doing the things that other children his age do. His father explains how his day is structured: "He comes home from school, does homework first, takes a little break– eats, of course – and then plays two games, just two. Then he goes in the pool, plays basketball… Then 8 o'clock comes, and he plays with the team from 8.00 to 10.00 pm."

FACE TO FACE WITH THE WORLD'S YOUNGEST PROFESSIONAL GAMER

Born on 6 May 1998, Victor De Leon III – aka LiL Poison – started gaming at the age of two, and took part in his first competition at the age of four. Major League Gaming recruiters signed him as a Pro Gamer when he was just six, making LiL Poison the world's youngest signed professional gamer. We asked him about the first game he ever played.

I started playing a basketball game, *NBA 2K* ①, for the Dreamcast but I only really remember playing the *Star Wars Episode I* ② game. I was still two years old at that time.

So what's your favourite game?
My favourite game now is *Halo 3* ③. I do play other games too but I like that one the most right now.

How have you been getting on with *Halo 3*? What do you think of it?
To me it's easy. I like it a lot. They made it more fun to play.

Even basic video games require great hand-eye coordination, so for a two-year-old to be playing is incredible. Did video-gaming just seem to come naturally to you?
I guess. My daddy said it did.

Your father and uncle are both gamers, so presumably they helped you out in the beginning?
My daddy and my uncle Gaby [who plays under the name of Poison] both show me things to do and not to do in the game and at tournaments.

And now you are beating them?
Yup, and they hate it! Just kidding – but I do beat them.

Your first tournament was in New York when you were four. Can you tell us a bit about it?
I don't remember a lot of that day. I know we came in fourth place and I was doing better than my uncles and my daddy.

And you've just gone on from strength to strength. You signed a sponsorship deal with a corporate company, how does that work out?
The sponsors help get me and my daddy to tournaments around the country. We have one main sponsor each year, but if anyone is interested in sponsoring me they can look at www.lilpoison.com.

And you even teach people how to play *Halo 2*! How did you get into that?
My dad and I taught people to be better *Halo 2* ④ players but I stopped because it got too busy. I have to do homework and practice for myself.

How many hours of gaming practice do you do a day?
I always played about two hours a day. Maybe more if there is nothing else to do but my daddy and mom don't let me play too much.

> **"** He kind of passed me when he was four. **I just couldn't keep up with him**. I became sort of a coach, but every time I told him something, he'd say, 'I know, daddy' **"**
>
> Victor De Leon II,
> LiL Poison's father

FACT

LiL Poison has taken the world by storm, appearing in countless magazines and newspaper interviews, as well as a handful of TV programmes. A full-length documentary about his life is due for theatrical release in 2008.

You have lots of other interests, too, such as sports, drawing and your pets, not to mention your school work. How do you fit it all in?

I like to swim in the summer and play basketball. I draw a lot and play with my toys and watch *SpongeBob* 5 . Me and my uncle know all the episodes by heart, it's so funny. I have two dogs and a hamster. My dogs' names are Rocky and Scruffy and my hamster is called Cortana. And I do my homework all the time. I have to or else my daddy and mommy won't let me play.

Do you think you'll be playing video games when you're 18?

I don't know what I am going to do then, but if there are cool games I think I will be playing them.

Have you got any tips that you can pass on to other gamers?

To remember that it's a video game and video games have glitches. So if something doesn't happen the way you want it to happen don't get mad, just try again.

SHOOTING GAMES

OUTLINE

Shooting games are often first-person, in which the action is viewed from the protagonist's perspective (below), but overhead or on-rails shoot-'em-ups continue to be a vibrant sub-genre.

SHOOTING GAMES, IN THEIR VARIOUS GUISES, ARE THE OLDEST AND MOST ENDURING OF THE VIDEO GAME GENRES, AND THEIR POPULARITY HAS NEVER BEEN GREATER THAN IT IS TODAY.

For as long as we've had video games we've had shooting video games. There's some debate about what exactly constitutes the **first ever video game** – contenders include A. S. Douglas's *OXO*, a noughts and crosses game developed for the EDSAC computer in 1952, or William Higinbotham's *Tennis for Two*, created in 1958 on an oscilloscope. But it's clear that the very **first shooting game** also reaches back to the earliest days of the medium: *Spacewar!* was created in 1961, by MIT students Martin Graetz, Steve Russell and Wayne Wiitanen on a DEC PDP-1, and consists of two spaceships firing missiles at each other, viewed from an overhead perspective.

Since then, the genre has evolved and blossomed across countless worlds and inspired a multitude of niche sub-genres. Early shooters, like *Space Invaders* 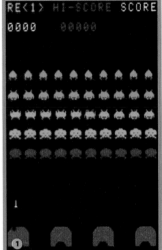, *Galaxian* and *Scramble*, all saw the action viewed from overhead or from the side. These have given way to several modern variants that are undergoing a renaissance thanks to the ability to download and play such games on the PlayStation 3, Xbox 360 and Wii.

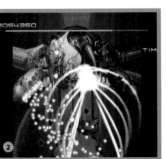

On-rail shooters, in which the action progresses in 3D along a predetermined path, include titles such as *Panzer Dragoon* and *Rez*. Arena shooters, such as *Robotron: 2084* and *Geometry Wars: Retro Evolved*, take place in a fixed arena with the action viewed from overhead. But the most popular of these types of games are scrolling shooters, where the action is either viewed from overhead, as in *Radiant Silvergun* or *Ikaruga* ②, or from the side, as in *Gradius V* ③ or *R-Type*. There's even a further sub-genre: the danmaku shooter – a Japanese offshoot of the scrolling shooter in which players weave through screens that are almost literally full of bullets, such as *Giga Wings* or *DoDonPachi*.

TIMELINE

1961	**1971**	**1980**	**1993**	**1997**
1961: A group of MIT students create *Spacewar!* – the first ever shooting game	1971: Nutting Associates produces *Computer Space*, the first arcade video game	1980: Williams releases *Defender* 5	1993: id Software releases *Doom*	1997: Rare's *GoldenEye: 007* is released
		1984: Nintendo releases *Duck Hunt*	1994: Sega releases *Virtua Cop*	1998: ESP releases *Radiant Silvergun*
	1978: Cinematronics releases *Space Wars*	1992: id Software releases *Wolfenstein 3D*	1996: Apogee Software releases *Duke Nukem 3D*	1998: Sierra Studios releases *Half-Life*

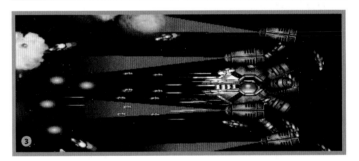

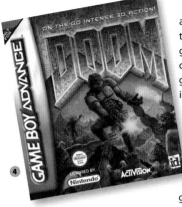

ON-THE-GO INTENSE 3D ACTION!

DOOM

GAME BOY ADVANCE

LICENSED BY Nintendo

ACTIVISION

id

4

It was id Software's *Wolfenstein 3D* and *Doom* **4** that really defined the FPS as we know it today. Those games laid down a template that continues to form the basis of the genre. It's a genre that, thanks to improved technology, has been used to recreate historical conflicts with pinpoint accuracy, or conjure up exotic sci-fi worlds with rather less respect for realism. It's a genre that allows players to experience high-octane, intense gunfights, or stealthily sneak around; to play on their own or in teams. It's a genre that has reached its apogee with games like *Halo* and *Half-Life 2*.

But the mainstay of the genre today is undoubtedly the first-person shooter (FPS), in which players see the action through the eyes of the game's protagonist. (In third-person shooters, players look over their character's shoulder.)

TRIVIA

➲ The US Army released *America's Army* **9**, a first-person shooter in 2002. It was designed as a recruitment tool.

➲ Perhaps the most famous shooting game never to have been released is *Duke Nukem Forever*. Development started in April 1997 and is still ongoing, which has helped it to win top spot in *Wired* magazine's Vaporware Awards in 2001, 2002, 2005 and 2006.

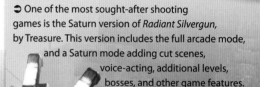

9

➲ One of the most sought-after shooting games is the Saturn version of *Radiant Silvergun*, by Treasure. This version includes the full arcade mode, and a Saturn mode adding cut scenes, voice-acting, additional levels, bosses, and other game features.

8

5 1

1999

1999: Electronic Arts releases *Medal of Honor*

1999: First public beta of *Counter-Strike*

2000: Eidos releases *Deus Ex*

6

2001

2001: Microsoft releases *Halo: Combat Evolved*

2001: Sega releases *Rez*

2002: Electronic Arts releases *Battlefield 1942* **6**

2002

2002: The US Army releases *America's Army*

2002: Nintendo releases *Metroid Prime* **7**

2003: Activision releases *Call of Duty*

2006

2006: Sony releases *Resistance* **8**

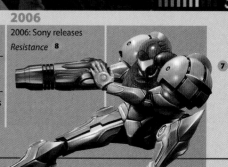

7

DOOM

PLATFORMS

PC
XBOX 360
PS
XBOX
PS2
DS
PS3
GBA
Wii

SPEC

Developer:
id Software
Publisher:
Various
Initial release:
Doom *(1993), PC*

GAMEPLAY

This first-person shooter is experienced through the eyes of the main character: the only surviving human on the Martian moon Phobos, where a series of secret experiments by a military-industrial conglomerate have unleashed the hordes of Hell. This sole survivor is faced with the task of fighting his way through unrelenting waves of demonic entities to make it out alive.

Fastest collaborative speedrun for *Doom*

The fastest collaborative speedrun (where all four levels of the game are recorded separately) of the original *Doom* ❶ is "Doom Done Quicker", a run through by an anonymous group of gamers that takes just 16 min 5 sec, set on 10 December 2000.

Fastest completion time for *Doom 2*

The shortest time taken to complete *Doom 2* ❷ by a single player on the "Ultra-Violence" skill level is 26 min 9 sec, set on 28 December 2003 by Radek Pecka of the Czech Republic. Radek also holds the record for the fastest two-player time, along with Vincent Catalaa. The pair completed the game in 22 min 27 sec on 7 April 2005.

Fastest time for *Doom* 3

With the skill level set at "Marine", French engineering student Jérôme Bouzillard set a time of 1 hr 9 min 37 sec for the completion of *Doom 3* ❸ on 18 November 2006. (For speedrun purposes, timing stops after each fade-to-black at the end of a level and resumes after the loading screen disappears.)

Most Powerful gun in the *Doom* series

The most powerful gun in the *Doom* series is the BFG9000. BFG is commonly believed to be an abbreviation for "Big Fragging Gun", though in the paperback novel it is referred to as the "Big Freaking Gun", and in the Hollywood movie it is described on a computer monitor as a "Bio Force Gun".

First networked deathmatch

Doom was the first FPS that enabled players to engage in a deathmatch (where each player tries to kill as many other players as possible) over a network. Indeed, the creators of *Doom* were responsible for creating the word "deathmatch".

TRIVIA

➲ It's difficult to determine the most modded first-person shooter, but it's fair to say that *Doom* is probably a serious contender. The id Software FTP archive contains over 13,000 WAD files, created by users to modify the original game in some way. Indeed, the *Doom* engine was built from the ground up to support user modification, with game data such as levels, graphics, sound effects and music stored separately from the game engine in these WAD files, which, according to the game's initial design document, stands for "Where's All the Data?"

➲ In addition to inspiring several novels and comic books, *Doom* also inspired a Hollywood movie starring Rosamund Pike, Karl Urban and The Rock. Its soundtrack was written by Clint Mansell, the former lead singer and guitarist of the British band Pop Will Eat Itself.

THE NAME OF THE GAME

John Carmack ④ , the creator of *Doom,* claims that the inspiration for the name of the original game came from the 1986 Tom Cruise movie *The Color Of Money.* In a scene where Cruise's character Vincent Lauria arrives at a pool hall and is asked what he has inside his cue case, the cocky hustler replies with a grin: "Doom".

QUAKE

PLATFORMS

PC | XBOX 360
PS3 | XBOX
PS2 | DS
PS1 | PSP
PSP | Wii

SPEC

Developer:
id Software
Publisher:
Activision
Initial release:
Quake (1997), PC

GAMEPLAY

A series of fast-paced first-person shooters take you – an anonymous soldier – on a journey through a portal into unknown dimensions in an attempt to stop an alien race (known as the Strogg) from capturing Earth. The gameplay takes place across multiple storylines in multiple games and sends you to a variety of sci-fi and gothic worlds.

First FPS to offer online multiplayer on a console

Quake III Arena 1, released for Sega's Dreamcast on 24 October 2000, was the first major release (and first FPS) to allow real-time networked gaming. It was also possible to connect Dreamcast and PC, allowing console gamers to take on owners of the PC version.

Largest free LAN party

QuakeCon takes place every year in Dallas, Texas, USA. The first was held in August 1996, attended by around 100 people, including a surprise appearance by the id Software development team. It wasn't until the following year, however, that id Software took an active role in the organisation of the event. The most recent event, *QuakeCon 2007*, was attended by over 7,000 gamers, took up 6,500 m² (70,000 ft²) and featured two tournaments, each with a cash prize of $50,000.

The first example of machinima animation

Diary of a Camper was created in 1996 by United Ranger Films, using id Software's *Quake* 3. Machinima is a term coined in 1998 to describe the use of game engines to create animated films. *Diary of a Camper* tells a rather simple story, by the

FIRST GAME ENGINE TO FEATURE SPLINE-BASED CURVED SURFACES

id Tech 3, the engine behind *Quake III Arena*, was the first to allow spline-based curved surfaces in a game. This technology renders and slots together a series of small geometric shapes in order to create the impression of a smooth surface, so gone are the flat, 2D sprites of its predecessors. Other features of the engine include improved animation (thanks to the use of vertex movements), a high-level shader language and a method for rendering volumetric fog.

standards of current machinima, in which a team of marines engages in battle with a lone sniper – who turns out to be *Quake* co-creator John Romero.

Fastest *Quake* speedrun The quickest *Quake* finish was achieved not by an individual but by a group. The video "Quake Done Quick" splices these Nightmare difficulty speedruns together to create a total time of 19 min 49 sec.

It has spawned several sequels that have improved that time. **The fastest is "Quake Done Quick With A Vengeance"**, a Nightmare run in 12 min 23 sec! It was created on 13 September 2000 by Markus Taipale, Peter Horvath, Attila Csernyik, Sergi Cami, Aleksander Osipov, Ingmar Poerner and Ilkka Kurkela.

TRIVIA

➲ *Quake* was one of the earliest shooters to popularise "rocket jumping" (where players fire rockets at their own feet). However, the **first game to feature rocket jumping** was *Rise of the Triad*, released in 1994.

➲ Up until *Quake IV* **2** the series had its own dedicated engine; this was replaced in *Quake IV* with the *Doom 3* (id Tech 4) engine.

➲ At the Red Annihilation *Quake* tournament in 1997, co-creator John Carmack gave his 1987 Ferrari 328 GTS to the winner, Dennis "Thresh" Fong.

HOT TIP

Games in the *Quake* series feature various Easter eggs and hidden secrets. There's a secret credits room in *Quake*, found in The Underearth level by shooting all of the pictures of demons. And, in *Quake II*, you can view pictures of the development team in a secret room after destroying the final boss; just look for the crack on the wall after the battle.

THE FIRST ALL-FEMALE *QUAKE* TOURNAMENT **4**

In July 1997, more than 100 entrants competed in the first all-female *Quake* tournament for a share of the $10,000 prize pot. The overall winner was Kornelia "Queen of Quake" Takacs **4** from Budapest, Hungary.

COUNTER-STRIKE

PLATFORMS

PC · XBOX 360 · PS · XBOX · PS2 · DS · 3 · Wii

1

3

3

SPEC

Developer:
Valve
Publisher:
Vivendi Universal (PC),
Microsoft Game Studios
(Xbox)
Initial release:
Counter-Strike: Beta
(1999), PC

GAMEPLAY

In what began life
as a modification of
Valve's Half-Life, a gang
of terrorists face-off
against a team of
counter-terrorists across
a series of rounds. This
is considered, by many
PC players, to be the
ultimate online shooter.

Most successful game mod
ever Counter-Strike **1** was
originally a modification of Valve's
Half-Life game. It was first unveiled
as a public beta on 18 June 1999
and went on to sell over 9 million
retail copies worldwide on two
different platforms (PC and Xbox).
A game mod is a modification to an
original game made by members
of the public.

Most widely played online
first-person shooter
Since early 2000, Counter-Strike has
been the most widely played online
first-person shooter in the world.
It generates over 6 billion player
minutes every month, and averages
at least 270,000 simultaneous
players at any one time.

First gaming clan to legally
bind their players to a clan
On 1 February 2003 the Swedish
clan SK Gaming issued contracts to
several Counter-Strike players. SK
Gaming was also the first western
electronic sports club to receive a fee
for a player transfer, when on 18 May
2004 rival clan – Team NoA –
bought Ola "elemeNt" Moum (born
Krivopalov Evgeniy, 17 January 1986)
out of his contract.

Most action gamers
playing on a single server
On 27 November 2004, at
DreamHack Winter in Jönköping,
Sweden, a team from Microsoft and
Unisys sustained 1,073 gamers
playing Counter-Strike on a single
Unisys ES7000 server. At DreamHack
2006, the same organisers set the
record for the **largest LAN (local
area network) party**, with 9,184
participants on 8,521 machines.

2

FIRST GAMING CLAN
TO BE REPRESENTED
BY A SPORTS AGENT
Swedish Counter-Strike clan Ninjas in Pyjamas
(or NiP) **2** has been represented by sports agent
Johan Strömberg since January 2005. Johan has
also represented soccer and hockey players
across Sweden.

First game engine to be optimised for 64-bit processors

Valve's *Source* engine debuted in October 2004 with *Counter-Strike: Source* ③. The "game engine" is the software used to craft a virtual world – a suite of tools that help designers create the core game and determine the logic and structure of the gameplay.

ELECTRONIC SPORTS WORLD CUP

The Electronic Sports World Cup is an international professional gaming championship that has been held since 2003. Winners of the *Counter-Strike* competitions include Pentagram ④ (Poland) in 2007 and SK Gaming (see opposite) in 2006.

COUNTER-STRIKE LEADERBOARD 07

	TEAM		POINTS
1	Pentagram (Poland)	▲1	480
2	fnatic (Sweden)	▼1	452
3	Made In Brazil (Brazil)	▲7	298
4	SK Gaming (Sweden)	new	234
5	69°N-28°E (Finland)	▲1	162
6	H2K.Thermaltake (Denmark)	new	115
7	Meet Your Makers (Norway)	▼4	90
8	X7-Hacker (China)	▼3	89
9	eSTRO (S. Korea)	▼2	49
10	Team NoA (Denmark)	new	33

Source: Gotfrag.com (19 April 2007)

TRIVIA

➲ *Counter-Strike* originally featured real-world weapons, presented with their actual names and manufacturers (such as the Glock 18, or Colt M4A1). They were given fictional names from version 1.6 onwards in order to avoid trademark infringement.

➲ In 2001, Japanese publisher Namco released *Counter-Strike Neo*, a version of the game that was adapted for use in arcades. Several changes were implemented to make it more suitable to the tastes of Japanese gamers, including modifying the character models and implementing a "karma" system that punishes players for hiding and sniping.

FACTS

The Cyberathlete Professional League is a professional gaming organisation that holds tournaments open to all registrants. Past *Counter-Strike* World Champions include fnatic (New Zealand, 2006), SK Gaming (Germany, 2002, 2003 and 2005) and Team NoA (Norway, 2004).

In 2007, the league announced that they would be hosting two 64-team *Counter-Strike* tournaments (*Source* and *1.6*) at their Extreme Winter Championships, due to take place in December 2007.

HIGHEST-EARNING COUNTER-STRIKE TEAM (2007)

The Polish team Pentagram ④ (aka Pentagram G-shock aka PGS) – comprising Filip "Neo" Kubski, Jakub "kuben" Gurczynski, Lukas "LUq" Wnek, Mariusz "Loord" Cybulski and Wiktor "TaZ" Wojtas – made more money playing *Counter-Strike* in 2007 than any other competing clan, earning over $50,000 in prize money from winning the 2007 Electronic Sports World Cup ($40,000) and coming second in the shgOpen (€10,000).

> **"** *It's definitely hard, you got to* **keep playing**. **"**
>
> David "Zid" Chin, *Counter-Strike* Electronic Sports World Cup qualifier

HALF-LIFE

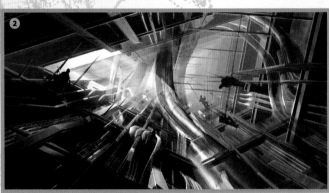

HλLF-LIFE

PLATFORMS

PC
XBOX 360
XBOX
PS2
PS3
DS
Wii

SPEC

Developer:
Valve
Publisher:
Various
Initial release:
Half-Life (1998), PC

GAMEPLAY

This award-winning first-person shooter follows the adventures of Dr Gordon Freeman on his first day in a new job at an underground research facility.

Best-selling first-person shooter of all time (PC)

Half-Life 1 has sold over 8 million copies since its release in 1998, making it the best-selling first-person shooter on the PC. Together with sequels and spin-offs, the franchise has sold over 16 million copies, and its narrative-inspired design has influenced subsequent generations of shooters ever since.

Largest digital distribution channel for games

Half-Life 2 2 was one of the most popular games available through Valve's *Steam* service – a digital distribution and digital rights management platform that opened in 2002. The service is now used by third-party publishers and is available in 18 languages by 13 million active users. As of September 2007, over 200 PC titles

were available for purchase and download. *Steam* also monitors your hardware specification, allowing publishers to target games to specific customers and offer after-sales rewards. The **first after-sales offer from *Steam*** was for users with a Radeon graphics card, who were given free copies of *Half-Life 2: Lost Coast* and *Half-Life 2: Deathmatch*.

FASTEST *HALF-LIFE 2* SPEED RUN

As with many other first-person shooters, *Half-Life* and *Half-Life 2* have been used by dedicated gamers to create "speed runs" – attempts to play through as quickly as possible. The fastest complete-game *Half-Life 2* speed run is 1 hr 36 min 57 secs, achieved by the "*Half-Life 2* Done Quick" (HL2DQ) team on 8 March 2006.

❚❚ *The* **right man in the wrong place** *can make all the difference in the world.* **❚❚**

G-Man, *Half-Life 2*

1

2

TRIVIA

➲ *Half-Life* appears in season 1 of TV series *Lost*. Sayid's friends discuss the effectiveness of Gordon Freeman's crowbar as a weapon. As a nod to this Valve added hidden "Dharma" logos from *Lost* in *Half-Life 2*.

➲ The Black Mesa security office is located in Sector 7G. Coincidentally (or not), Homer Simpson is Safety Inspector for Sector 7G at Springfield's Nuclear Power Plant.

➲ *Half-Life*'s script was written by Marc Laidlaw, a sci-fi author who has also written several novels. Two of them – *The Orchid Eater* and *The 37th Mandela* – can be found in Gordon Freeman's locker.

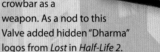

engine, which simulates Newtonian physics, taking into account mass, gravity, friction, and so on, of each object in the game.

First PC game to feature developer commentary An additional level of *Half-Life 2: Lost Coast* was available for download shortly after release. This level incorporates floating speech bubbles (known as commentary nodes) in the game world. Interacting with these nodes plays an audio commentary in which the developers discuss the creation of that area. The 2007 *Orange Box* version contains over two-and-a-half hours of commentary activated in this way.

First game to feature a Gravity Gun In *Half-Life 2*, players can use the Gravity Gun to pick up virtually anything in the environment before shooting that object as a projectile. This complex functionality demonstrates the versatility and fidelity of the sophisticated Havok

HIGHEST RATED SHOOTER BY *PC GAMER* MAGAZINE

Half-Life 2 received an incredible score of 98% from *PC Gamer* magazine (US edition), equalling their highest ever score (awarded to *Sid Meier's Alpha Centauri*). In the magazine's August 2007 poll of the Top 100 games of all time, it sits at No. 3. Readers of *Computer Gaming World* also voted *Half-Life 2* as their best game of all time in their 200th edition, and Gamespy.com awarded the game a perfect score in their review ("arguably the best first-person shooter ever"), as did the *New York Times* (25 November 2004).

HALO

PLATFORMS

PC   XBOX360

PS3   XBOX

PS2   3DS

3   GAMECUBE

GBA   Wii

SPEC

Developer:
Bungie Studios
Publisher:
Microsoft
Initial release:
*Halo: Combat Evolved
(2001), Xbox*

GAMEPLAY

*Players take on the role
of the Master Chief,
a power-armoured
commando on a bid
to save Earth from
the alien forces of the
Covenant. But on a
mysterious ring-shaped
world, a far more sinister
threat emerges…*

**Best-selling game on the
Xbox** *Halo 2* ⑥ has so far sold
over 8.3 million copies. The second
best-selling game on the Xbox is
Halo: Combat Evolved, which has
sold over 5.7 million copies.
Halo 3 ②, became the **fastest-
selling preordered game** by
the time of its initial release on
26 September 2007, with pre-sales
of 1.7 million units in the US alone.

HIGHEST GROSSING GAME (ONE DAY)

On 25 September 2007, the release of *Halo 3* generated $170 million worth
of first-day sales in the USA alone – nearly triple the $60 million that *Spider-
Man 3* made on its first day of release. Even in its opening weekend, *Spidey-3*
failed to beat *Halo 3*, achieving "just" $151 million! The "Midnight Madness"
launch at 10,000 stores made the *Halo* threequel the **most successful
entertainment product launch** in history.

And, according to Microsoft, over 1.4 million Xbox Live users
played it online during the first
24 hours, giving the company
another record for
the **busiest day
in Xbox Live
history**.

Longest ban from Xbox Live
An anoymous US gamer using
the gamertag | Scar | managed
to unwittingly download *Halo 3
Epsilon*, a version of the shooter
used by Bungie and Microsoft
employers to test and refine the
gameplay. | Scar | played the
game with his console connected
to Xbox Live, and quickly came
to the attention of Microsoft. In
September 2007, his gamertag and
console account was banned until
31 December 9999.

Most successful Machinima
series "Machinima" is the term
given to movies compiled using
actual game footage edited
together to form a new coherent
story. A production entitled *Red
vs. Blue* created using the
multiplayer modes in *Halo:
Combat Evolved* ③, and later
Halo 2, generated estimated
annual revenues of $200,000,
with between 650,000 and
1,000,000 viewers "tuning
in" weekly to see the online
episodes. Originally created
independently, it soon gained
the blessing of developer
Bungie, who later
commissioned special
promotional episodes.

820,000 – the number of gamers who took part in the free multiplayer beta-testing for *Halo 3* in 2007, according to *USA Today*

HALO RUNS (LEGENDARY)

source: speeddemosarchive.com

LEVEL	TIME	DATE	NAME
Pillar of Autumn	5 min 51 sec	27 Feb 2005	Cody Miller
Halo	15 min 29 sec	1 Jul 2004	Brandon Raffensperger
Truth and Reconciliation	24 min 21 sec	1 Jul 2004	Cody Miller
Silent Cartographer	4 min 18 sec	1 Jul 2004	Andrew Halabourda
Assault on the Control Room	6 min 53 sec	1 Jul 2004	Sean Oehrle
343 Guilty Spark	7 min 41 sec	1 Jul 2004	Tristan Cahill
The Library	20 min 57 sec	1 Jul 2004	Cody Miller
Two Betrayals	25 min 03 sec	1 Jul 2004	Taylor Jones
Keyes	9 min 23 sec	11 Mar 2005	Andrew Halabourda
The Maw	10 min 00 sec	27 Jan 2005	Cody Miller

Fastest completion: *Halo 2* In August 2005, America's Cody Miller completed *Halo 2* on the Xbox (at Legendary difficulty) in 3 hr 17 min 50 sec, without dying. Cody is the first champion to finish the game on the "Legendary" setting without losing a life.

TRIVIA

⮌ The history of the game's protagonist, Master Chief, and several aspects of the universe, have been fleshed out in a series of spin-off books and graphic novels ⑤. Other merchandising includes action figures ①.

⮌ Although there is no officially confirmed link between Bungie's *Marathon* trilogy and its later *Halo* series, there are several points of continuity. The *Marathon* logo can be found throughout *Halo: Combat Evolved*, including on the Pillar of Autumn starship and on Captain Keyes' chest. Master Chief also wears Mjolnir ④ armour and Mjolnir-equipped soldiers are mentioned several times in *Marathon*.

❝ Halo 3 *is a cultural touchstone,* **a Star Wars for the thumbstick** *generation.* **❞**

Wired *magazine, September 2007*

FIGURES

10,000 – the number of US retailers who opened their doors at 12.01 am on 25 September 2007 – *Halo 3* launch day.

20,000 – an estimate, in pounds, of the weight of pizzas eaten by Bungie staff over the 36 months it took to create *Halo 3*.

UNREAL

PLATFORMS

PC   XBOX 360

XBOX

PS2   DS

3

Wii

SPEC

Developer:
Epic Games
Publisher:
Atari/Midway Games
Initial release:
Unreal (1998), PC

GAMEPLAY

A series of futuristic story-driven and arena-based first-person shooters originally developed for the PC and now available on console. The game is renowned for its multiplayer capabilities and exciting player vs player deathmatches, where the aim is to be the last man standing!

First game to be created using the Unreal engine

The various iterations of the Unreal engine have been used to power over a hundred games, from *Harry Potter and the Philosopher's Stone* to *Rainbow Six: Vegas*. Perhaps unsurprisingly, its first outing was the original *Unreal* game in 1998.

First computer-controlled deathmatch opponent

The Reaper Bot, created for *Quake* by programmer Steve Polge , who would go on to work for Epic Games on the *Unreal Tournament* series, was the first computer-controlled deathmatch opponent. Indeed, *Unreal* was the first game to officially include deathmatch bots created by the programmers.

Quickest *Unreal* speed run

On 4 April 2005, Mark Freyenberger blazed through the original *Unreal* on the easy skill level in the lightning time of just 49 min 18 sec.

First console game to receive a downloadable patch

Unreal Championship on the Xbox featured a small software update patch that was issued to address performance issues with the game.

First beat-'em up character to star in a first-person shooter

The character Raiden, originally one of the cast members of the *Mortal Kombat* series of beat-'em ups, went on to star in *Unreal Championship 2: The Liandri Conflict* ②. The game also featured commentary by the *Mortal Kombat* announcer, Shao Kahn.

First console game to support player modifications

Although several previous console games have allowed players to customise content or create maps for shooters using an in-game editor, *Unreal Tournament 3* ③ on the PlayStation 3 is the first console game to support full user-defined "mods". This sort of sophisticated creation of content and wholesale modification has become a hallmark of first-person shooters on the PC.

1.5 million – number of downloads of the demo version of *Unreal Tournament 2004*, one week after it was released on 11 February 2004

> **❝** *The boys at Epic learned from their mistakes in* Unreal, *and it **really shows in** Unreal Tournament… they more than compensated by including **some great teamplay**.* **❞**
>
> Gonzo, Ars Technica

WORLD CYBER GAMES

Unreal Tournament was one of the games featured at the World Cyber Games (WCG) in 2001 and 2002, allowing players to fight it out to become the best *Unreal Tournament* player in the world.

RANK	WCG 2001	WCG 2002
1	GitzZz (Germany)	GitzZz (Germany)
2	XSPain (UK)	Shaggy (UK)
3	Xan (South Korea)	eVeNfLoW (Australia)

Most overall kills in a 30-minute *Unreal Tournament 3* deathmatch

To celebrate the November 2007 European launch of Epic's *Unreal Tournament 3*, clans Team Dignitas (two player) and Four Kings (three players) gathered in Birmingham, UK, to play a 30-minute deathmatch. In a tense and closely fought battle, Frederiek van Gammeren (aka Frantic) of Dignitas emerged the ultimate victor with 131 kills. He respawned 74 times during the match.

GAME MODS

One of the factors behind the enduring popularity of the *Unreal* series is the ease with which gamers can create mods. Tools like the *UnrealEd* map editor and the *UnrealScript* scripting language have been embraced by gamers and used to create an ever-growing array of content, from "mutators" that make small tweaks to gameplay, such as *Counter-Strike* clone *Tactical Ops* ④, to total conversions that replace almost the entire game.

HOT TIP

For an instant kill, use the ASMD shockrifle and fire an orb. If you then hit the orb with the beam function just as it reaches your target you will create a lethal explosion.

TOM CLANCY

Tom Clancy's

PLATFORMS

PC	XBOX 360
PLAYSTATION	XBOX
PS3	DS
3	
PSP	Wii

GAMEPLAY

A series of stealth action and squad-based tactical shooters that take place in a universe conceived by best-selling author Tom Clancy. Although all of the Clancy games take place inside the same universe, it's very rare for the storylines to cross over. Titles include popular franchises such as Rainbow Six, Ghost Recon and Splinter Cell. Typically, each game requires you to take on the role of an elite US Special Forces team on a mission to save the world from terrorists or evil military groups.

Fastest *Splinter Cell* speedruns
Oskar Lundquist completed the original *Splinter Cell* in 1 hr 21 min 45 sec on 27 August 2006. The fastest time on *Splinter Cell Pandora Tomorrow* [1] is held by Wesley Corron, who blazed through normal difficulty in 1 hr 11 min 45 sec on 11 December 2004. The best completion time for *Splinter Cell Chaos Theory* is just 1 hr 16 min 34 sec, made by Mathew Thompson on 30 August 2006. This record is made even more impressive by the fact that Mathew played the game on the "expert" difficulty.

Best-selling squad shooter
Tom Clancy's Rainbow Six [2] has consistently out-performed every other title in the squad shooter genre. To date this franchise has seen over 20 retail releases with over 15.5 million sales worldwide.

Largest foreign-owned games studio in China
The Shanghai UBI Computer Software Co. Ltd opened in 1996 and is responsible for several Tom Clancy titles, including the PlayStation 2 version of *Ghost Recon Advanced Warfighter* [3] and the Xbox version of *Pandora Tomorrow*. The team has over 500 employees.

First game to use dynamic lighting technology on PS2
Ubisoft were proud to announce that *Tom Clancy's Splinter Cell Pandora Tomorrow* was the first PlayStation 2 game to use moving dynamic lighting. This came in the form of a torch, wielded by the ARGUS mercenaries, picking out details in the darkness.

MEET THE FOUNDER
Tom Clancy is a best-selling US author of political thrillers who has sold more than 80 million books. In 1996, he co-founded Red Storm Entertainment, a video-game development house, with former British Royal Navy captain Doug Littlejohns.

First video game launched at a movie festival

Splinter Cell Pandora Tomorrow received its premiere at the 2004 Sundance Film Festival, the first time a video game has debuted at a movie festival. This unique launch – organised by Ubisoft, Motorola and Xbox Live – illustrated the ever-converging movie and games industries.

Largest mobile gaming launch

Mobile-phone versions of *Tom Clancy's Splinter Cell Pandora Tomorrow* were launched on an unprecedented 48 different handsets in over 30 countries in 2006, making this the largest mobile gaming launch. It also remains the UK's highest-rated shoot-'em-up in mobile gaming history, scoring, for example, 9.1/10 on Gamespot.com.

> **"** I wanted a different way in which to tell my stories. Coming up with **concepts for computer games gives me another avenue of creative expression**. **"**
>
> Tom Clancy

TRIVIA

➲ Tom Clancy's work has inspired several Hollywood blockbusters, including *The Hunt for Red October*, *Patriot Games*, *Sum of All Fears* and *Clear and Present Danger*.

➲ *Splinter Cell* protagonist Sam Fisher uses Krav Maga. Developed in Israel, this real-world fighting style is intended to kill or disable an opponent as quickly as possible. It is currently used by government agencies around the world, but is illegal to teach to civilians in many countries.

➲ A movie adaptation of *Rainbow Six* is due for release in 2010. John "Hard Boiled" Woo was originally down to direct, but rumour is that Zack Snyder will be handling both writing and directing. His previous work includes the *300*.

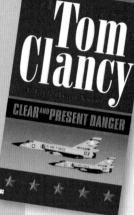

Best "Game of the Year" 2006 (BAFTA)

Tom Clancy's Ghost Recon Advanced Warfighter (on Xbox) picked up the 2006 video game BAFTA for "Game of the Year", plus the award for "Best Technical Achievement". At the 2006 Golden Joystick Awards, it also picked up the Editors' Choice award for Best Game. "... with its gritty realism, intense atmosphere and over-the-shoulder cam, it has to be one of the most absorbing war games in recent years," said CVG. "It got us playing our 360's."

FIGURES

$180 million – the declared value of sales by *Tom Clancy* game developers Ubisoft for the financial quarter ending 30 June 2007.

200 – number of staff working on *Tom Clancy* games during the most intensive periods of development.

22 – countries that Ubisoft operates from, including Canada, Switzerland, South Korea and Finland.

GEARS OF WAR

PLATFORMS

PC · XBOX 360 · XBOX · PS3 · 3DS · 3 · Wii

SPEC

Developer:
Epic Games
Publisher:
Microsoft
Initial release:
Gears of War *(2006)*,
Xbox 360

GAMEPLAY

A third-person shooter set on another planet in a dystopian future, in which players control Marcus Fenix, a member of Delta Squad, and attempt to save humanity from an unremitting alien threat: the Locust Horde.

> **▐▐** *We always held **high hopes** for Gears of War, but we never expected such an overwhelmingly **positive response** from **critics and gamers** all over the world.* **▐▐**
>
> Michael Capps,
> President, Epic Games

Fastest selling original game (Xbox 360)
On 15 December 2006, *Gears of War* became the fastest-selling next-generation game of that year and was the fastest-selling Xbox game at that time. The game, which can be played online, sold more than two million copies in its first six weeks.

First Xbox 360 shooting game to sell out in Japan
Gears of War was released in Japan on 18 January 2007, and became the first Xbox shooting game to reach the top ten chart there. It was also the first shooter to sell out in Japan – a surprise given the lack of popularity for shooters there.

INTERVIEW WITH... CLIFF BLESZINSKI

At the age of six, Cliff Bleszinski saw *Space Invaders* at a neighbour's house and knew what he wanted to do with his life. Now aged 32, "Cliffy B" is lead designer at Epic Games. We asked him about what he was most proud of in *Gears of War*.

I'm most proud of the Lancer, which has a chainsaw bayonet on the end of it. I had wanted to see a weapon like this in a video game for years and we were finally able to realise that vision in *Gears of War*.

What was your day-to-day involvement in the creation of the game?
As designer, I was responsible for the creation of much of the universe, as well as spearheading the fun factor in the title. Basically, making sure that the game is as entertaining and exciting as humanly possible.

What's your high score?
I have slaughtered millions of evil Locust and thus lost count. I'm simply doing my part to help save humanity!

What's next for the GoW trilogy?
Currently we've got the game shipping for Windows XP and Vista.

Biggest driver to usage (Xbox Live) *Gears of War* has proved to be the biggest driver to new paid subscriptions to Xbox Live. Microsoft claim that the game has driven a 50% increase in usage, and Xbox Live is now host to over a million online players. Within two weeks of its launch, *Gears Of War* overtook *Halo 2* as the most played Xbox Live game.

First music single to top the chart after promoting a video game Originally a No.1 Christmas hit in 2003/4, Gary Jules' version of "Mad World" topped the download chart in November 2006 after his version of the Tears for Fears classic was used as background music during the TV commercial for *Gears Of War*.

First console game to use the Unreal 3 engine *Gears of War* was the first console game to use Epic Games' award-winning engine. The engine has proven so popular that many other developers have signed up to use it for future games.

GEARS OF WAR XBOX LIVE LEADERBOARD (SEPT 07)

On the right is the **Warzone Leaderboard** of the top-ranking Xbox Live *Gears of War* players (as of 19 Sept 2007). The games were set up in the following manner:
• A minimum of six players must play "Ranked Games", but only individual scores count
• Game type: Warzone
• Map: Gridlock, Fuel Depot, Escalation, Mansion, Mausoleum, Rooftops, Tyro Station, War Machine, Canals, Clocktower and the two downloadable maps
• No. of rounds: 1–19
• Bleed out time: 5, 10, 20, 30, 60 sec

	NAME	SCORE
1	DatzWassup	500,040
2	man slay3r	462,454
3	IXIWargasmIXI	459,380
4	JayLeo08	446,707
5	iC3 KiMoZ	439,260
6	ManOfProphecy	437,886
7	PFS PrOsTyLe	436,609
8	PhantomFox4	434,523
9	Ender x21x	434,404
10	ETsnipers	433,626

HOT TIP

Littered throughout the game are cog tags (the *GoW* equivalent of dog tags), which can boost your gamerscore points. Finding the 30 tags is tricky, but you will know one is nearby when you see the red cog and skull symbol spray-painted on a wall or object. The small blue tags are found chained together in pairs on the floor.

SHOOTING GAMES ROUND-UP

Most successful first-person shooter ever

Game: *GoldenEye 007*
Publisher: Nintendo

The 1997 James Bond spin-off for the Nintendo 64 continues to feature in the Top 100 (if not Top 10) games of all time, scoring highly for its varied objectives, multiplayer options and original stealth gameplay. It has sold over 8 million copies, ranking it alongside *Halo 2* as the biggest-selling FPS of all time.

Least violent FPS

Game: *Deus Ex*
Publisher: Eidos

It is possible to complete Ion Storm's *Deus Ex* ➊ having killed only three enemies. The game is renowned for its open-ended design, which makes it possible to approach it in a variety of ways, including – thanks to non-lethal weaponry and various stealth options – non-violence.

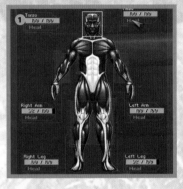

First video game to log high scores

Game: *Sea Wolf*
Publisher: Midway

Released in 1976, *Sea Wolf* was an arcade game that simulated a submarine naval battle. Players viewed the action through a periscope mounted on the machine and fired torpedoes at enemy targets. The high-score appeared on the bottom of the screen, below the current player's score.

First video game to include a personalised high-score table

Game: *Asteroids*
Publisher: Atari

Atari's classic shooter, released in 1979, was the first game to allow players to create a personalised top 10 table for that day's scores.

Highest *Giga Wing* score ever

Game: *Giga Wing*
Publisher: Capcom

J. C. Padilla (USA) achieved a score of 260,805,365,030 on the Sega Dreamcast version of *Giga Wing* ➍ in 2003. The record for the arcade version is 2,954,296,261,700, (2 trillion 954 billion 296 million 261 thousand 700) by Alex Landeros (USA) on 18 June 1998.

FIRST XBOX 360 GAME TO SELL 1 MILLION UNITS IN THE US

Game: *Call of Duty 2*
Publisher: Activision

The second instalment of the *Call of Duty* ➌ franchise was a launch title for the Xbox 360 and the first game on this platform to sell more than 1 million units in the USA alone. To this day, it continues to rank as one of the most successful first-person shooters ever.

$120,000 – the cost in 1960 of the PDP-1 computer, the only machine capable of playing *Spacewar!*, the world's **first shooting game**

Highest ever *Space Invaders* score

Game: Space Invaders
Publisher: *Taito*
The highest verified score ever reached in a game of *Space Invaders* is 55,160 points, set by Donald Hayes (USA) on 7 June 2003. The **highest ever *Space Invaders Part II* score** was set in 1982 by Matt Brass (USA) with 425,230 points. *Space Invaders Part II* (also known as *Space Invaders Deluxe*) was the **first game to include an intermission** – at the end of each level, the last invader flies off on a spaceship that broadcasts an SOS message.

First console-based first-person shooter

Game: *Wolfenstein 3D*
Publisher: id Software
A modified version of Wolfenstein 3D was the first FPS on a console platform. Previously, the massive computational power required to run an FPS game limited the genre to the PC platform. The game was released for the Super Nintendo Entertainment System in Japan on May 5 1993.

⑥

Highest ever *Asteroids* score

Game: *Asteroids*
Publisher: Atari
The highest score ever reached in a game of *Asteroids* by a single individual is 41,336,440, set in 1982 by Scott Safran (USA).

Best-selling first person shooter franchise

Game: *Medal of Honor*
Publisher: Electronic Arts
Originally published for the PlayStation in 1999, *Medal of Honor* ⑤ spawned 11 sequels – including *Medal of Honor: Pacific Assault* ⑥ – and spin-offs which, combined, went on to sell over 27 million copies.

Most players supported by a console first-person shooter

Game: *Resistance: Fall of Man*
Publisher: Sony
The PS3 title *Resistance: Fall of Man* ② allows up to 40 players to participate in a single game, running at 30 frames per second.

First to feature bullet time

Game: *Requiem: Avenging Angel*
Publisher: Ubisoft
Ubisoft's *Requiem: Avenging Angel* was the first game to feature bullet time, a feature that slows down time to allow a player to dodge bullets.

⑤

TRIVIA

↪ The 1997 *DoDonPachi Campaign Version* is believed to be the world's **rarest shooting game** – and a contender for the world's **rarest video game** – as it was released as a limited competition prize. While it is thought that 100 copies of the arcade game are in existence, there is only one genuine board that is on display in an amusement arcade in Tokyo, Japan.

↪ Among the **rarest pieces of video game memorabilia** are the 300 tea cups that were made to promote *Panorama Cotton*, a shoot-'em-up published in 1994 by Japanese publisher Success. To obtain one, players had to enter a random draw by sending in a registration card.

FACTS

The **first shooting game to include a boss character** is arguably the *Galaxian* arcade game ⑦, published in 1979 by Namco. It featured successive waves of attackers, and each wave included a larger flagship that was increasingly hard to shoot down.

PLATFORM GAMES

OUR EXPERT

Oli Welsh started out as a media analyst and translator (he speaks fluent French). He began writing for *Edge* magazine in May 2004 and still contributes to the magazine every month. Oli also writes regularly for games websites Eurogamer.net and GamesIndustry.biz, and his work has appeared in *Official Xbox 360 Magazine* and *NGamer*.

OUTLINE

Platform games are all about jumping. Typically, you need to get from A to B by jumping to platforms over dangerous obstacles. You're at risk from falling and there are usually enemies to avoid or defeat. Many platform games mix in elements from other styles of game: exploration, combat, vehicles and racing, puzzles and minigames.

THE PLATFORM GENRE IS RESPONSIBLE FOR SOME OF THE MOST SUCCESSFUL VIDEO GAMES OF ALL TIME. IT ALSO GAVE BIRTH TO GAMING'S TWO MOST FAMOUS CHARACTERS – MARIO AND SONIC.

The **first true platform game** was the 1981 Nintendo arcade game *Donkey Kong* **1**. It was the first game to star Mario – though he was called Jumpman at the time – and the first game created by legendary Japanese designer Shigeru Miyamoto.

Larger and more sophisticated games started appearing in 1984: *Impossible Mission* influenced later adventure platformers such as *Tomb Raider* with its exploration and puzzles. *Knight Lore* **2** by Ultimate was the **first example of a 3D world** – if not actual 3D graphics – in platform gaming.

In 1985, Nintendo released *Super Mario Bros.* on the NES. Its large, complex scrolling levels changed 2D platformers forever, and it remains the **best-selling video game of all time**, with over 40 million copies sold.

Seeking a mascot to rival Nintendo's Mario, Sega created *Sonic the Hedgehog* **3** in 1991. It was much faster than the Mario games and was a big success. But by 1995 2D platformers were going out of style, although that year Ubisoft's *Rayman* became one of the **best-selling PlayStation games of all time in the UK.**

It was a while before the genre worked in 3D. *Jumping Flash*, a 1995 PlayStation launch game, was the **first platformer in true 3D**, but it was hard to play and didn't sell well. The 1996 game *Crash Bandicoot* **4** had beautiful 3D graphics and some simple 3D gameplay elements, but mostly worked like a 2D game.

It was the same year's *Super Mario 64* for the Nintendo 64 that created the 3D platformer we know

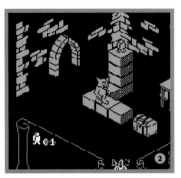

GUINNESS WORLD RECORDS

TIMELINE

	2D PLATFORMERS	ACTION PLATFORMERS	ADVENTURE PLATFORMERS	3D PLATFORMERS
	Jumping action, viewed from the side only	*Platform games featuring combat and/or multiplayer*	*Including puzzles, exploration, story and combat, in 2D or 3D*	*Jumping around in full 3D worlds*
1981	Donkey Kong			
1982	Pitfall!			
1983	Manic Miner	Mario Bros.		
1984	Jet Set Willy		Impossible Mission Knight Lore	
1985	Super Mario Bros.	Ghosts'n'Goblins		
1986		Bubble Bobble	Metroid*	
1987	Rainbow Islands	Mega Man	Head Over Heels	
1988	Super Mario Bros. 3	Contra		
1989		New Zealand Story	Prince of Persia	
1990	Super Mario World			
1991	Sonic the Hedgehog	Turrican		
1992	Kirby's Dream Land		Flashback	
1993		Super Star Wars		
1994	Donkey Kong Country			
1995	Rayman	Earthworm Jim		Jumping Flash!
1996	Yoshi's Island		Tomb Raider*	Crash Bandicoot Super Mario 64
1997		Metal Slug	Oddworld	
1998				Banjo Kazooie Sonic Adventure
1999				Ape Escape Rayman 2 Donkey Kong 64
2000				
2001				Jak and Daxter
2002				Super Mario Sunshine Sly Cooper
2003		Ratchet & Clank*	Prince of Persia: the Sands of Time	
2004	Donkey Kong's Jungle Beat			
2005			Psychonauts	
2006	New Super Mario Bros.			
2007				Super Mario Galaxy

* see Action-Adventure section for more details

TRIVIA

➲ *Donkey Kong's Jungle Beat*, for the GameCube, is the only platform game you control with a musical instrument: it uses the bongo controller from the *Donkey Konga* music game **8** with the player hitting the drums and clapping to run and jump.

➲ Since its release in 1986, arcade platform game *Bubble Bobble* has been converted to run on an impressive 24 different computer and console systems.

➲ Thanks to Mario and Sonic, platform games are the all-time number one titles on five consoles: NES, SNES, N64, Megadrive and Dreamcast. By contrast, there's no platform game in the all-time top five for the PlayStation or the top 10 for PlayStation 2.

today, with its varied gameplay, free camera and emphasis on item collection. Most 3D platformers follow this style, although 1999's *Rayman 2* **5** and 2001's *Jak and Daxter* **6** combined it with stronger storylines and simpler levels to great effect.

Platform games are less popular today than they used to be, with the biggest-selling titles tending to be in the action or adventure sub-genres. Nintendo, the great innovator of the genre, has mostly returned to making 2D platformers, but perhaps 2007's *Super Mario Galaxy* **7** for the Wii can reinvent the joy of jumping.

CREATOR

Celebrated designer **Shigeru Miyamoto** **9** (Japan) counts classic platformers *Donkey Kong* and *Super Mario* among his many creations. Considered by his peers to be the greatest video game designer in the world, Miyamoto's titles are renowned for their imaginative worlds that encourage exploration and discovery. In 1998, Miyamoto became the first person to be inducted into the Academy of Interactive Arts and Sciences' Hall of Fame.

SUPER MARIO

PLATFORMS

PC
XBOX360
PlayStation
XBOX
PS2
3DS
3
GBA
PSP
Wii

SPEC

Developer:
Nintendo
Publisher:
Nintendo
Initial release:
Super Mario Bros.,
(1985), NES

GAMEPLAY

Super Mario Bros. games are platform adventures featuring several worlds made up of many large levels, in which Mario must rescue the princess from the fat dragon Bowser **3**. Mario can run and jump, bop enemies on their heads, throw items and use power-ups. The games are packed with secrets, puzzles, crazy characters and intense tests of platforming skill.

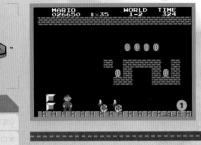

BEST-SELLING VIDEO GAME OF ALL TIME (INCLUDING BUNDLES)

The best-selling video game ever is *Super Mario Bros.* **1**, released by Nintendo for its NES console (called Famicom in Japan) in 1985. It has sold 40.2 million copies worldwide, 10 million more than the second best-selling game (the Game Boy version of *Tetris*). This figure includes copies of the game "bundled" with Nintendo systems.

Best-selling video game of all time (excluding bundle sales) First released in Japan in 1988, *Super Mario Bros. 3* **2** is the best-selling video game of all time that has never been bundled with console hardware, having sold over 17.2 million copies.

Best-selling video game series of all time Total sales for the Super Mario platform games series have exceeded 145 million copies worldwide, including remakes, making it the best-selling video game series of all time. Seven of the top 20 best-selling console titles of all time are Super Mario games. Every one of those seven has sold over 10 million copies.

Highest score for a game of Super Mario Bros. The highest score for a game of *Super Mario Bros.* **1** is 1,044,950, set by Brian Sulpher of Ottawa, Canada on 18 September 2005. The scale of this achievement becomes clearer when you realise that Sulpher's mark is almost twice as

high as the second-highest score on record: 570,150, set by Jon Taber of the USA on 3 September 2006.

First "free" camera in a video game The first video game to allow the user to control the camera independently of the character was *Super Mario 64* **4**, created by Nintendo in 1996. Instead of a

17 million – units sold of *Super Mario World* on the SNES, making it the **biggest-selling 32-Bit game** of all time

SUPER MARIO SERIES FASTEST COMPLETION TIMES

source: speeddemosarchive.com

GAME	PLAYER	TIME	DATE
Super Mario Bros.	Andrew Garkidis	5 min 00 sec	10 Apr 2007
Super Mario World	Scott Kessler	10 min 54 sec	9 Jul 2004
Super Mario Bros. 3	Freddy Anderssom	11 min 03 sec	2 Jun 2007
Super Mario 64	Eddie Taylor	19 min 47 sec	28 May 2005
Super Mario Sunshine	Peter Branam-Lefkove	1 hr 59 min 49 sec	22 Jul 2004

fixed perspective from behind the main character, like previous 3D games, *Super Mario 64* allowed the camera to be rotated around Mario, and zoomed in an out. This has now become standard in third-person gaming.

First movie based on an existing video game The 1993 release *Super Mario Bros.*, starring British actor Bob Hoskins as Mario the plumber and Colombian-born John Leguizamo as his brother Luigi, was the first example of a major motion picture to be based on an existing video game. Although not a huge critical or commercial success at the time, the film has gone on to attain cult status.

TRIVIA

◑ Not content with being platform games' biggest star, Mario has appeared in almost every type of game you can think of. He's had long-running and popular series of his own in several genres: there are five Mario Kart racing games, 12 Mario Party games and six RPGs featuring the plucky plumber. He's even starred in a typing tutorial.

◑ Mario has been voiced, since 1995's *Mario's Game Gallery*, by the actor Charles Martinet, who has made brief appearances in TV shows such as *ER, NYPD Blue* and *Nash Bridges*. He also provides the voices of Luigi, Wario, Baby Mario and Baby Luigi.

◑ Mario's first love interest was Pauline, the damsel-in-distress in the original *Donkey Kong* game. Poor Pauline was soon put in her place with the arrival of Peach (aka Princess Toadstool), Princess of Mushroom Kingdom. His original love reappeared in the Game Boy *Donkey Kong* of 1994 and *Donkey Kong 2: March of the Minis* in 2006, by which time they had become "just friends".

MOST PROLIFIC VIDEO GAME CHARACTER

The character who has appeared in the largest number of video games is Mario 5, created by Shigeru Miyamoto of Nintendo, in Kyoto, Japan, in 1982. Mario has appeared in 116 distinct titles (not including remakes or re-releases). He featured in 13 new games in 2005 alone.

DONKEY KONG

FASTEST COMPLETION TIME FOR *DONKEY KONG COUNTRY* ON THE Wii

The fastest recorded completion time for *Donkey Kong Country* ① is just 32 minutes, achieved by Timothy Peters on 23 June 2007. Peters used the Wii Virtual Console. The **fastest completion with saves on the SNES** is 47 minutes by Tom Votava and Carlos Krueger.

PLATFORMS

PC | XBOX 360
PlayStation | XBOX
PSP | DS
3 | GBA
PSP | Wii

SPEC

Developer:
Nintendo
Publisher:
Nintendo
Initial release:
Donkey Kong (1981),
Arcade

GAMEPLAY

The player controls Jumpman (later named Mario) as he tries to rescue his girlfriend Pauline from the giant ape Donkey Kong. Jumpman must dodge or smash obstacles and jump over gaps. When the game's four screens are complete it restarts on a harder difficulty.

First use of visual storytelling in a video game The first example of a complete story, with beginning and end visually portrayed within a game is the original *Donkey Kong*. It was designed by Shigeru Miyamoto (Japan) and released by Nintendo in July 1981. It is also the **first example of the use of cutscenes to tell a story** in a game: for example, an introductory animation shows Jumpman/Mario's girlfriend being abducted by Donkey Kong.

Most collectable items in any platform game The most collectable items in any platform game is 3,821, held by UK developers Rare for *Donkey Kong 64*, released in 1999. Players can collect

201 golden bananas, 3,500 coloured bananas, 40 banana medals, 20 banana fairies, 40 blueprints, 8 boss keys, 10 battle crowns, 1 Nintendo coin and 1 Rareware coin. There

are also many infinite-supply items to gather, such as banana coins, watermelons and headphones.

Fastest completion time for *Donkey Kong 64* On 20 December 2006, Tom Votava of the USA completed *Donkey Kong 64* in 4 hr 26 min. Votava is a major video game record-holder with many NES game records to his name.

DONKEY KONG ARCADE: TOP 10

RANK	% SCORE	POINTS	PLAYER	DATE
1	100%	1,050,200 pts	Billy Mitchell	13 Jul 07
2	99.90%	1,049,100 pts	Steve Wiebe	23 Mar 07
3	83.72%	879,200 pts	Timothy Scerzby	17 Aug 00
4	76.34%	801,700 pts	Stephen Boyer	31 Oct 07
5	73.10%	767,700 pts	Tim Jackson	1 Feb 83
6	56.29%	591,200 pts	Jeffrey Brandt	25 Oct 82
7	54.12%	568,400 pts	Brian Kuh	5 Jun 00
8	53.45%	561,300 pts	Shawn Beard	24 Jul 82
9	45.56%	478,500 pts	Scott Talmage	10 Jul 82
10	37.90%	398,000 pts	Leo Daniels	11 Jun 04

$1.8 million – damages paid to Nintendo in 1984 by Universal City Studios after losing a court case claiming *Donkey Kong* infringed *King Kong*

MOST SUCCESSFUL VIDEO GAME DOCUMENTARY

The most successful documentary film about a video game is the 2007 release "*The King of Kong: A Fistful of Quarters*" ②. Directed by Seth Gordon, the movie follows Steve Wiebe's successful attempt to beat Billy Mitchell's *Donkey Kong* high score. However, Mitchell went on to reclaim the record just weeks before the documentary was released to cinema.

Highest score on an original *Donkey Kong* arcade game using the "No hammer" challenge

Shawn Cram of the USA achieved a world record score of 317,000 points playing the original *Donkey Kong* coin-slot arcade machine ③ without using the hammer (which usually allows Jumpman to smash oncoming barrels thrown at him by Kong). Cram achieved this gaming milestone on 5 May 2006.

Highest score on Donkey Kong (arcade)

The highest score ever recorded is 1,050,200 points, set by legendary American gamer Billy Mitchell ④ on 13 July 2007, in a game lasting 2 hr 39 min. He beat previous record holder Steve Wiebe by just 1,100 points, but unlike Wiebe, did not play the game through to completion. Mitchell, who set the very first world record *Donkey Kong* score in 1982, offered $10,000 to anyone who could beat his score at the 2007 Classic Gaming Expo.

TRIVIA

➲ Legend has it that the name Donkey Kong was thought up by the game's creator, Nintendo design genius Shigeru Miyamoto (Japan). Apparently Miyamoto originally wanted to call the game "Stubborn Gorilla", but settled on *Donkey Kong* after flicking through a Japanese-English dictionary and discovering that donkeys were synonymous with stubborness, and Kong synonymous with gorillas.

➲ Donkey Kong's nemesis, Jumpman ⑤, was given a moustache because the resolution of the arcade screens in the early 1980s wouldn't allow a space between his nose and mouth. He was also given a hat because technology at the time wouldn't allow for realistic movement of hair.

➲ Jumpman was later named "Mario" by Nintendo of America's staff, in honour of his resemblance to their landlord Mario Segali and, as a result, a video game legend was born.

➲ In *Donkey Kong Junior* ⑥, the 1982 successor to the original *Donkey Kong* ③, the central roles were reversed – Kong found himself caged, with Mario as his captor. This is the only game in the *Donkey Kong* series that sees Mario cast as a villian.

FIGURES

$30 – amount collected by the first *Donkey Kong* arcade cabinet in its first night on test in the Sport Tavern in Seattle.

❝ Donkey Kong *without question is* **the toughest game**... *The average* Donkey Kong *game doesn't last a minute.* **It's absolute brutality.** ❞

Billy Mitchell ④, *Donkey Kong* world record holder

SONIC THE HEDGEHOG

PLATFORMS

PC
PSP
PS3
PS2
PSP
XBOX 360
XBOX
DS
GAME BOY ADVANCE
Wii

SPEC

Developer:
Sega Sonic Team
Publisher:
Sega
Initial release:
Sonic the Hedgehog (1991), Mega Drive

GAMEPLAY

Sonic is all about speed. The games mix spectacular stunts with ring-collecting and enemy-bopping. Most games feature supporting playable characters, like Tails, Knuckles **3** *and Shadow.*

Best-selling game on Sega Systems
The best-selling game on any Sega console has been Sonic Team's *Sonic the Hedgehog 2* **2**, released for the Sega Mega Drive in November 1992. It sold 6 million copies worldwide. Only 180,000 of these were sold in Japan, where Sonic is much less popular than he is in the US and Europe, despite the fact that the games are made in Japan. The *Sonic* series as a whole has sold over 45 million copies worldwide.

Fastest completion time
Joe Stanski of Michigan, USA, completed the original *Sonic the Hedgehog* **1** in a fastest-ever time of 17 min 52 sec on 11 June 2007. This was done using, not the 1991 classic, but the Xbox Live Arcade version.

Fastest video game character
Sega claims that Sonic is capable of running, unassisted, so fast that he breaks the sound barrier. This is what happens when an object travels faster than the speed of sound – 1,237 km/h (769 mph) – and creates a "sonic boom".

Highest score for *Sonic the Hedgehog 2*
The highest score on record for *Sonic the Hedgehog 2* **2** is 433,600, recorded by Heather Corcoran of Glendale, Arizona, USA, on 23 November 2001. Heather set her unprecedented score by Twin Galaxies rules: start with three lives, five-life limit, no continues.

Best-selling retro game compilation
The best-selling compilation of classic games ever released is Sega's *Sonic Mega Collection*, released in 2002 for the GameCube and 2004 for the PlayStation 2, Xbox and PC. It has sold over 4.3 million copies. The *PS2* version includes no less than

LONGEST-RUNNING COMIC BASED ON A VIDEO GAME

The longest-running comic series based on a video game character is the American comic *Sonic the Hedgehog* **5**, published by Archie comics. It has now been running for 14 years and over 180 monthly issues, having first appeared in July 1993. The UK's *Sonic the Comic*, which was published fortnightly, ran for 223 issues between 1993 and 2002.

> **"** In order to really enjoy Sonic, **2D is truly the way to do it."**
>
> Yuji Naka **6**, *Sonic* co-creator

6

TRIVIA

➲ *Mario and Sonic at the Olympic Games* **4**, 2007's sports game for the Wii, marks the first time the old rivals Mario and Sonic have ever appeared in a game together. Sonic first appeared on Nintendo after Sega stopped making its own consoles in 2001, but it was another six years before the company mascots shared the screen.

➲ There is no high score record for the original *Sonic the Hedgehog*, since it has a maximum score of 9,999,990 points. To date, this score has been achieved by 23 people on the Xbox Live Arcade scoreboards.

➲ Sonic was originally called "Mr Needlemouse". He was created when Sega was looking to replace its original mascot character, Alex Kidd. Sega also considered an armadillo, a dog, a rabbit and a fat cartoon of the former American President Theodore Roosevelt wearing pyjamas. The latter eventually became Sonic's nemesis, Eggman, aka Dr. Robotnik **7**.

20 vintage games, including *Sonic the Hedgehog 1–3*, puzzle game *Dr. Robotnik's Mean Bean Machine* and lesser-known Sega platformers *Flicky* and *Ristar*.

7

Most playable characters in any platform game *Sonic Heroes* by Sega, released in 2004 for the GameCube, PlayStation 2, Xbox and PC, has 12 playable characters – a record for platform games. Players compete in four teams of three:

Team Sonic features Tails and Knuckles; Team Dark features Shadow, Rouge and E-123; Team Rose features Amy, Cream and Big; and Team Chaotix features Espio, Charmy and Vector.

PRINCE OF PERSIA

PLATFORMS

PC | XBOX 360
PlayStation | XBOX
PS2 | 3DS
3 | GAME BOY ADVANCE
PSP | Wii

SPEC

Developer:
Ubisoft
Publisher:
Ubisoft
Initial release:
Prince of Persia
(1989), Apple II

GAMEPLAY

An adventure platformer set in the world of the Arabian Nights. In the original 2D game the Prince has just one hour to save the Princess from evil Vizier Jaffar. Ubisoft revived Prince of Persia with a 3D series starting in 2003, and kept the gameplay's mix of swordfighting and fiendish traps.

First motion-capture animation in a video game

The first example of animation created by capturing real human motion (rotoscoping) in a video game is *Prince of Persia* **1**, created in 1989. Designer and programmer Jordan Mechner **6** used an early motion-capture technique called rotoscoping, where he filmed his brother David performing the Prince's acrobatic moves. He then traced over each frame to create the Prince's smooth, realistic animation.

Fastest completion of *Prince of Persia Classic* (Xbox 360 Live Arcade)

The fastest completion time for *Prince of Persia Classic* **2** on the Xbox 360 is 11 min 59.67 sec, achieved by ZMANIAK. He also has the highest score on record – 1,196,637. *Prince of Persia Classic* is a remake of the original with enhanced graphics, available for download on Xbox Live Arcade.

Highest-rated platformer on PS2 and Xbox

The platform game with the highest average review score on PlayStation 2 and Xbox is *Prince of Persia: The Sands of Time*, created by Ubisoft with original *Prince of Persia* designer Jordan Mechner in 2003. It scores 92% on review database website Metacritic.com. On GameCube, it ties with *Super Mario Sunshine*, which also scores 92%.

Shortest time limit in a *Prince Of Persia*

The shortest time limit in a *Prince Of Persia* is the original *Prince of Persia*, which gives players just one hour of real time to save the Princess before she is forced to marry the evil Vizier Jaffar **5**, or die. The Xbox 360 Live Arcade remake *Prince of Persia Classic* imposes the same time limit.

FASTEST COMPLETION OF PRINCE OF PERSIA: THE SANDS OF TIME

The fastest completion time for the first of the 3D Prince of Persia games, *The Sands of Time* **4**, is 2 hr 6 min 3 sec, set by Paul Wagener of Geldrop, the Netherlands, on 1 October 2005. Wagener used the Nintendo GameCube version.

6

"Game of the decade" (1990s)
Pre-eminent among the many plaudits won by *Prince of Persia* – which include "Best Arcade Game" by MacWorld and "Action Game of the Year" (1993) by Computer Gaming World – was the "Game of the Decade" award by film and TV distributor Canal+.

❝ *Although the Prince sometimes sounds a little effiminate,* **leading some wags to rename him 'the mince',** *he does eventually partner up with a Princess…* **❞**

Matt Fox, *The Video Games Guide*

7

TRIVIA

➲ The *Prince of Persia* series is inspired by *The Book of One Thousand and One Nights*, aka the *Arabian Nights* – the source of tales such as "Aladdin" and "Ali Baba and the 40 Thieves". Programmer Jordan Mechner set his version in Persia.

➲ Brother David wasn't the only member of programmer Jordan Mechner's family to help him create the first *Prince of Persia* in 1989. Father Francis composed the music! This small operation is quite impressive when you consider over 200 people worked on *Prince of Persia: Warrior Within*.

🎬 *Prince of Persia: The Sands of Time* is being made into a movie. Disney is making the film with producer Jerry Bruckheimer, the man behind the *Pirates of the Caribbean* series, TV's *C.S.I.* (the **most popular TV show of 2006**), the classic action movie *Top Gun*, *The Rock*, *Pearl Harbour* and many more.

HOT TIPS

Prince of Persia: The Sands of Time (PS2)
To play the first level of classic *Prince of Persia* in 3D, start a new game and stay on the balcony. Hold L3, then quickly press X, square, triangle, circle, triangle, X, square, circle.

Prince of Persia: The Two Thrones 7
To unlock the chainsaw, take out your dagger, but don't equip a secondary weapon. Then pause the game and press up, up, down, down, left, right, left, right, up, down, up, down.

JAK & DAXTER

PLATFORMS

PC XBOX 360
PlayStation XBOX
PS2 DS
3 GameCube
PSP Wii

SPEC

Developer:
Naughty Dog
Publisher:
Sony
Initial release:
Jak and Daxter (2001),
PlayStation 2

GAMEPLAY

Jak and Daxter *is a series of 3D platformers known for their huge size, beautiful cartoon graphics and epic sci-fi plots. They star Jak and his friend Daxter, who's been transformed into a weasel-like creature. Sequels* Jak II *and* Jak 3 *introduced shooting and* Grand Theft Auto-*style city and vehicle elements, while* Daxter *was a spin-off for PSP.*

Most successful platform game developer

Naughty Dog, the creators of *Jak and Daxter*, developed the two top-selling platform games on the PS2 with the original *Jak and Daxter* second behind the all-conquering *Crash Bandicoot: Wrath of Cortex*. Total sales for the *Jak and Daxter* series on the PS2 now stand at over 7 million copies, making it one of the best-selling games series for that console.

First seamless 3D world in a console game

Jak and Daxter: The Precursor Legacy ② was the first console game to present the player with a single, unbroken 3D world. Thanks to Naughty Dog's advanced "streaming" technology, the game world could be explored without any loading times between areas. Even *Grand Theft Auto III*, released two months before *Jak and Daxter*, featured loading times between Liberty City's islands.

Most successful single-format platform series

With combined sales of 7.1 million copies, the *Jak and Daxter* series – *The Precursor Legacy*, *Jak II* and *Jak 3* – is the most successful platform game series not to be ported onto another platform. *Daxter*, for the PSP, is considered a spin-off, not a sequel. Although a PS3 *Jak and Daxter* had been rumoured, Naughty Dog's commitment to making *Uncharted: Drake's Fortune* makes it unlikely. *Jak and Daxter* is likely to remain one of the few platform games that is exclusive to the PS2.

LARGEST NUMBER OF CUTSCENES IN A PLATFORM GAME

The largest number of cinematic cutscenes in a platform game is 131 in Naughty Dog's *Jak II: Renegade* ③, released in 2003. There are 51 cutscenes in the first act alone. *Jak and Daxter* games are known for their involved stories and funny dialogue, more in keeping with an RPG or action-adventure than a platform game. However, in the first game, Jak did not speak at all.

> *First and foremost, **the AI needs to be fun**. That should always come before realism, because after all, we are making games!*
>
> Evan Wells, Co-Designer on *Jak and Daxter*

FACTS

➲ The *Official PlayStation Magazine* review of *The Precursor Legacy* awarded the game 10/10!

➲ The series has spun off into various other genres of game: *Jak X: Combat Racing* is a driving/combat game featuring both characters, while *Daxter* is a platformer for the PSP in which you control just Daxter.

TRIVIA

➲ Though many RPGs allow you to change your character's appearance, Naughty Dog's *Jak II* is the first platform game in which you can shave! For five Precursor Orbs, you can toggle Jak's goatee beard on or off.

➲ Daxter is an "ottsel" – a mixture of otter and weasel – but started off life as a normal boy; according to the game's backstory, he was knocked into a vat of Dark Eco by his friend Jak, which transformed him into a furry creature.

➲ Naughty Dog co-founders Andy Gavin and Jason Rubin published their first video game, *Ski Crazed*, whilst still at school.

First game to use the GOAL programming language
Naughty Dog co-founder Andy Gavin lead the creation of the Game Oriented Assembly Lisp (GOAL) programming tool, the first application of which was the original *Jak and Daxter* game. GOAL was built using the Allegro CL and Lisp languages and allowed the creation of over 500 types of game object, each with a particular set of complex elements. The smooth animation, beautiful vistas and bright colours are all characteristic of the GOAL engine.

Fastest completion of Jak and Daxter
The fastest completion time for *Jak and Daxter: The Precursor Legacy* 2 is 2 hr 20 min 3 sec, achieved by Ben "Mkt2015" Fichter on 14 February 2005. It is a particularly difficult game to complete quickly because of its lack of shortcuts or glitches for experienced gamers to exploit.

Fastest completion of Jak II
Ben Fichter also holds the record for the fastest completion of *Jak II* 3. Playing on "Hero" mode with "warp" saving, Fichter completed the speed run in 4 hr 42 min on 30 June 2006, doing so in just 56 different segments.

PLATFORM GAMES ROUND-UP

FACTS

➲ The **best-selling platform game on the Atari 2600** was the revolutionary *Pitfall!* (1982). It was one of the first platform games to feature in a TV show when, in 1983, an animated version called *Pitfall Harry* appeared on the CBS show *Saturday Supercade* (1983).

➲ The shooting arcade game *Moon Patrol* was an early example of how genres can cross-pollinate, combining elements of platform gaming with a traditional shooter. It was also the **first game to feature parallax scrolling**, in which objects farther away scroll slower than those closer to the foreground.

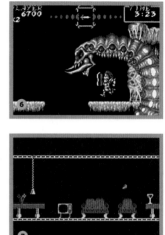

First orchestral recording of a video game soundtrack
Game: *Heart of Darkness*
Publisher: Amazing Studio
The music for the 1998 platformer *Heart of Darkness* was composed by Bruce Broughton and performed by the Sinfonia of London.

Most successful Western game series in Japan
Game: *Crash Bandicoot*
Publisher: Naughty Dog
Crash Bandicoot ❶ games have sold 4.5 million copies in Japan – an impressive feat given how poorly non-Japanese games sell there.

Shortest video game release
Game: *Great Giana Sisters*
Publisher: Rainbow Arts
The shortest period of release for a video game was one week, for the 1987 platform game *Great Giana Sisters*. Publisher Rainbow Arts was forced to withdraw it from sale pending legal action from Nintendo, because the game was a very thinly disguised copy of Nintendo's *Super Mario Bros.* (the Commodore 64 version of the game even included the tag line "the brothers are history" on the cover). The game spread by illegal pirate copies but originals remain rare.

Best-selling French game
Game: *Rayman*
Publisher: Ubisoft
The 2D side-scrolling platformer *Rayman* ❹ for the Atari Jaguar and the PlayStation, designed by Michel Ancel and produced by Ubisoft in 1995, sold 4 million copies; the *Rayman* series as a whole has sold more than 11 million around the world. The game is also the **best-selling PlayStation title in the UK**. It is thanks to the success of *Rayman* that Ubisoft is a large and successful publisher today.

LARGEST NUMBER OF GAMES IN A SINGLE SERIES

The largest video game series – not including spin-offs in other genres – is the Capcom platform game series *Mega Man* ❷, starring the character designed by Keiji Inafune ❸. There are 17 games in the "classic" series starring the original character. There are also 11 *Mega Man X* games, four *Mega Man Zero* games, two *Mega Man ZX* games, three *Mega Man Legends* games, six *Mega Man Battle Network* games plus three *Mega Man Star Force* games making a total of 46.

CAPCOM

39.2 million – total units sold over the past 11 years of the seven games in the Crash Bandicoot series

HIGH SCORE TABLE – CLASSIC ARCADE PLATFORMERS

GAME	SCORE	PLAYER	DATE
Bubble Bobble	5,823,600	Tom Gault	4 Mar 1988
Contra	1,546,600	Chad D. Johnson	15 Jul 2002
Ghosts 'n Goblins	811,000	Steve Donaldson	11 Jun 2004
Pac-Land	4,150,400	Mark Mendes	14 May 1986
Flicky	4,548,540	Jonathan Long	26 Jun 1986
Bomb Jack	20,010,960	Giauco Bondavalli	3 Nov 1984

❝ *Platform games are one of the consummate gaming exercises and will most likely always be with us in some form or another.* **❞**

Brian Schwab, author, *AI Game Engine Programming*

First console game to require twin analog
Game: *Ape Escape*
Publisher: Ubisoft
The first console game controlled with two analog sticks was *Ape Escape* ⑤, a 3D platformer for PlayStation released in 1999. It was released alongside the DualShock analogue controller and was the first title to require it. The player would use the left stick to move and the right to use various gadgets.

Rarest ZX Spectrum game
Game: *Frank the Flea*
Publisher: Megasoft
The rarest game for the Sinclair ZX Spectrum is the platform game *Frank the Flea* ⑦, released in 1986. Only 28 copies were ever produced. Richard Welsh, the game's 15-year-old programmer, sold them for £2 each, or £1 if you supplied your own cassette and postage.

Fastest perfect run on *Super Ghouls 'n Ghosts*
Game: *Super Ghouls 'n Ghosts*
Publisher: Capcom
Scott Kessler completed *Super Ghouls 'n Ghosts* ⑥ on the SNES in 45 min 41 sec on 17 November 2005. Not only was this the first and fastest complete game on record without using continues, Kessler finished the game without losing a life or even taking a single hit.

⑤

INTERVIEW WITH...
WALTER DAY

TRACKING VIDEO GAME HIGH SCORES FROM AROUND THE WORLD FOR NEARLY A QUARTER OF A CENTURY.

Walter Day ① is the founder of Twin Galaxies, an official body that records high scores for thousands of arcade games and home consoles. We spoke to Walter about how and when he got into video gaming...

I was an oil broker in Houston, Texas, in 1980 when a friend introduced me to *Space Invaders*. Before long I was a devotee of *PAC-Man*, *Centipede*, *Robotron* ② and *Frogger*.

Why did you decide to start Twin Galaxies, and where does the name come from?
I loved video games so much that in 1981 I decided to open up an arcade ③ in Ottumwa, Iowa, as an excuse to be able to play more games! While renovating the space for our proposed arcade in September 1981, the name Twin Galaxies burst into my brain. At first I thought I was merely remembering someone else's brand name. However, in time it became clear that the name was original – so we claimed it.

What was the first game you ever adjudicated at?
In February 1982, I refereed a world record high-score attempt on the Williams *Defender* arcade game. This record attempt happened in Twin Galaxies in Ottumwa and it was during this event that I discovered that the gaming industry needed a scorekeeper. Our subsequent offer to keep track of the industry's high score records was accepted by the manufacturers of the time and we have been the scorekeepers ever since.

Do you have to be present at every adjudication? If not, what evidence do you accept?
All gameplay has to be watched, either in person ④ or via videotaped submission. As a result, we have a significant library consisting of thousands of videotaped performances, some dating back decades. Each game is different. We analyze each game and then create custom-made rules that apply on a game-by-game basis. Some games have no weaknesses that can be exploited by the player. Others, however, must be videotaped from the very beginning to the very end. And, for a videotaped game performance to be accepted, it has to be watched carefully to ensure that there is no cheating.

What kinds of tricks do players use to cheat?
A presiding referee must be completely familiar with any game they are called upon to referee so he or she can recognize if cheating occurs. And, if the game is new to them, they can send the videotape to other Twin Galaxies referees for supplemental reviews. Because of Twin Galaxies' diligent verification processes, a gaming attempt submitted on videotape may take weeks or even months to win the seal of approval. Some cheats are so subtle that we may even have to watch a tape frame-by-frame to determine if they employed an illegal strategy.

the ultimate conflict between man and machine

ROBOTRON: 2084

Upright model shown. Also available in cocktail table, cocktail table with base and compact cabinet.

For the service back-up that keeps you out-front, call Williams toll-free at 800/323-7182. In Illinois, call toll-free at 800/572-1226.

Williams
ELECTRONICS, INC.

2

3

FACT

Twin Galaxies holds pinball statistics dating from the 1930s and video game statistics from the early 1970s.

What's your favourite game? What game are you best at playing?

Running Twin Galaxies now takes up all my time, so I sadly no longer have time to play video games. But, back when I did have time, I was best at games like *Centipede*, *Robotron* **2** and *Make Trax* – games popular in the early 1980s. Still, I do like modern games like *Crazy Taxi* and *Tony Hawk Pro Skater*, I just don't have the spare hours to play them!

What's your favourite record?

Abdner Ashman broke both the Junior *PAC-Man* and *Robotron* world records, back-to-back, on the same night. It happened at the "Legends of the Golden Age" championship in Humble, Texas, on 2 December 2005.

So what's next for TG?

We will be developing a series of gaming tournaments **5** to crown champions on thousands of game titles that currently have no champions.

1

> **❜❜** *Walk down Main Street in this southeast Iowa town and you'll pass a shoe store, a men's clothing shop, a hamburger joint **and the world's most famous video game arcade. That's not a misprint.** ❜❜*
>
> *Quad City Times*, Moline, Illinois, 15 December 1982

GUINNESS WORLD RECORDS GAMER'S EDITION 2008

The ultimate gamer's a

SPORTS GAMES

WITH THE RULES OF PLAY ALREADY IN PLACE, TURNING SPORTS INTO VIDEO GAMES WAS A NO-BRAINER. ADD IN THE ALLURE OF BIG-NAME SPORTS CELEBS AND YOU HAVE THE PERFECT PACKAGE.

OUR EXPERT

Martin Korda is a leading games consultant and one of Europe's most widely published games journalists, with his extensive writing credits including *The Guardian*, IGN. com, Eurogamer.net, GamesIndustry.biz, *PC Zone*, *PSW* and *Official Xbox Magazine*.

OUTLINE

Sports games constitute one of video-gaming's broadest genres. Ranging from brutal impact sports such as American Football to gentler challenges like billiards or golf. Sports games often pit players against virtual recreations (or placing them in the shoes) of their real life sporting heroes. Gameplay is often self-determined and open-ended.

3

The inception of the sports genre, as with so many other video games, was a modest one. In the late 70s and early 80s, many sports games provided scaled down versions of the sports they represented, such as 1978's *Basketball* with its one-on-one gameplay, and 1980's *Championship Soccer's* blocky players, a far cry from the modern day adherence to authenticity, licensing agreements and supreme graphical polish.

By the mid- to late-80s, the genre was slowly awakening to the power of franchises, iconic figures and official licensing agreements. 1984 saw arguably the first sports game appearance for a plumber named Mario in Nintendo's *Golf* **3**. Who could have foreseen the impact the character would have on the sports gaming world, appearing in lots of award-winning titles, including 2007's *Mario and Sonic at the Olympic Games*?

> **❝** *Madden NFL Football is no longer just a video game. **It has become a pop-cultural phenomenon**. Each year in August, the launch date is treated like a national holiday by millions of people.* **❞**
>
> Todd Sitrin, VP of Marketing, EA SPORTS

After the titanic success of TV's Wrestlemania III in 1987 put pro wrestling on the international map, the video game industry was quick to realise the sport's potential, and in 1988, the world got its taste of virtual grappling with the **first wrestling game**, *WWF: Wrestlemania* on the NES. The WWF (later WWE) games would never look back, remaining one of the industry's strongest-selling sports franchises.

1988 would prove to be a landmark year for the genre, signalling the birth of the licensed sports game with the release of *WWF: Wrestlemania*, *John Madden Football* and the hugely popular *Wayne Gretzky Hockey*, while 1989 saw basketball attract a big name signing with the release of *Magic Johnson's Fast Break*.

1

2

In the early 90s, the world witnessed the first truly titanic football video game rivalry, as two top-down soccer games went head to head. *Kick Off* and *Sensible Soccer* split public opinion in an unprecedented way, although the rivalry between gamers didn't run quite as deep as the ongoing face-off that exists today between Electronic Arts' **best-selling and longest-running** *FIFA* series **2** and Konami's *Pro Evolution Soccer*.

By the mid 90s, a dominant force in the genre was beginning to emerge in the shape of EA Sports, due in no small part to the publisher's drive to attain a large number of sporting licenses, most notably NBA, NFL, FIFA, PGA and NHL, and by the turn of

6

TIMELINE

1978	1988	1990	1992
1978: *Basketball*	1988: *John Madden*, *Wrestlemania* **5** and *Wayne Gretzky* released	1990: *Player Manager*, *Links: The Challenge of Golf* and *Greg Norman's Ultimate Golf* released	1992: *Sensible Soccer*, *Jack Nicklaus Golf*
1980: *Golf* and *Championship Soccer*			1993: *Madden NFL '94* and *FIFA International Soccer* released by EA
1981: *Ice Hockey*	1989: *Magic Johnson's Fast Break* **6** and *Kick Off* released	1991: *NHL Hockey*	1995: *NBA Live '95*
1984: *Golf* (Nintendo)			

5

17 – percent of total console game sales in 2006 in the sports game genre, according to market research firm NPD's figures

TRIVIA

➲ *Wii Sports* has won several prestigious games media awards, including IGN's Best Sports Game of 2006 and the E3 Game Critics Award for Best Sports Game, also in 2006.

➲ In 2001, the World Wildlife Fund sued the World Wrestling Federation over the use of the initials WWF. The trial would eventually lead to the wrestling organisation rebranding itself and its games to WWE (World Wrestling Entertainment) in 2002.

➲ The "EA Sports" brand was created in 1993 with the slightly clumsy motto: "If it's in the game, it's in the game", voiced by Andrew Anthony. This was later shortened to the now familiar "EA Sports: it's in the game".

FIGURES

104 – officially licensed snooker and pool players featured in Sega's *World Snooker Championship 2007*.

the millennium, the publisher had become the **world's top-selling sports game publisher**.

However, the likes of *Virtua Tennis*, *Pro Evolution Soccer*, *Top Spin* and the 2K sports ④ series ensured that sports game enthusiasts were still spoilt for choice. And with

the advent of the Nintendo Wii's interactive controller and 2006's *Wii Sports* revolutionising the way sports games are currently played, the future of the genre is guaranteed to be more exciting than at any other time in its long and illustrious history.

1996	2000	2003	2006
1996: *Olympic Summer Games* ⑦ released	2000: *Mario Tennis* and *SSX* all hit the shelves	2003: *Top Spin* and *MVP 2003* released	2006: *Wii Sports* ⑧
1998: *Tiger Woods '99*	2001: *ESPN Hockey Night*, *ESPN NFL Primetime* and *NBA Street* released	2005: *Super Mario Strikers* ❶ and *FIFA Street* make their debut	2007: *Mario and Sonic at the Olympic Games*, *FIFA '08* and *Pro Evolution Soccer 2008* all released
1999: *NFL 2K* and *Tony Hawk's Pro Skater* introduced for first time			

BASKETBALL

PLATFORMS

PC | XBOX 360
PS2 | XBOX
PS3 | DS
3 | GBA
PSP | Wii

GAMEPLAY

Basketball simulations and arcade games, offering 1v1 to full 5v5 matches, featuring either real life licensed teams or fictional ones. Older games feature 2D graphics, but since 1992 most basketball games released have featured a full 3D environment, with TV camera style views.

> *NBA Europe Live, presented by EA Sports, creates an authentic platform for fans of all ages to enjoy **real life and virtual basketball experiences.***
>
> Jan Bolz, EA

First basketball game The aptly named *Basketball* was released on Atari 2600 in 1978. The simple one-on-one matches, that lasted just four minutes, were played from a side-on 2D perspective **1**, featuring basic stickmen characters.

Longest basketball series

The *NBA Live* **2** series is the longest-running basketball series of all time. The first game, *NBA Live 95*, was released in 1994, and the release of *NBA Live 08* in 2007 signalled the franchise's 13th year. The annual releases also ensure that the franchise now contains more games than any other basketball series.

Highest winning margin in a game of *NBA Jam: Tournament Edition* (arcade version) On 2 June 2007, Canadian Kelly R. Flewin won a match on the arcade version of *NBA Jam: Tournament Edition* **3** by 13 points to set the world record for the highest winning margin for the basketball game. Flewin achieved the record at Funspot, a family entertainment centre based in Weirs Beach, New Hampshire, USA.

FIRST GAME TO FEATURE A SINGLE PROFESSIONAL BASKETBALL PLAYER

The first basketball game to carry a professional player license was *Magic Johnson's Fast Break* (also known as *Magic Johnson's Basketball* **4**), which was released on PC and Amiga in 1989 and on the Amstrad CPC, Commodore 64, NES and ZX Spectrum the following year. The earlier 1983 release of *Dr. J vs. Larry Bird* for the Apple II and Commodore 64 featured two licensed players.

20,000
– lines of speech spoken by match commentators Marv Albert and Steve Kerr during *NBA Live 08* gameplay

First winner of *NBA Live season* simulator

In 2006, the Dallas Mavericks became the first winners of the EA *NBA Live Season* 5 simulation, beating the Cleveland Cavaliers in six games to emerge as champions. The simulation of the 2006/2007 season was generated by *NBA Live 07* and represented the first time that an entire season had been officially generated by an NBA Live game.

Highest margin of victory in *Bulls vs Blazers and the NBA Playoffs* (SNES)

On 15 January 2006, Rudy Ferretti set a record for the highest margin of victory in a game of *Bulls Vs Blazers and the NBA Playoffs* on the Super Nintendo. Verified by a video recording of his game, Ferretti's record saw him winning by a 61-point margin against his computer opponent during the 12-minute-per-period game.

TRIVIA

➔ *Basketball* 1 (released 1978), the world's first ever basketball game, made a very brief appearance in the movie *Airplane!* (1980).

➔ Former Chicago Bulls shooting guard Steve Kerr 6 took over as announcer for *NBA Live 07* when his predecessor, Mike Fratello, became the coach of the Memphis Grizzlies. Fratello had provided commentary since *NBA Live 2004*.

➔ Unlockable characters in *NBA Live 2003* featured many of the rappers who also had songs in the game. These included Busta Rhymes, Just Blaze and Snoop Dogg.

BASKETBALL
VIDEO COMPUTER SYSTEM
GAME PROGRAM
2 VIDEO GAMES
ONE PLAYER · TWO PLAYERS
ATARI
CX 2624

First 3D basketball game

Nintendo's 1992 game *NCAA Basketball* (by Sculptured Software) was the first to feature 3D graphics. For the first time ever, players could see the action from a player-level 3D perspective. This graphical style has been copied by countless subsequent basketball games and remains the industry standard perspective to this day.

HIGHEST MARGIN OF VICTORY OVER AN AI OPPONENT

Canadian Brian Sulpher played a 12-minute-per-quarter game of the SNES version of *Tecmo NBA Basketball* 7 (set to the Expert difficulty setting and played on Normal speed) and secured a victory margin of 331 points on 18 September 2005.

TECMO SUPER NBA BASKETBALL
Nintendo
SUPER NINTENDO

AMERICAN FOOTBALL

2

3

PLATFORMS

PC   XBOX 360
PS1   XBOX
PS2   DS
3   GBA
PSP   Wii

GAMEPLAY

High-impact sports games in which the player controls their favourite American Football team and attempts to pick the right field plays to lead them to Superbowl glory. The most popular franchise, and by far the longest-running, is the Madden *series, created by EA Sports. The series is endorsed by the famous ex-player, ex-coach and sports commentator John Madden* ①*.*

Highest first week sales of an NFL game

The quickest-selling NFL game of all time was *Madden NFL 07* ②, which shifted an impressive 2 million copies in its first week of sales. This eclipsed the previous record of 1.8 million sales held by *Madden NFL 06.*

Most Madden Bowl wins

The highest number of Madden Bowl victories (an annual elimination tournament using the latest version of *Madden NFL*) is two, a record held jointly by four professional football players. Former Washington Redskins running back Reggie Brooks won the title in 1995 and 1996, Jacquez Green, former Tampa Bay Buccaneers wide receiver, won it in 2001 and 2002, Indianapolis Colts defensive end Dwight Freeney won in 2003 and 2004, while Buccaneers tight end Alex Smith ③ (left), won the title in 2006 and 2007.

Most sacks in *NFL Blitz 2000* (arcade)

Mike Landt of Missouri, USA, holds the record for the most sacks (tackling a quarterback as he passes) in one game of the arcade version of *NFL Blitz 2000* (factory default setting). He pulled off a stunning nine sacks on 30 April 2000 at Putt Putt Golf course in his hometown of Ypsilanti.

①

EA SPORTS

MADDEN

NFL 2001

E

EDITION

2.8 million – first week sales of *Madden 06*, America's best-selling game of 2006

FIGURES

95 – Score, out of 100, awarded to *Madden NFL 2003* on the PS2 by games review aggregator metacritic.com: the highest score by any game in the Madden franchise.

1.1 million – copies sold in the USA of *Madden NFL 07* on Xbox 360, making it the most popular sports game in the USA.

Highest score in *NFL Blitz* against a computer opponent

The holder of the highest score against a computer opponent in the PlayStation version of 1998's *NFL Blitz* is the USA's Mark Moore, who put an impressive 57 points past his AI opponent in default mode on 11 April 1999.

Most games in an NFL franchise

Electronic Arts' *Madden NFL* series has produced 16 games. In its earlier days, the series was called *John Madden Football*, but this was later abbreviated to *Madden NFL* for the series' 1993 release *Madden NFL 94*.

TRIVIA

➲ The Nintendo Wii version of *Madden NFL 07* was the first game in the series to feature motion control. Players could use the motion-sensitive Wii nunchucks to pull off a variety of moves and plays.

➲ *Madden NFL 2001* is rumoured to have started the alleged EA cover curse – which involved the player featured on the game's cover suffering bad luck – after NFL 2001's cover player Eddie George saw his form slump from 1,962 all-purpose yards with 16 touchdowns the previous year to just 1,218 yards and five touchdowns.

➲ The Dreamcast version of *NFL Blitz 2000* was released twice because the original release contained several bugs. These were rectified for the second release, which could be distinguished by the presence of the words "Hot!" and "New!" on the game's cover.

FIRST ESPN-LICENSED NFL GAME

ESPN Sunday Night NFL was the first American football game to become affiliated with the sports channel ESPN. Only a few other NFL games would carry the ESPN logo in their titles – including *ESPN NFL Football*, *ESPN NFL Primetime 2002* and *ESPN NFL 2K5* – before Electronic Arts brought the ESPN rights for its *Madden NFL* series soon after *2K5* was released.

FOOTBALL

PLATFORMS

PC | XBOX 360
PS1 | XBOX
PS3 | DS
3 | GBA
PSP | Wii

GAMEPLAY

Players can play a variety of different football formats ranging from four-a-side games to eleven-a-side matches. Games feature teams of either real life licensed players, players based on real-life or fictional players.

Most consecutive football series releases on a single platform The *FIFA* football series ❶ holds the record for the highest number of consecutive yearly releases on a single platform. A FIFA-branded game was released every year for 10 years on the Sony PlayStation from 1996 to 2005.

First five-a-side football game In 1985, Mastertronic's *Five-a-Side Indoor Soccer* ❹ became the world's first five-a-side football video game when it was released on the Commodore 64.

First top-down football game

In 1980, Atari released *Championship Soccer* ❾ on the Atari 2600. It was the first football game with a top-down perspective. *Championship Soccer* featured four-a-side matches. This playing viewpoint

remained popular for many years and went on to influence the likes of *Sensible Soccer* ❸ and *Kick Off.*

First football game to be played from a side perspective The first football game to allow players to control their team from a side perspective (stadium viewpoint) was *International Soccer* ❷. The game – also known as *NASL Soccer* – was released on the Atari 2600 in 1980. This side-on playing perspective has since become the default view for many leading football games, including the *FIFA* and *Pro Evolution Soccer* games.

> ❝ *The lasting appeal of Sensible Soccer is the **ocean of hidden, realistic and subtle depth** beneath its cartoony, instantly playable and accessible surface.* ❞
>
> Jon Hare, designer/director of the *Sensible Soccer* series

5,000 – the number of ideas and comments made to Electronic Arts via the fifaplay.com website for improving gameplay in *FIFA 08* before its release

TRIVIA

➔ Electronic Arts' *FIFA 2001* ⑧ was the first game of the series to carry sponsor names on player shirts. However, Manchester City (UK) and Lyon (France) did not carry the names of their sponsors (Eidos and Infogrames), as they were rivals to EA.

➔ German goalkeeper Oliver Kahn sued Electronic Arts over the use of his name and likeness in FIFA World Cup 2002. The judge ruled in his favour.

➔ *Sensible Soccer's* ③ distinct graphical style was first used in a game called *Sensible Olympics*, which was due to be out in time for the 1992 Olympic games. Sadly, the game was never released.

Most points in *FIFA Street*

On 7 August 2006, Andrew Mee of Denbighshire, Wales, scored 222,774 points on the Xbox version of *FIFA Street* ⑥. Playing on the Easy setting, Mee achieved this highest-ever total while playing a 12-minute game.

Proving that soccer skills can run in the family, another member of the Mee clan, Jonathan, holds the record for the highest margin of victory in *FIFA Street* (Xbox). On 8 June 2007, he beat his computer opponent (set to the Easy setting) by a 22-goal margin in a 12-minute match.

First action/strategy football game

Player Manager ⑦ (released 1990) was the first ever football game to allow players to simultaneously play as both a manager and a player. The action section of the game used the *Kick Off* engine, while the playing/management formula would go on to influence playing modes like Master League in the *Pro Evolution Soccer* series.

Highest margin of victory in *Worldwide Soccer* (Sega Saturn)

Elijah Parker of the USA holds the record for the highest margin of victory in a game of *Worldwide Soccer* (Sega Saturn). On 21 August 1997, he beat his computer-controlled opponent by a 14-goal margin.

LONGEST-RUNNING FOOTBALL FRANCHISE

The longest-running football franchises of all time are the *FIFA* and *Sensible Soccer* series. The first *Sensible Soccer* game, known simply as *Sensible Soccer*, was released in 1992. The release of *Sensible Soccer 2006* marked the franchise's 14th year. The first *FIFA* game was *FIFA International Soccer*, which was released in 1993. In 2007, the franchise equalled *Sensible Soccer's* record of 14 years with the release of *FIFA 08* ⑤.

HOT TIP

You can unlock some natty hairstyles for custom players in *Sensible Soccer 2006* on PlayStation 2 by winning the various championships and titles on offer: Win the Super Cup to unlock a bouffant hairstyle; triumph in the Dutch League to unlock dreadlocks; become English Shield champions and unlock a mullet; win the Scottish League Cup to unlock receding hairline; secure the French League Cup and unlock a monk-style haircut; triumph in the Spanish Shield to unlock a ponytail.

GOLF

TEE UP WITH MARIO AND HIS FRIENDS!

PLATFORMS

PC | XBOX 360
PS1 | XBOX
PS2 | DS
3 |
PSP | Wii

GAMEPLAY

Golf and mini golf games featuring real-life or fictional players and courses. Control systems range from mouse clicking to mouse/controller swinging. Celebrity-licensed golf games have been common since the early 1990s, with golf's greatest icon, Tiger Woods, currently dominating the golf scene in video-gaming as he has in real life.

GOLF
VIDEO COMPUTER SYSTEM™
GAME PROGRAM™
9 HOLE COURSE
ONE TO TWO PLAYERS

ATARI
A Warner Communications Company

CX 2634

Longest-running golf series

The record for the longest-running golf game franchise is 13 years, held by the *Links* golf game series. The first game, *Links: The Challenge of Golf*, was released in 1990. The most recent release was *Links 2004* **1**, released in 2003 for Xbox.

First PGA-licensed game

The first PGA-licensed golf game was *Mattel's PGA Golf* **3**, released for Intellivision in 1980. The game was played from a basic top-down view and allowed up to four players to compete against each other.

First Tiger Woods game

In recent years, the Tiger Woods-licensed golf series has dominated the market. The first golf game to carry the champion golfer's name was *Tiger Woods 99*, released in 1998.

❝ *Since 1998, Tiger Woods PGA Tour has provided an authentic golf experience, with an emphasis on innovation that **has enabled gamers to literally put themselves in the game** and challenge gamers around the world.* **❞**

Tom Goedde, Director of Marketing, EA

First golf game to feature Mario

One of the world's favourite and most recognisable video game characters, Mario, first appeared on the Japan course of *Golf* for the Famicom in 1987, though some gamer's claim that Mario was the golfer with a moustache in the 1984's *Golf* on the NES. Mario has gone on to star in a variety of golf games, including *Mario Golf* (N64, 1999) and *Mario Golf: Advanced Tour* (Game Boy Advance, 2004).

FIRST COMMERCIALLY RELEASED GOLF GAME

The world's first ever golf game was the aptly named *Golf* **4**, which was released in 1980 for the Atari 2600. However, although this was the first golf game, it wasn't the first to let you swing a club. A year earlier in 1979, *Miniature Golf* (also for the Atari 2600) became the first ever golf-themed game to receive a commercial release and the **first ever miniature golf game** to be released.

Best score in Reflection Bay course of *Tiger Woods PGA Tour 06*

Douglas Loyd of the USA set the record low round of 49 strokes on the Reflection Bay course of *Tiger Woods PGA Tour 06* **5** for the PlayStation 2. He set the record on the same day as his Doral course record (15 February 2006, see right). The game was set to Easy, with hole settings set to 18 and Mulligans turned off.

Best total score for Castle Pines (Ladies) course of *Jack Nicklaus Golf* on Game Boy/ Game Boy Colour

On Friday 14 October 2005, Tom Duncan (USA) completed the Castle Pines (Ladies) course of *Jack Nicklaus Golf* on Game Boy Color in just 60 strokes. Duncan played the 18-hole course on beginner level.

$3.09 billion – 2007 revenue of EA, the makers of *Tiger Woods PGA Tour*. In that year, they had 24 titles that sold more than 1 million copies each

Top score on Maple Course 1: Toad Highlands (stroke mode) of *Mario Golf* for N64

The best recorded score for a round of the Maple Course 1: Toad Highlands course in the 1999 title *Mario Golf* 2 on the Nintendo 64 is -12. The record was set by Chris DeMichael of Kent, Ohio, USA, on 28 May 2006, who played the course in stroke mode and with the factory default settings in place. The record was confirmed by a video recording of DeMichael's record-breaking round submitted to Twin Galaxies.

TEE OFF WITH TIGER 08

Type these codes into the password screen to unlock some great features…

CODE	UNLOCKS
ALLSTARS	All players
RIHACHINRIZO	Mizuno items
LIGHTNING	PGA items
JANNARD	Oakley items
INTHEGAME	EA items
JUSTDOIT	Nike items
SNAKEKING	Cobra items
SHOJIRO	Bridgestone items

FACTS

➲ In *Mario Golf* on the Nintendo 64, Boo Classic is misspelled "Boo Clasic" on the Tournament screen.

➲ The first three games in the *Hot Shots / Everybody Golf* golf series on the PlayStation and PSP have sold more than 7.5 million copies.

➲ *SimGolf*, released by Maxis in 1996 for the PC, is the only golf game so far to feature a real golf ball tucked away in the packaging.

➲ *Minna no Golf Portable: Coca-Cola Special Edition* 7 was released in 2005 by Sony for the PSP. The game features extensive Coca-Cola branding; billboard ads, clubs shaped like Coke bottles and themed packaging. Only 1,300 copies were made as prizes for a Coke competition.

BEST SCORE IN DORAL COURSE OF *TIGER WOODS PGA TOUR 06* ON PS2

On 15 February 2006, Douglas Loyd of Hazelwood, Missouri, USA, completed the Doral golf course in *Tiger Woods PGA Tour 06* on the PlayStation 2 (easy mode) in just 47 strokes. He achieved this feat with hole settings set to 18 and Mulligans turned off. His record was verified by a video recording of all 18 holes.

TRIVIA

➲ *Mario Golf: Toadstool Tour* was the first ever game to feature both Mario and Diddy Kong, after Nintendo bought the character rights from Rare.

➲ Famous for its serious re-creation of golf, the *Links* 6 series took a strange detour in 1999 with the release of *Links Extreme*, which allowed players to hit exploding golf balls at their opponents.

➲ Before Tiger Woods' domination of the market, several other golfers had lent their names to games. They included *Jack Nicklaus Golf* (PC, 1988), *Arnold Palmer Tournament Golf* (Megadrive, 1989), *Greg Norman Ultimate Golf* (Amiga, 1990) and *Nick Faldo's Championship Golf* (Amiga, 1993).

TENNIS

> **❝** *The reason we think Virtua Tennis became popular was because* ***we made players play like superstars.*** **❞**
>
> Mie Kumagai, Producer on the *Virtua Tennis* series

PLATFORMS

PC | XBOX 360
PS1 | XBOX
PS2 | DS
PS3 | GBA
PSP | Wii

GAMEPLAY

Tennis games that mix realism and arcade-style gameplay, featuring a wide variety of court surfaces and players and often giving the game player the opportunity to test their skills by taking part in tournaments or championships.

Best-selling tennis game

Mario Tennis on the Nintendo 64 in 2000 sold over 2.3 million units worldwide, making it one of the most popular stand-alone tennis video game ever. *Wii Sports Tennis* has reached 8.32 million homes, but the tennis element comprises just one-fifth of the total game (which itself came bundled with the Wii in most territories).

Highest-rated tennis game

The tennis game consistently rated higher than any other is *Top Spin*, for the Xbox. It secured an average score of 90% across the major game aggregator sites. "The most well-rounded, feature-rich game of tennis to be found anywhere, on any system," said GameSpot.com.

First 3D tennis game

Released in 1990, *International 3D Tennis* was the first tennis game to use 3D graphics. Nine years later, *Virtua Tennis* provided a far more realistic, natural and enjoyable simulation of tennis, thanks to the realism of the player movements and the use of complicated ball physics.

MOST PLAYABLE "REAL" CHARACTERS

Virtua Tennis 3 ③ boasted the highest number of playable characters based on real tennis stars in the series, offering 12 male and seven female players, including Roger Federer ④, Maria Sharapova ⑤ and Venus Williams.

190,000 – the number of *Pong* table tennis arcade games sold to bars and amusement parks following its release by Atari in 1972

TRIVIA

➲ The original Xbox release of *Top Spin* contained a bug that allowed players to use a shot known as the Deathdrop. It was ostensibly a drop shot, but it was impossible to return. This led to countless problems when players competed against each other via Xbox Live. The bug was later fixed by a patch.

➲ *Mario Tennis* on the Nintendo 64 was the first outing for Luigi's moustachioed rival Waluigi. While he was a playable character, there are some suggestions that his inclusion was merely to provide Wario with a doubles partner.

➲ *Virtua Tennis 2* was released on the Dreamcast in November 2001 and proved to be one of the final games released for the console system. Most Dreamcast software production halted a few months later.

➲ *Virtua Tennis 2*'s King and Queen boss characters can be unlocked by winning all of your matches in Tournament mode without dropping a single game, and then beating either King or Queen in the final.

FIGURES

20 – the number of homing pigeons spray-painted with the *Virtua Tennis 2* logo. The birds were used in the game's marketing campaign and were trained to fly in and out of Wimbledon courts during the 2003 championships.

1958 – the year *Tennis for Two* debuted. Possibly the world's first tennis video game, it was played on an oscilloscope.

Most consecutive wins on Wii Sports Tennis

Staś Kostrzewski ② played the most consecutive one-game singles matches on *Wii Sports Tennis* at a live competition held on 7 November 2007. The event was held at the Champs-Élysées branch of Virgin Megastore in Paris, France. Kostrzewski managed a run of 21 consecutive singles match victories before he was finally beaten.

Most points in *Mario Tennis* (N64, ring or points mode)

On 13 August 2002, Jason Whalls of Haslett, Missouri, USA succeeded in scoring an impressive 569 points in the Ring/Points mode (set time limit) of the Nintendo 64 version of *Mario Tennis* ①. Jason's feat was verified by a video recording of all 569 points.

Highest score in *Virtua Tennis* (Dreamcast) exhibition mode

Jan-Erik Spangberg of Sweden clocked up a total of 44,000 points on his way to achieving the highest score in the Exhibition (Los Angeles) singles mode of the Sega Dreamcast version of *Virtua Tennis*. Spangberg set the record on 14 February 2001 with the game set to "Very Hard" difficulty.

MOST POLYGONS PER PLAYER MODEL IN A TENNIS GAME

Each *Virtua Tennis 3* player model contained a staggering 25,000 polygons, giving them an incredibly lifelike look as well as highly realistic movements. Pictured here is Maria Sharapova in the flesh and as rendered in the game ⑤.

EXTREME SPORTS

FS NOSEBLUNTSLIDE

PLATFORMS

PC	PS1
PS2	XBOX
3 PS3	DS
Wii	PSP
XBOX 360	GAME BOY ADVANCE

GAMEPLAY

Players test their skills in a variety of mostly urban, youth-oriented, adrenalin-fuelled sports such as skateboarding, snowboarding and BMX biking. Points are usually scored by players demonstrating their abilities in performing tricks and stunts. Later arcade versions of the games used "real" equipment controllers, such as stand-on skate- or snowboards, to add authenticity.

First extreme sports game

Released in 1986 to the arcade and then the following year at home on the ZX Spectrum and Commodore 64, *720°* **1** was the first extreme sports video game experience. A skateboard simulation, it, like modern extreme releases, required the player to prove their worth on the streets before advancing to skating tournaments at local parks. Successful players would also be able to upgrade their skating equipment with money won from these tournaments. The **highest score attained on the arcade version** was 527,100 points by Ron Perelman (USA) in Anaheim, California, USA, on 17 June 1987.

Highest score for *SSX* "show off"

The highest trick score on the show off mode across all six tracks on snowboarding game *SSX* **4** is

3,641,581 points, held by Californian Laurent Daubas. This feat was achieved on 31 August 2001. On the same day, Laurent also managed to land the best trick score on all six tracks featured in the game. However, he has since lost the top spot on two of those tracks (Pipedream and Snowdream). In both cases he was beaten by Steve Bates of Wisconsin, USA.

Highest score on *California Games* (half-pipe)

An all-time extreme sports classic, *California Games* **2** was originally released for the Commodore 64 in 1987, featuring surfing, half-pipe, BMX and footbag modes. The highest score achieved on the half-pipe section is 33,129 by American Marc Cohen on 5 October 2007. If you manage to stay in the half-pipe long enough, an earthquake will knock the "H" from the Hollywood sign in the background, turning it into the skate-themed "ollywood".

Best-selling extreme sports game

After the success of the original *Tony Hawk's* there was never any doubt that the sequel would perform well. However, it's surprising to learn that no other extreme sports game has managed to surpass the unit sales of *Tony*

PlayStation 2

SSX

EA SPORTS BIG

TRIVIA

➲ The Tony Hawk's series is famous for its secret skaters. Each release has featured a variety of hidden characters, including a couple of Star Wars faces; Darth Maul appeared in *Tony Hawk's 3* **7** and Jango Fett in *Tony Hawk's 4*. Other guest stars so far have included Shrek, Wolverine, Spider-Man, KISS and Iron Maiden's undead mascot Eddie.

➲ *BMX XXX* **6** is the only extreme sports game to have been censored. Featuring several nude BMX riders, this was modified in the PlayStation 2 version to include black bars covering exposed body parts. Ironically, the version on the family-centric GameCube remained unchanged. *BMX XXX* was originally part of the Dave Mirra series, until Dave realised the nature of the content and requested his name be removed.

Hawk's Pro Skater 2 **3**, which sold over 2 million in the USA alone. The success of the first two games led to a huge fan base for the series and also secured Tony Hawk's position as the longest-running extreme sports franchise. There have been 12 titles released so far since the series started in 1999.

Most popular extreme location

The most popular location for extreme stars to ride in video games is New York City. So far the Big Apple has been emulated as a session location for 10 extreme games: *BMX XXX*, *Grind Session*, *Mat Hoffman's Pro BMX*, *Rolling*, *SSX Tricky*, *Thrasher* and four separate episodes of *Tony Hawk's Pro Skater* have all recreated the feel of tearing up the "city that never sleeps".

TOP SKATER!

The **highest score on the Easy/Novice course** of 1997 arcade classic *Top Skater* **8** is 1,160,526 points, by Tai Kuang Neng of Malaysia, on 27 May 2003. Tai Kuang also has the **highest score on the Hard/Expert course**, with 836,733 points, and the **highest score on the Secret course**, with an amazing 1,406,239 points.

PLATFORMS

PC | XBOX 360
PS1 | XBOX
PS2 | DS
3 |
PSP | Wii

GAMEPLAY

From the earliest days of ice hockey games, the aim has been pretty much the same: get the puck into your opponent's goal more often than he gets it into yours. Of course, the complexity of graphics and the level of skill required to play has increased dramatically since the early days, so that now players control teams in incredible 3D and can execute moves and shots the pros would be proud of.

First ice hockey game The first ice hockey game to receive a commercial release was *NHL Ice Hockey* ❶ on the Intellivision, released in 1979. The game, the first to be licensed by the NHL, had no single player mode and pitted two player-controlled teams against each other.

Longest-running ice hockey series The longest-running ice hockey video game series is Electronic Arts' *NHL* series. The franchise's first release,

NHL Hockey, hit the shelves in 1991 for the PC, Mega Drive and Game Gear. The series enjoyed its 16th anniversary in 2007 with the release of *NHL 08* ❸.

First ice hockey game to feature the ESPN license While several ice hockey games have carried the ESPN license over the years, the first one to be endorsed by the sports broadcasting channel was the 1994 *ESPN National Hockey Night* for the SNES and Sega Mega Drive. ESPN announcer Bill Clement provided commentary in the game.

Most ice hockey game records Serial record-breaker Rudy Ferretti of East Manhattan,

New York, USA, is the most prolific ice hockey record-breaker on the planet, holding an impressive 11 ice hockey world records. His records include unsurpassed achievements on a wide range of ice hockey games including titles from the *NHL*, *NHLPA* and *Wayne Gretzky* series.

Highest winning margin in *NHL 98* (SNES) One of Rudy Ferretti's most recent records was set on 14 November 2006, when he managed to beat a computer-controlled opponent on the SNES version of *NHL 98* by a 13-point margin. The game was played with 10-minute periods. Ferretti was allowed to pick any teams.

Highest winning margin in *NHLPA Hockey 93* (SNES) 14 November 2006 was clearly a very good day for Rudy Ferretti, as after securing his record in *NHL 98* (see above), he went on to achieve another highest margin of victory record. This time, the game was *NHLPA Hockey 93* ❻ on the SNES. Once again, Ferretti's margin of victory was 13 points in a game of 10-minute periods and with Ferretti able to pick any teams.

FIRST ICE HOCKEY GAME LICENSED BY A PRO PLAYER

Back in 1988, Wayne Gretzky ❹ became the first professional player to lend his name to an ice hockey game, when Bethesda Softworks LLC released *Wayne Gretzky Hockey* for PC, Atari ST, Macintosh and NES. Its lightning-quick top-down action recreated all the thrills of the real life sport, right down to scuffles between the players.

TRIVIA

➲ The so-called EA Cover Curse (usually associated with the publisher's NFL series) is also said to apply to the NHL series. The most harrowing example was when *NHL 2004*'s cover player Dany Heatley **5** was involved in a horrific car accident that killed his friend and teammate, Dan Snyder, shortly after the game's release.

➲ The European release of *NHL Hockey* (the first game in the longest running NHL series of all time) featured 22 European teams rather than the 24 NHL teams featured in the US release.

Highest winning margin in *NHL 94* (Sega Genesis)

The highest margin of victory in a 10-minute per period game of *NHL 94* **2** (played in regular season mode) is 16, achieved on 21 August 2006 by Terence O'Neill of Staten Island, New York, USA.

Highest winning margin in *NHL 2004* (PlayStation 2), exhibition mode

The USA's Terence O'Neill (see above) achieved the highest recorded margin of victory in an exhibition mode game of *NHL 2004* for PlayStation 2. He thrashed his computer-controlled opponent by an impressive 12-point margin on 10 September 2006, with game settings on default and team line edits allowed.

> **"** The NHL *games are designed and developed by a collection of **passionate and knowledgeable** hockey fans.* **"**
>
> Kevin Wilkinson, Executive Producer, NHL

HOT TIP

Boost your Gamerscore on the Xbox 360 version of *NHL 2K8*:

"Are we there yet?" – win 100 games to net yourself 150 points.

"No Favourites" – play one game with each team for 50 points.

"Online gamer" – if you play 30 ranked matches online you'll earn yourself another 100 points.

"Dynasty" – win three Stanley Cups in a row, at pro difficulty level, for 100 points.

"Dominance" – win the Stanley Cup and the President's Trophy in the same year to get 75 points.

SPORTS GAMES ROUND-UP

HOT TIP

How to unlock secret features for added fun in the *Wii Sports* "Bowling" game:

Diamond bowling ball: Reach pro level.

Red bowling ball: Press and hold LEFT on the control pad while the screen is fading to black before you start bowling.

Gold bowling ball: Press and hold RIGHT on the control pad while the screen is fading to black before you start bowling.

Blue bowling ball: Press and hold UP on the control pad while the screen is fading to black before you start bowling.

Green bowling ball: Press and hold DOWN on the control pad while the screen is fading to black before you start bowling.

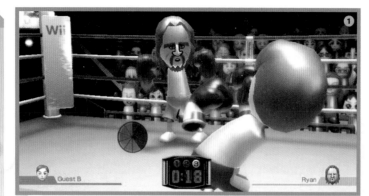

Fastest knockout in *Wii Sports – Boxing*

Game: *Wii Sports – Boxing*
Publisher: Nintendo

The fastest ever recorded knockout in a single-player match of the boxing game ① of *Wii Sports* on the Wii is the lightning-fast 49 seconds (into round one), a record which was set on 25 May 2007 by William Willemstyn III of the USA. According to records website Twin Galaxies, Willemstyn also holds the records for working the bag in training, with 18 points, and most punches thrown in training with 29.

Fastest knockout in *Riddick Bowe Boxing* (SNES)

Game: *Riddick Bowe Boxing*
Publisher: Extreme Entertainment

On 27 September 2004, Rudy Ferretti of East Manhattan, New York, USA, knocked out his computer-controlled opponent in just 47 seconds (into round one) in a single-player match of *Riddick Bowe Boxing* on the SNES.

Fastest time for 100 Qbit sprint in *Alien Olympics*

Game: *Alien Olympics*
Publisher: Mindscape, Inc.

Prolific record-breaker Tom Duncan of New Castle, Indiana, USA, set the fastest recorded time for the 100 Qbit sprint in *Alien Olympics* ⑤ on the Game Boy/Game Boy Color. Duncan completed the race in 15.36 seconds on 8 May 2006.

Fastest 100-metre sprint in *Carl Lewis Athletics 2000*

Game: *Carl Lewis Athletics 2000*
Publisher: Ubisoft

On 25 November 2006, Tom Duncan recorded the fastest-ever time for the 100-metre sprint in *Carl Lewis Athletics 2000* on the Game Boy/Game Boy Color, completing the race in 9.2 seconds.

MOST WWE THQ SUPERSTAR CHALLENGE TITLES

Game: *SmackDown vs. Raw*
Publisher: THQ

For the past five years at WrestleMania, THQ has held an annual tournament called the Superstar Challenge, in which WWE wrestlers compete for the title of best *SmackDown vs. Raw* player. The highest number of tournament victories so far is four, a record held by Shelton Benjamin ②. The only other winner of the Superstar Challenge has been Elijah Burke, who won the title in 2007 at WrestleMania 23.

1,095 – days worth of real-world statistics that were used to build realistic AI for every single player featured in *Major League Baseball 2K6*

TRIVIA

➲ Due to alleged coding issues, it's apparently impossible to break the archery and skeet records in the Mega Drive's *Olympic Summer Games* 7 .

➲ If you look at the background behind the court while playing the tennis game 6 on *Wii Sports*, you'll see a white building. This is a recreation of Nintendo's headquarters in Kyoto, Japan.

➲ 2003's *WWE Raw 2* featured a dynamic signboard mechanic, whereby the crowd would hold up signs bearing slogans which were either for or against the wrestler when he shifted his attitude from good guy to bad guy or vice versa.

Furthest javelin throw in *Carl Lewis Athletics 2000*

Game: *Carl Lewis Athletics 2000*
Publisher: Ubisoft
By successfully throwing a javelin 87.03 metres in *Carl Lewis Athletics 2000* 3 on the Game Boy/Game Boy Color, Tom Duncan recorded the furthest-ever javelin throw. Duncan achieved the feat on 24 December 2006, thus rounding off an incredibly successful year of video game record-breaking with another superlative sports record.

Quickest victory in *WWF No Mercy* on Nintendo 64

Game: *WWF No Mercy*
Publisher: THQ
On 1 June 2001, Jesse Krueger of Minnesota, USA, set the world record for the fastest victory in a single bout of *WWF No Mercy* 4 on the Nintendo 64. Krueger won his Exhibition mode match against an AI opponent set to Expert level in just 57 seconds, with count outs set to 20 seconds and with no TKO, DQ or rope break.

*"WWE's **the greatest form of sports entertainment in history,** and the audience loves it for that. "*

Vince McMahon, Chairman of WWE

Quickest 100-metre dash in *Olympic Summer Games* (PlayStation)

Game: *Olympic Summer Games*
Publisher: US Gold
On 30 June 2000, Carlos Kruegar of Penha, Brazil, set a world record of 6.980 seconds for the 100-metre dash event in *Olympic Summer Games* on PlayStation. The game was set to factory default when he achieved the record.

HIGHEST SCORE IN *WII SPORTS – BOWLING*

Game: *Wii Sports – Bowling* **Publisher:** Nintendo
Carl Aspinwall of Derry, New Hampshire, USA, holds the highest recorded score of 300 points (the score needed for a "perfect game") for the Bowling section of *Wii Sports* on the Nintendo Wii. Aspinwall set the record on 26 April 2007 with the game set to the default settings.

FACT
The realistic sound effects in *Fight Night Round 3* come from recordings of someone punching a dead pig!

RACING GAMES

OUR EXPERT

After editing the award-winning website Arcade Perfect, **Duncan Harris** became games editor for *Edge* magazine, the UK's most respected multi-platform print title. Duncan now contributes to *Edge*, *PC Gamer*, *PSM3*, *Official PlayStation Magazine* and *Games Master*. He has also worked for *NGamer*, *ImagineFX*, Nvidia and *FHM*.

OUTLINE

Played either in the first or third person, racing games can feature any kind of vehicle, from a basic go-kart through to a futuristic weapon-equipped hovercraft, and can be set anywhere from real-life racing circuits to fantasy worlds. But whatever you're driving and wherever you are, the aim is usually the same: use your driving skills to get to where you need to be as quickly as you can.

WHETHER IT'S PULLING 360-DEGREE SPINS PAST THE LONDON EYE, RACING AGAINST THE CLOCK OR JUST SMASHING INTO YOUR FRIENDS, RACING GAMES HAVE EVERYTHING THE SPEED FREAK NEEDS.

In 1974, the racing genre was nothing more than a block of pixels, speeding around a dot-defined track against the clock. The game was *Gran Trak 10* **1**, the **first arcade cabinet to feature a combination of gear-stick, steering wheel and foot pedals**. Not for another eight years would *Pole Position* **2** add the next piece to the puzzle, as one of the first games to feature artificially intelligent opponents on a 3D circuit. Knowing that you could race in a virtual world, developers then started asking

the whats, hows and wheres of this virtual space. On both computers and consoles were driven trucks, bikes, Batmobiles – anything that could stretch the boundaries of the genre using the current technology. Popular driving games of the 1980s include Psion's 1984 *Chequered Flag* (technically the **first racing simulator**, although it lacked opponents) and the runaway success of Sega's 1986 arcade title *Out Run*.

With 1993's *Ridge Racer*, however, technology took the lead. The late-1990s marked the dawn of a new age of realism in racing games, and the struggle to bring both vehicles and worlds closer to those TV broadcasts and real-world showrooms. Many

£20 million – the estimated cost of the F1 racing car simulator developed by the McLaren Mercedes team – the ultimate video racing game!

releases (such as *Burnout* and *OutRun 2*) stuck to the earlier principles of arcade driving with their lightning speed and simple thrills. But, despite these familiar mechanics, advances in technology and visuals remain high priority.

Now, with each revolution in special effects, analogue controls and physics come sexier, tougher and cleverer ways to drive. If it isn't *Test Drive Unlimited* squeezing an entire island paradise on to one disc, it's *Project Gotham Racing* ③ capturing every brick and rivet of the world's great cities. As the latest *Wipeout* ④ embraces PS3's tilt-sensitive controller, *TrackMania* embraces its fans by letting them lay the roads. *Gran Turismo* and *Forza Motorsport*, meanwhile, vie for the position of most realistic simulator. In this video game genre, more than any other, the race to be best is always on.

TRIVIA

➲ Despite claiming little interest in motorsport, Geoff Crammond became one of the most important names in video game racing during the 1980s and 1990s. A background in physics gave his racing simulators exceptional car handling models and driver AI, evident in titles such as *Stunt Car Racer* (1989) and the Microprose *Grand Prix* series (1992–2002).

➲ Japan has *Gran Turismo* and the USA has *Forza Motorsport*, but it's the UK that's proved to be the major racing force so far. *Burnout, GTR2, Project Gotham Racing, Driver, Motor Storm, Colin McRae Rally* and *Wipeout* are all titles developed in the UK. Even *Sega Rally* is now with a team based in the UK. ⑤

❚❚ *Games must not rely on hardware specifications, but on the creativity of the developers.* **❚❚**

Kazunori Yamauchi,
series creator of *Gran Turismo*

TIMELINE

1974: *Gran Trak 10*	**1974**
1982: *Pole Position*	
1983: *Pitstop*	
1986: *Out Run*	
1989: *Hard Drivin'*	**1989**
1989: *Indianapolis 500* ⑦	
1992: *Virtua Racing*	
1992: *Super Mario Kart*	**1992**
1993: *Ridge Racer*	
1993: *Daytona USA* ⑤	
1995: *Sega Rally Championship*	**1995**
1995: *Wipeout*	
1997: *Gran Turismo*	
1998: *Colin McRae Rally*	**1998**
1999: *Driver*	
1999: *Crazy Taxi* ⑥	
2000: *Metropolis Street Racer*	**2000**
2002: *Burnout 2: Point of Impact*	**2003**
2003: *TrackMania*	
2005: *Project Gotham 3*	
2007: *Forza 2*	**2007**

GRAN TURISMO

GRAN TURISMO®
THE REAL DRIVING SIMULATOR

PLATFORMS

PC
PlayStation
PS2
3
Wii
XBOX 360
XBOX
DS

SPEC

Developer:
Polyphony Digital
Publisher:
Sony
Initial release:
Gran Turismo (1997),
PlayStation

GAMEPLAY

Players use credits to first buy and then tune their cars, which they can enter into certain vehicle-specific events. Players progress by honing their driving skills, winning races and using the credits they win as prize money to develop a garage of cars.

Largest number of cars in a racing game With 721 available cars from 90 marques – the **largest number of manufacturers in a racing game** – *Gran Turismo 4* [1] has the largest variety of cars. Creator Kazunori Yamauchi (Japan) reportedly wanted to rival that with its upcoming PlayStation 3 sequel, but demands of PS3 development made this impossible.

Highest-selling PlayStation game Sales of 10.85 million units make the original *Gran Turismo* [3] the highest-selling game on the PlayStation. Its sequel, *Gran Turismo 2*, is the third-highest with 9.37 million units sold.

Highest-selling PlayStation 2 racing game Sales of 14.88 million units make *Gran Turismo 3: A Spec* the best-selling racing game on PlayStation 2. Were it not for *Grand Theft Auto* instalment *Vice City*, it would be the highest-selling game overall.

Highest-rated modern racing game According to aggregator website Metacritic.com, the first *Gran Turismo* has received the highest review scores of any racing game released since 1995, with an average score of 96%.

First high-resolution console racing game Running at a maximum resolution of 1080p (1,920 x 1,280 pixels), the *Gran Turismo HD Concept* demo has the highest image resolution of any console racing game. This downloadable demo is a preview of *Gran Turismo 5*, due Spring 2008.

Largest prize fund for a racing game tournament At $40,000, the prize fund for the *Gran Turismo 4* tournament at 2006's Electronic Sports World Cup [4] stands as the highest for a racing game tournament. The prizes for the top three positions were $13,000, $9,000 and $6,000.

LARGEST INSTRUCTION GUIDE FOR A RACING GAME

In China and Japan, the first editions of *Gran Turismo 4* included a 212-page reference guide [2]. The book featured a car index, an introduction to racing physics and various professional tutorials.

5,000 – the number of polygons used to render each one of the 150 cars that feature in *Gran Turismo 3 A-Spec*

GRAN TURISMO TOURNAMENT TIMES

While *Gran Turismo*'s emphasis on AI-powered single-player races has made it unpopular with professional gaming leagues, large tournaments have occasionally taken place. On 21 April 2005, retailer Game Crazy announced the ten finalists of its "Race Your Way to Vegas" event, which challenged players from across America to achieve a fastest lap of the same *Gran Turismo 4* circuit. The finalists were:

	NAME	FROM	TIME
1	Josh Lewis	Columbus, Ohio	1 min 26.982 sec
2	Steven Murphy	Derwood, Maryland	1 min 27.621 sec
3	Peter Peters	Vallejo, California	1 min 27.623 sec
4	Stephen Lau	Sugarland, Texas	1 min 27.726 sec
5	Andrew Holtz	Fairborn, Ohio	1 min 27.808 sec
6	Ray Lee	Houston, Texas	1 min 27.915 sec
7	Jonathan Mason	Brooklyn, New York	1 min 28.121 sec
8	Troy Dozler	Vancouver, Washington	1 min 28.158 sec
9	William Stephens	Indianapolis, Indiana	1 min 28.238 sec
10	Ramiro Galindo	Hutto, Texas	1 min 28.313 sec

TRIVIA

➲ No fewer than four "concept" versions preceded the release of *Gran Turismo 4*. They were the 2001 Tokyo Collection, 2002 Tokyo-Seoul edition, 2002 Tokyo-Geneva edition and a more substantial demo, with 50 cars and five courses, entitled *Gran Turismo 4 Prologue*.

➲ The first *Gran Turismo* is the only racing game to receive a 10/10 score from *Edge* magazine since it was first published in 1993.

➲ Swedish rock band The Cardigans have twice referenced *Gran Turismo* in their work. Their fourth album shares its name, while the track "My Favourite Game" refers to its popularity during tour bus journeys.

HOT TIP

Gran Turismo 4 starts you out with just 10,000 virtual credits – not much when you consider that later cars cost hundreds of thousands. To get underway in the quickest possible time, head for the Historic Showroom and pick up the Mazda MX-5 Miata. At 6,000 credits, it leaves you with sufficient money for upgrades and shots at several early contests.

PROJECT GOTHAM RACING

PROJECT GOTHAM RACING

PLATFORMS

PC | XBOX 360
PlayStation 2 | XBOX
PSP | 3DS
PlayStation 3 | Game Boy Advance
PlayStation | Wii

SPEC

Developer:
Bizarre Creations
Publisher:
Microsoft
Initial release:
Project Gotham Racing (2001), Xbox

GAMEPLAY

A visually astonishing racing series played out in incredible supercars in real-world, photorealistic locations. As with most racing games, the aim is to finish the course in the fastest possible time, but in *PGR*, drivers can also advance by scoring Kudos points awarded for driving skill.

Most complex race environment With 1 million polygons making up its Brooklyn Bridge alone, *Project Gotham Racing 3*'s (PGR3) ❶ New York City is the most complex environment in a racing game. The bridge has roughly the same polygon-count as an entire track in *PGR2* ❷.

Largest licensed soundtrack included in a racing game 90 licensed songs across 9 genres make up *PGR3*'s soundtrack, the largest of its kind in any racing game.

First console racing game to integrate online data into offline play By combining Xbox Live player information with offline scoreboards and menus, *PGR* was the first racing game on a console to integrate online data with offline play. This feature has since evolved in later installments.

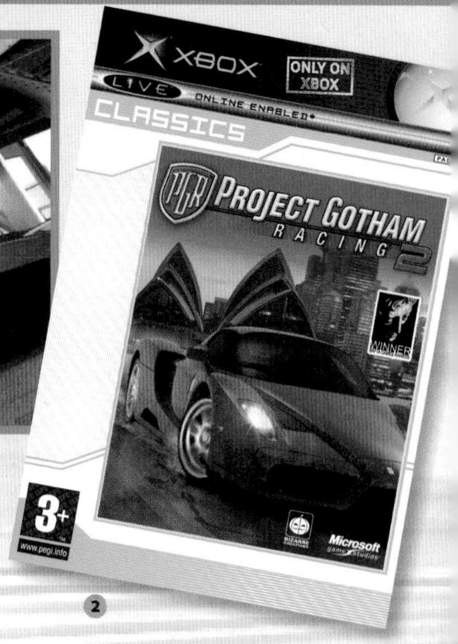

❷

30,000 – the number of spectators who could view any given *PGR3* race live online by watching Gotham TV on the Xbox Live

XBOX LIVE *PGR3* NÜRBURGRING TRACK BEST TIMES

With its replay broadcasts and global leaderboards, the Gotham TV feature of *PGR3* inspired thousands of players to log race times on Xbox Live. The most dedicated players inevitably focused on the game's arduous, breakneck rendition of the famous Nürburgring Nordschleife. Here are the best of the best, as recorded on Xbox Live. All times were recorded using the Ferrari F50 GT.

	XBOX LIVE GAMETAG	TIME	DATE
1	VVV Neo Jake	6 min 48.28 sec	18 Apr 2007
2	D2C Handewasser	6 min 48.7 sec	22 Feb 2007
3	FERRARI F50 GT	6 min 49.62 sec	23 Jan 2007
4	N0RM5KI	6 min 50.7 sec	24 Dec 2006
5	D2C Ch0mpr	6 min 51.76 sec	4 Sep 2006
6	acX Arma360	6 min 51.84 sec	24 Jan 2007
6	R1R RiCH	6 min 51.84 sec	9 Aug 2007
8	VVV VeNoM	6 min 51.94 sec	3 Jun 2007
9	acX Schneemann	6 min 52 sec	6 May 2007
10	acX BigSchnigg	6 min 52.25 sec	14 Feb 2007
11	TTR Avesta	6 min 52.88 sec	13 Apr 2007
12	CODI VEYRON	6 min 53.13 sec	25 Aug 2006
12	digitalmovement	6 min 53.13 sec	20 Jan 2007
14	TTR McLaren F1	6 min 53.62 sec	10 Mar 2006
15	D0NT WALK	6 min 53.71 sec	10 Jan 2007
16	TzZ M3NTALIST	6 min 53.92 sec	3 May 2007
17	VVV Hyperion	6 min 54 sec	2 Sep 2006
17	VVV Daveyskillz	6 min 54 sec	19 Jan 2007
19	TTR Chief	6 min 54.01 sec	25 Mar 2006
20	NAVALHAWKEYE	6 min 54.32 sec	5 Feb 2006

*"Anyone can make a good-looking game but **the top games blow you away by being super-realistic**, adding things that you didn't expect and surprising you."*

Ged Talbert, lead designer *PGR4*

FACT

The latest game in the series, *PGR4*, features a dynamic theme tune by The Prodigy, entitled "Shadow". By breaking the song down and sequencing it in real-time, the game alters the music as players navigate through its menus.

FIGURES

50 ft – the size of the lettering of the "good luck" message given to Formula One racing driver Lewis Hamilton by *PGR* developer Bizarre Creations. The message was written in skid marks by professional stunt drivers who burned through **3** sets of tyres!

3 – the number of *PGR2* soundtracks released by The Malaco Music Group. Each CD contained **15** tracks.

Most complex car models in a racing game *PGR4*

has the most complex car models of any racing game; each is made of around 70-100,000 polygons. This includes the interiors, which account for nearly half that total.

Most commercially successful mini-game With

200,000 trial downloads and 45,000 paid downloads in its first two months on release, *Geometry Wars: Retro Evolved* (also included with *PGR3)* is the most commercially successful mini-game. *PGR4* includes the sequel, *Geometry Wars Wave*.

First console racing game to feature streaming race replays *PGR3* was the

first console racing game to allow the in-game viewing of online race replays. The feature was integral to its Gotham TV component, which broadcast live data from the Xbox Live servers to players around the world. The TV service also meant players could become spectators and watch races being played out live around the world.

TRIVIA

➲ Although *Metropolis Street Racer* didn't share the same publisher, name or format – it was released by Sega for its Dreamcast console – it's unarguably the first in the series from the developer. It establishes the core elements which set the *PGR* series apart from all other racing games.

➲ *Metropolis Street Racer* was originally intended for release alongside Sega's US launch of the Dreamcast on 9 September 1999. Repeat delays and technical problems, however, delayed the project for over a year. It was eventually released, still with glitches, but to wide acclaim, in November 2000.

TRACKMANIA

PLATFORMS

PC · XBOX 360 · PS3 · XBOX · DS · 3 · PSP · Wii

SPEC

Developer:
Nadeo
Publisher:
Focus Interactive/ Digital Jesters
Initial release:
Trackmania (2003), PC

GAMEPLAY

Players race on standard tracks to earn "Coppers", the special TrackMania currency that allows them to buy blocks of track so that they can create and modify their own raceway. Described as "part sim, part arcade and part puzzle", the game has a massive following online, where fans race against each other.

BIGGEST ONLINE RACE

The biggest race ever staged online was in *TrackMania*, where 132 players took part in a single time trial. In addition to standard races, the game uses a turn-based system to achieve such large numbers of racers.

Largest content base of any racing game The largest amount of content available in any racing game is the pool of tracks and cars downloadable in *TrackMania*. The *TrackMania* Exchange website boasts 176,506 user-created tracks, the *TrackMania* Car Park website boasting 228 unique cars.

First publicly available game developed specifically for an online competition The first publicly available game made specifically for an online competition was *TrackMania Nations*, developed for the 2006 Electronic Sports World Cup (ESWC). In the run-up to the competition, this enhanced, stadium-based version was free to download from the ESWC website.

Most popular online racing sim The *TrackMania* series is the most popular online racing sim franchise, with 3,398,745 online player registrations as of 22 October 2007. All versions of the game can compete on the same servers.

Most nationalities in an offline racing competition Participants from a record 34 nations entered the *TrackMania* event at 2007's Electronic Sports World Cup.

Design It. Build It. Drive It!

PC CD-ROM

NADEO

TrackMania®

$40,000 – total prize pot at the 2006 Electronic Sports World Cup *TrackMania Nations* face-off in Paris, France

TRACKMANIA AT ESWC 2007

Having been specially developed for the Electronic Sports World Cup in 2006, *TrackMania Nations* returned to the ESWC at the 2007 event. Held at the Parc des Expositions de la Porte de Versailles in Paris, France, over the weekend of 7–8 July 2007, the *TrackMania Nations* event generated a huge amount of interest in the gaming community. The final was raced over three tracks, with the winner of each race collecting 30 points and scores combined for the three races to find the overall champion.

POSITION	NAME	POINTS	PRIZE MONEY
1	Freek Molema (XeNoGeaR)	86	$10,000
2	Dorian Vallet (Carl)	76	$6,000
3	Simon Ferreira (Lign)	68	$3,000
4	Charles Devillard (selrahc37)	63	–

Most popular user-created video The most popular video created by a gamer using in-game materials is *1K Project II* by Blackshark.

A composite of 1,000 different *TrackMania* replays, it has been viewed over two million times on the website GameTrailers.com.

TRIVIA

➲ There's little that can't be customised in *TrackMania*, especially in its more recent versions. In addition to their own track layouts and cars, players can create animated avatars (for use on the game's internet forums), car horn noises, music tracks, billboards, tournaments and car clubs.

➲ According to creator Florent Castelnerac, *TrackMania* wasn't even inspired by an existing racing game. Instead, it took its cues from classic management game *Sim City*. Other inspirations included *Lemmings*, *Super Monkey Ball* and *Quake*.

➲ A persistent controversy surrounding *TrackMania* has been its use of the notorious StarForce copy protection system. Many users have claimed the software, which checks to see if the original game disc is in your drive, damages PCs. No conclusive proof exists, however, and the StarForce version included with *TrackMania United* has been updated from previous versions.

HOT TIP

Owners of *TrackMania United* looking to get involved in the *TrackMania* community should look at ManiaLinks, the game's inbuilt community browser. Here you'll find links to the very best cars, tracks and videos.

COLIN MCRAE RALLY

colin mcrae™

PLATFORMS

PC | XBOX 360
PS1 | XBOX
PS2 | DS
3 | GAME BOY ADVANCE
PSP | Wii

SPEC

Developer:
Codemasters
Publisher:
Codemasters
Initial release:
*Colin McRae Rally
(1998)*, PlayStation

GAMEPLAY

Developed with the involvement of the late Colin McRae, the 1995 World Rally Champion, the Colin McRae series boasts a high level of realism that makes the player feel like they are driving a high performance rally car. A huge number of gameplay options, including single and multiplayer modes, championship and customised rallies, add to a hugely satisfying driving experience.

Most complex audio in a racing game With up to 96 active sound effects per car at any one time, *Colin McRae: DiRT* ① features the most complex audio in any racing game. The total number of audio samples featured is 16,121, which form 1,005,772,154,467,879,035,136 (over one sextillion) different combinations during crashes.

First BAFTA for a rally game At the British Academy of Film and Television Arts (BAFTA) Game Awards of 2005, *Colin McRae Rally 2005* on the N-Gage won Best Handheld Game.

Most corners in a single racetrack (cars) The largest number of corners on a racetrack for a car-based racing game is 156, as featured in the Pike's Peak Hill Climb ② in

Colin McRae: DiRT. In comparison, the Nürburgring used in *Gran Turismo* boasts just 73.

Most camera views in a racing game The largest number of camera views in a racing game is 1,012, as featured in *Colin McRae: DiRT*. That total comprises 22 different cameras (including six available while driving) for each of the game's 46 cars.

MOST CO-DRIVER PACE NOTES IN A RALLY GAME

Colin McRae: DiRT features 1,920 co-driver pace notes (the advice given by the co-driver to help the driver negotiate the rally course) – the most for any rally game.

– the number of different combinations of sound effects possible in *Colin McRae: DiRT*

PIKE'S PEAK HILL CLIMB TIMES

The Pike's Peak Hill Climb is the jewel in the crown of the Colin McRae franchise, an epic time trial that snakes its way to the peak of the Rocky Mountains. Here are its top 10 racers, together with their cars and times, recorded from the Xbox 360 Live leaderboards.

	NAME	CAR	TIME
1	DDD Torsby	Toyota Celica	6 min 52.02 sec
2	MEGA NG MAN	Toyota Celica	6 min 53.32 sec
3	Gerard Martinez	Toyota Celica	6 min 54.48 sec
4	Michal Basta	Toyota Celica	6 min 59.04 sec
5	Ulquoirra BE	Toyota Celica	7 min 00.14 sec
6	Gyro Fett	Toyota Celica	7 min 01.18 sec
7	Coolspirit	Toyota Celica	7 min 01.54 sec
8	FAF Candy	Toyota Celica	7 min 01.87 sec
9	OLLE THE FISH	Toyota Celica	7 min 02.53 sec
10	FAF Skyline GTR	Suzuki Escudo	7 min 02.68 sec

FASTEST PHYSICS ENGINE IN A RACING GAME

The fastest physics engine in a racing game is that of *Colin McRae: DiRT*, which updates at 1,000 hz (1,000 times a second). In comparison, *Forza Motorsport 2*'s physics update at only 360 hz.

❝*I have played lots of crap games. We wanted this one to be **as realistic and as close to reality as possible.*❞**

Colin McCrae, speaking before the release of the second *Colin McRae Rally* game in 2000.

TRIVIA

➲ The early Colin McRae titles featured some of the racing genre's more interesting cheats. Examples include turning co-driver Nicky Grist into an elf and turning your car into either a Micro Machine or a giant wobbling blob of jelly!

➲ Neon, the technology behind *Colin McRae: DiRT*, is powerful enough to render near-photorealistic visuals. Paint is scratched off as cars clip the scenery, barriers bend during impact and the tracks are composed of over 65 different surfaces.

➲ Only the first three Colin McRae titles bore the official name and liveries of the World Rally Championship (WRC), a licence that then moved to Sony and Evolution Studios.

FIGURES

366 – the number of racetracks featured in the six main games of the *Colin McRae Rally* series.

145 – the number of vehicles featured in the series.

MARIO KART

First console kart racing game
The first game in the kart-racing genre was *Super Mario Kart*, released in 1992. Games it has inspired include *Crash Nitro Kart*, *Lego Racers* and *Looney Tunes Racing*. It also spawned a series of Mario Kart games for the Nintendo 64, Game Boy Advance, GameCube, Nintendo DS and an arcade machine.

Best-selling Nintendo racing game
Sales of 8.47 million units make *Mario Kart 64* the highest-selling racing game on Nintendo 64. The platformer *Super Mario 64* is the only game to have outsold it.

The **best-selling racing game on the SNES** is *Super Mario Kart*, with sales of 8 million units; and the **best-selling racing game on the GameCube** is *Mario Kart: Double Dash!* **1**, which has sold over 6.6 million units.

Best-selling handheld racing game
Sales of 7.83 million units make *Mario Kart DS* **2** the highest-selling racing game on any handheld. In comparison, *Wipeout Pure* on the PSP has sold just 1 million units.

First Nintendo game to feature competitive online play
The first Nintendo-published game to feature competitive online play was *Mario Kart DS*, in 2005. While earlier online titles included *Animal Crossing* and *Phantasy Star Online Episode I & II*, none allowed players to battle each other.

PLATFORMS

SPEC

Developer:
Nintendo
Publisher:
Nintendo
Initial release:
Super Mario Kart
(1992), SNES

GAMEPLAY

The inventor and reigning champion of the kart-racing genre. Race as one of your favourite Nintendo characters in a variety of courses, challenges or face-offs, in both single and multiplayer games. Gameplay is boosted by a series of items left lying around the circuits – whether bonus objects to boost speed or to throw as projectiles, or hazards such as slippery bananas.

HIGH SCORES

In December 2005, fan website N-Sider staged an official 32-player *Mario Kart DS* tournament via the game's online network. Player groups – the game only allows eight players per race – were organised over the IRC (Internet Relay Chat) network, with all players required to submit results to ensure their authenticity. The tournament was sponsored by Nintendo of America and the prizes included consoles and limited edition merchandise. The top racers were:

PLAYER	POINTS
Taylor Yust	28
Kevin Caron	22
Robert Strutz	22
Adam Fletcher	16

MARIO ARCADE

Mario Kart Arcade GP **3**, an arcade cabinet co-developed by Nintendo and Namco, is the **only Mario Kart game to feature guest appearances by non-Nintendo characters**. PAC-Man, Blinky and Ms PAC-Man are all playable.

8.47 million – units sold of *Mario Kart 64*, the biggest-selling game in the series and the second biggest-selling game ever on the N64

TRIVIA

➲ *Mario Kart 64*'s working title was *Mario Kart R*, but the name was dropped following the release of *Sonic R*, a racing game featuring Sonic the Hedgehog. The duo provided gaming with its most memorable rivalry, one that was revived in 2007 with *Sonic & Mario at the Olympic Games*.

➲ Just as characters from other Nintendo games appear in *Mario Kart*, so *Mario Kart* has occasionally returned the favour. Remote-controlled karts are hidden in virtual pet game *Nintendogs*, while *Super Smash Bros. Brawl* for the Wii features an arena themed entirely around *Mario Kart*.

❝ With two players, Mario Kart *is the* **most racing fun to be had** *anywhere.* ❞

Edward Laurence,
Mean Machines magazine

FIGURES

35 – position reached by *Super Mario Kart* in *Game Informer* magazine's chart of the 100 greatest games of all time.

RACING GAMES ROUND-UP

FACTS

➲ *Pole Position*, the **most popular arcade game of 1983**, was also the **first to feature in-game advertising** – Marlboro, Martini, Pepsi and 7-Eleven were among the many brands promoted on billboards surrounding the race track. Namco released it in 1982.

➲ *Spyhunter* (1983), one of the most popular action-driving games ever, has been in movie development since 2003. Having gone through various treatments and directors, it's now due for release in 2009 by British director Paul W.S. Anderson.

First driving game (first-person)
Game: *Night Driver*
Publisher: Atari
This simple 1976 arcade game required the player to negotiate a road at night without hitting the roadside. The car itself was not computer-generated: it was a printed graphic stuck to the screen!

First "caRPG"
Game: *Final Lap Twin*
Publisher: NEC
Final Lap Twin (1989) for the PC Engine, was the first game to combine racing and role-playing elements ("caRPG"). Its Quest mode, in which a young boy dreams of becoming a world champion, features random battles and map-based adventuring.

First driving game to feature true force feedback
Game: *Hard Drivin'*
Publisher: Atari
Originally designed as a driving sim, *Hard Drivin'* ①, released to arcades in 1988, featured a motor that put force on the steering wheel to simulate feedback from the car's tyres.

Longest real-life circuit
Game: Various
Publisher: N/A
At 20.8 km (12.9 miles), Germany's Nürburgring Nordschleife is the longest real circuit to feature in a car racing game. Appearances include the 2005 release of *Gran Turismo 4* ②.

Largest driving game series
Game: *Need For Speed* (series)
Publisher: Electronic Arts
Need For Speed has lent its name to 17 different racing games since 1995.

First use of polygonal 3D
Game: *Drivers Eyes*
Publisher: Namco
The arcade game *Drivers Eyes* (1987) was the first to feature polygonal 3D environments.

First open-world driving game
Game: *Turbo Esprit*
Publisher: Durell Software
The first game to feature an open-world environment was the 1986 *Turbo Esprit* for the ZX Spectrum. The game is commonly held responsible for the success of the genre.

Most car classes in a single race event
Game: *Motor Storm*
Publisher: Sony
Motor Storm ③ features the most car classes in a single race event, with seven. The classes are MX Bikes, ATVs, Buggies, Rally Cars, Racing Trucks, Mudpluggers and Big Rigs.

MOST TRACK IN A SINGLE RACE ENVIRONMENT
Game: *Test Drive Unlimited*
Publisher: Atari
Featuring over 1,609 km (1,000 miles) of continuous road, *Test Drive Unlimited*'s version of Oahu, Hawaii ④ has the most track space in a single race environment.

3,182,535 – copies of *Gran Turismo* sold on its first day of release, the biggest-selling PlayStation 2 game ever, according to Sony

First multi-cabinet arcade game

Game: *Final Lap*
Publisher: Namco
The first racing game to support multiple players via linked cabinets was *Final Lap*, released to arcades in 1987. By linking four of the dual-screen machines, races of up to eight players – who controlled the cars using a steering wheel, pedals and a gear shift – could be supported around a representation of Japan's Suzuka Circuit.

Most comprehensive customisation suite

Game: *Forza Motorsport 2*
Publisher: Microsoft
Forza Motorsport 2 **5**, released in 2007, allows users to decorate their cars with over 4,000 layers of decals.

Most ported racing game

Game: *Pole Position*
Publisher: Atari
Ported to 20 different platforms following its 1982 arcade release, Atari's hugely popular *Pole Position* has appeared on the largest number of formats for an individual racing game. This figure is a combination of the number of games that were sold as stand-alones (12) and the number that were sold as part of a games pack (8).

Most profitable arcade cabinet

Game: *Sega Rally Championship*
Publisher: Sega
A 12-year-old *Sega Rally Championship* arcade machine is the most profitable arcade unit of all time, having taken £750,000 in coins during its lifetime.

First racing game withheld from release by UK censors

Game: *Carmageddon*
Publisher: SCI
Carmageddon **6** remains the first and only racing game to be initially refused a rating. Objectives included destroying other cars and being first to run over every pedestrian in the level.

Longest-running franchise

Game: *Test Drive* (series)
Publisher: Accolade/Atari
Debuting in 1987, *Test Drive* is the longest-running racing series. Its most recent title, *Test Drive Unlimited*, was released in 2006.

FACTS

➲ The first arcade game to feature steering wheel, gear shift and accelerator/brake pedals was Atari's 1974 *Gran Trak 10*. A hybrid race and maze challenge, the aim was to speed around the track in the fastest time while collecting points.

➲ American NASCAR star Dale Earnhardt Jr claims to use video games to help familiarise himself with a race track. In one interview, he stated that "the visuals are pretty close nowadays so I can refresh my brain and then, when I get in the real race car, I'm ready to go."

HIGHEST ATTAINABLE SPEED

Game: *Powerdrome* **Publisher:** Mud Duck Productions
The fastest speed in a racing game is 2,414 km/h (1,500 mph), achievable in *Powerdrome* **7**, which was released in 2004. A bug in the game *Big Rigs*, meanwhile, allows its trucks to accelerate indefinitely, but this doesn't fall within the intended rules.

ROLE-PLAYING GAMES

OUR EXPERT

Jon Hamblin's work has appeared in magazines such as *Edge*, *Official PlayStation 2 Magazine* and *SFX*. He has also worked in game development at Sega, and on ITV games show *Cybernet*. A long-term fan of RPGs, in 2005 Jon travelled to Japan to film cosplayers at the Tokyo Game Show for *Edge*.

OUTLINE

The role-playing game (or RPG) is one of the most popular genres in gaming today. RPGs focus on telling epic stories that can often take over 100 hours to unfold as the player progresses. They are generally built upon a quest structure, whereby the player undertakes many short missions while accomplishing their main goal.

WITH THEIR WELL-DEFINED CHARACTERS, STRONG STORYLINES AND BUTT-NUMBING GAME LENGTH, ROLE-PLAYING GAMES PROVIDE ALL THE ELEMENTS REQUIRED FOR AN EPIC ADVENTURE.

Computer and console role-playing games (RPGs) were largely a by-product of the huge popularity of tabletop gaming **1** in the 1970s, and particularly TSR's *Dungeons & Dragons* series. Often based around Tolkien-esque worlds full of wizards and demons, table-top games relied on the ability of a nominated dungeon master to invent compelling quests for the adventurers to take on.

As computer games took off, it didn't take long for people to realise that a computer could act as a dungeon master, generating quests for users to embark on. Arguably the **first computer-based RPG** was *dnd*, an entirely text-based game based on *Dungeons & Dragons* (hence *dnd*) that was developed at Southern Illinois University, USA, in 1974. (See page 168 for more details).

The first computer-based RPG series that really captured player's imaginations, *Ultima* **2**, didn't arrive until 1980. Designed by the eccentric programmer Richard Garriot, *Ultima*'s well-developed characterisation and use of graphics sparked a huge trend for adventure games.

TIMELINE

1974

1974: PLATO's *dnd* – one of the first computer-based RPG

1979: Edu-Ware issued *Space/Space II*, the first RPG to appear on a PC

1983

1980: *Ultima* **2** released – one of the first RPGs to feature graphics

1982: *Dragon Stomper* released for Atari 2600 – the first console RPG

1983: *Ultima III* released – the first RPG to feature animated graphics

1985: *The Bard's Tale* **3** released – the first RPG with 3D environments

1986

1986: The *Dragon Quest* series begins

1986: *Phantasy Star* series launched

1987

1987: *Dungeon Master* released

1991: The first version of *Neverwinter Nights* released – the first graphical MMORPG

1979 – the year that *Akalabeth: World Of Doom*, the predecessor to the popular *Ultima* series, was released

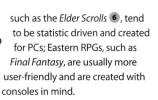

such as the *Elder Scrolls* **6**, tend to be statistic driven and created for PCs; Eastern RPGs, such as *Final Fantasy*, are usually more user-friendly and are created with consoles in mind.

Another difference between Eastern and Western RPGs is, of course, the language, which throws up its own problems. European and American fans of Japanese RPGs often find themselves waiting a year or more after a game's Japanese release until they are able to play them. This is because of the huge amount of time it takes to translate thousands of lines of text into English and other languages. *Dragon Quest VIII* **7**, for example, took two years to reach Europe, but most gamers agreed it was worth the wait.

The popularity of the *Ultima* series has grown over the years, and has become the **longest-running RPG franchise**.

In 1986, the first *Dragon Quest* game was released in Japan, popularising the genre to the Far East and inspiring hundreds of subsequent RPGs, including the highly popular *Final Fantasy* series, which began in 1987, and the *Pokémon* franchise, which was a massive success on its launch in 1996.

Western and Eastern RPGs have continued to evolve over the years with a few subtle differences – Western RPGs,

DESIGNER

Richard Garriot **9**, known as "Lord British" to his fans, built a house filled with traps and secret passage-ways with the proceeds of his highly successful *Ultima* role-playing game series. The house, known as Britannia Manor, was the scene of elaborate role-playing parties where guests, usually admirers of the designer, who queued for invitations, would interact with actors and the house itself.

TRIVIA

➲ Japanese gamers show their devotion to their favourite RPG games by indulging in "cosplay", a contraction of "costume roleplay" **8**. A phenomenally popular pastime, cosplayers dress as their favourite characters and meet at cosplay events. The hobby is exploding in the US and Europe now too, with the 2006 US Anime Expo attracting over 40,000 cosplayers. One of the largest cosplay events is Comiket in Japan, which can attract up to 100,000 cosplayers biannually!

1994

1994: *Elder Scrolls: Arena* released

1996: *Pocket Monsters Red & Green* **5** – the first Pokémon game and an instant success

1996

1996: *Elder Scrolls: Daggerfall* released, with largest RPG environment

1997: *Shemue* released – the most expensive RPG ever created

2002

2002: A re-imagined version of *Neverwinter Nights* **4** released

2003: *Knights Of The Old Republic* **10** released – the first *Star Wars* RPG

2003

2006

2006: *Elder Scrolls IV: Oblivion* released – the best-selling console RPG

2007: *Pokémon Diamond/Pearl* released

FINAL FANTASY

FINAL FANTASY.

SPEC

Developer:
Square
Publisher:
Various
Initial release:
Final Fantasy (1987), Famicom

GAMEPLAY

Statistics-based RPG series famous for its high production values.

SPEED RUNS

GAME	PLATFORM	COMPLETION TIME	PLAYER	DATE
Final Fantasy IV	Super Nintendo Entertainment System	3 hr 56 min (US Version)	Kevin Juang (USA)	19 Dec 05
Final Fantasy V	Super Nintendo Entertainment System	3 hr 26 min (PS1 Re-release)	Alex Eustis (USA)	1 Apr 06
Final Fantasy VI	Super Nintendo Entertainment System	5 hr 26 min (Japanese version)	Peter Tiernan (USA)	5 May 05
Final Fantasy IX	PS1	8 hr 32 min	Kari Johnson (USA)	3 Jun 07
Final Fantasy X-2	PS2	4 hr 9 min	Mike Janiak (USA)	23 Jan 06
Final Fantasy Tactics	PS1	5 hr 19 min	John Kearsley IV (USA)	15 Oct 06

*"Now! This is it! Now is the time to choose! **Die and be free of pain or live and fight your sorrow!** Now is the time to shape your stories! Your fate is in your hands!"*

Auron, Final Fantasy X

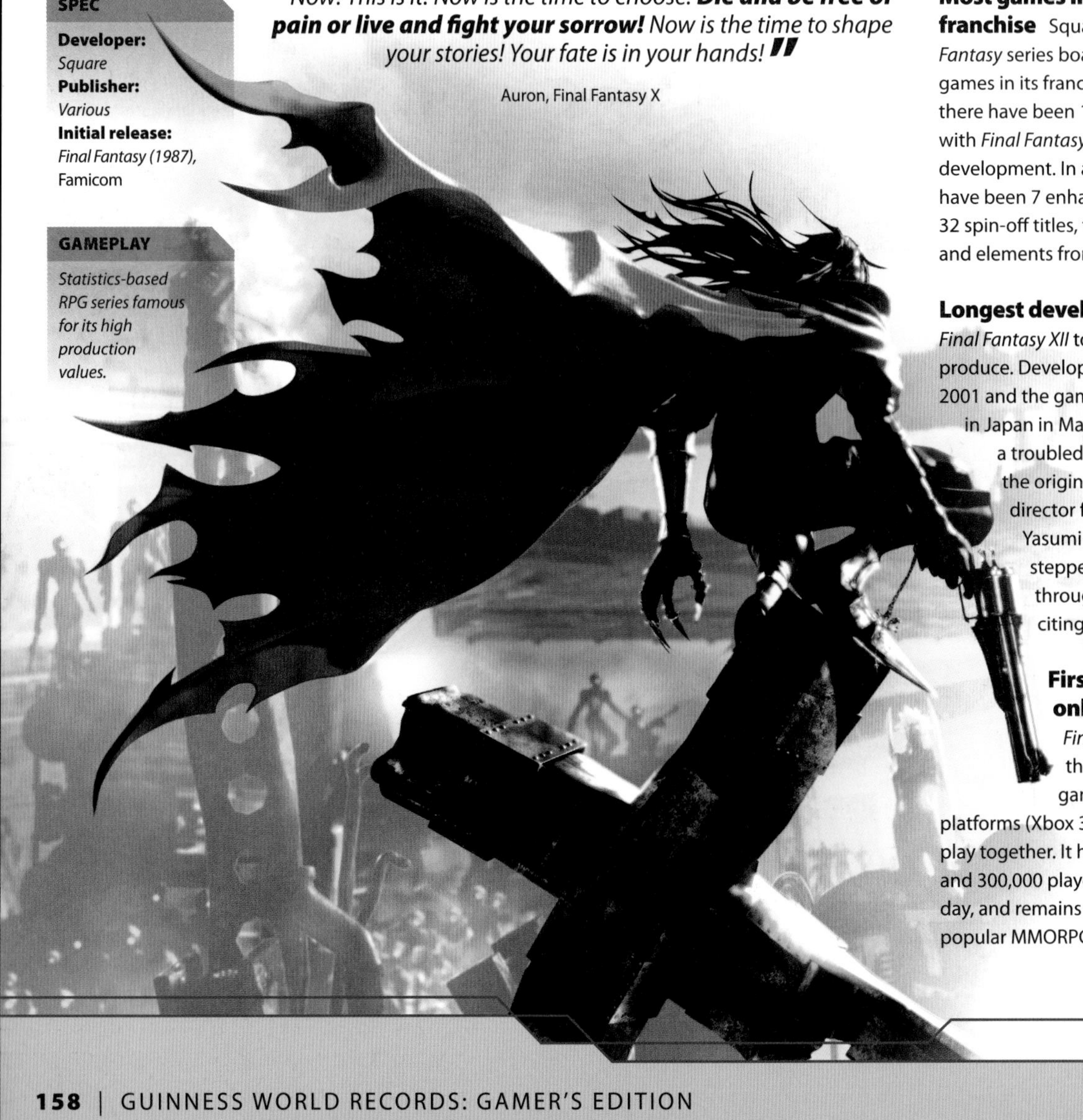

Most games in an RPG franchise Square-Enix's *Final Fantasy* series boasts a record 45 games in its franchise. Since 1987, there have been 12 main entries, with *Final Fantasy XIII* currently in development. In addition, there have been 7 enhanced games and 32 spin-off titles, featuring characters and elements from the main series.

Longest development period *Final Fantasy XII* took five years to produce. Development began in 2001 and the game finally shipped in Japan in March 2006. It was a troubled development – the original producer and director for the game, Yasumi Matsuno (Japan), stepped down half way through production, citing ill health.

First cross-platform online RPG *Final Fantasy XI* was the first game to allow gamers across multiple platforms (Xbox 360, PS2 and PC) to play together. It has between 200,000 and 300,000 players logging on every day, and remains the one of the most popular MMORPGs in Japan.

77 million – *Final Fantasy* games sold…
more than the Spice Girls, the biggest selling female group, who have sold 53 million records

PRODUCTS

The Final Fantasy franchise is well known for its collectable merchandise. *Final Fantasy VII* in particular has inspired hundreds of items – it even has its own limited edition drink, the *Final Fantasy XII Potion* ③, manufactured by Japanese drinks company Suntory.

Most expensive video game-inspired movie At a cost of $130 million (including marketing costs) *Final Fantasy: The Spirits Within* ① was the most expensive video game-inspired movie ever made. Released in 2001 by Columbia Pictures, it recouped just $32 million at the US box office, meaning it was also one of the least successful video game-inspired movies ever made. The film was the **first computer-generated animated movie with photo-realistic characters**.

Best-selling Final Fantasy game *Final Fantasy VII* has sales of over 9.8 million copies worldwide. It's the second best-selling game on PS1 (beaten by *Gran Turismo*) and is one of the best-selling console games of all time.

Most powerful monster in the Final Fantasy series Yiazmat ②, who appears in *Final Fantasy XII*, has 50,000,000 HP and is found in the Ridorana Cataract. Yiazmat is the ultimate boss and it can take several hours to kill it. It is necessary to have the best armour, weapons and accessories available, such as genji gloves and the Ultima Blade.

TRIVIA

➲ In the 2004 Summer Olympics, the US synchronised swimming duo Alison Bartosik and Anna Kozlova were awarded bronze for their performance to music from *Final Fantasy VIII*.

➲ *Aki Ross* was named #87 on *Maxim* magazine's "Hot 100" list for 2001, and was featured on the cover of the supplemental insert. She is the only nonexistent person to date to make the list.

➲ On 16 March 2006, *Final Fantasy XII* became the sixth game ever to receive a perfect 40/40 score from *Famitsu*, one of the most popular and respected games magazines in Japan.

FASTEST SELLING CONSOLE RPG GAME (ONE DAY)

The fastest selling RPG console game was *Final Fantasy X* (PS2), which sold 1,455,732 copies in one day on its Japanese release on 19 July 2001.

DRAGON QUEST

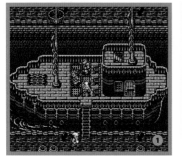

PLATFORMS

PC
XBOX 360
PS1
XBOX
PS2
DS
PS3
GAME BOY ADVANCE
PSP
Wii

SPEC

Developer:
Enix
Publisher:
Various
Initial release:
Dragon Quest
(1986), Famicom

GAMEPLAY

Japanese role-playing phenomenon originally created by Enix, before the company merged with Square. Best known for its extremely traditional structure and battle system.

Best-selling role-playing game on the Super Famicom

The best-selling RPG on the Super Famicom was *Dragon Quest VI* ❶, the final part in the Zenithia trilogy, which garnered over 3,200,000 sales after its release in 1995. This feat is made all the more remarkable when you consider it was never even released outside of Japan. A remake for the Nintendo DS is underway.

Best-selling *Dragon Quest* game

Dragon Quest VII on the PS2 has sold over 4.2 million copies worldwide.

Fastest-selling current-generation game in Japan

Dragon Quest Swords: The Masked Queen and the Tower of Mirrors for the Wii sold 305,254 in its first week of release in Japan (7–15 July 2007), making it the fastest-selling current-generation game in Japan. It was created by many members of the original *Dragon Quest* NES development team.

First video game concert

The first live music concert featuring tunes from video games was the "Family Classic Concert" performed by the Tokyo String Music Combination Playing Group on 20 August 1987 at the Suntory Hall in Tokyo, Japan. The show, which was a big success, was arranged and conducted by Koichi Sugiyama ❸, the official composer for the *Dragon Quest* series, and the music was taken from the soundtracks to the first two *Dragon Quest* games. To his many admirers, Sugiyama is affectionately known as the "Big Boss of video game music".

FASTEST-SELLING GAME IN JAPAN

The fastest-selling game in Japan was *Dragon Quest VIII* ❷, which sold over 3 million copies during the week of release in 2004. It is also the **biggest-selling Japanese PS2 game of all time**, with total sales of more than 3.6 million.

TRIVIA

➲ The series monster and character designs were produced by famed *Dragon Ball* manga artist Akira Toriyama. *Dragon Ball* ④ is one of the most successful manga series of all time, having sold more than 120 million copies.

➲ Japanese *Dragon Quest* fans can be obsessive about the game, sometimes dangerously so... A university student in Japan was once arrested for threatening to kill a friend after a disagreement over which *Dragon Quest* game was the best. The arrested student favoured *Dragon Quest VI*, but it's unknown what game his would-be victim preferred.

➲ *Dragon Quest* is not nearly as successful outside Japan, having been eclipsed by *Final Fantasy* and other RPG series. In Europe, only *Dragon Quest VIII: Journey of the Cursed King* and *Dragon Warrior Monsters* have been released.

*"Dragon Quest is the **biggest game series** in Japan; it is a **cultural status symbol**, enchanting adults, children, men and women."*

Tim Rogers, *Next Generation*

attacks!

First video game series to inspire a ballet The first video game series to inspire a ballet was *Dragon Quest*. Composed by Koichi Sugiyama and choreographed by ballet master Minoru Suzuki, it was originally written in 1995 and premiered in Tokyo, Japan, in 1996. Proving the game's cultural success, it has been performed several times since: in 1997, 1999, 2001 and 2002.

DRAGON ACCESSORIES

One of the more unusual bits of hardware associated with the *Dragon Quest* series is a plastic sword with a built-in game that plugged directly into a TV ⑤, allowing gamers to hack and slash through a slew of *Dragon* Quest monsters. A Japanese only release, *Kenshin Dragon Quest: Yomigaerishi Densetsu no Ken*, was well received – it was awarded the Digital Toy Award at the Digital Content Grand Prix (the gaming equivalent of an Oscar) in Japan in January 2004. A sequel (without sword) is currently being developed for the Nintendo Wii.

ELDER SCROLLS

The Elder Scrolls

" *Men are but flesh and blood.* **They know their doom, but not the hour.** **"**

Emperor Uriel Septim VII,
The Elder Scrolls IV: Oblivion

PLATFORMS

PC — XBOX 360
— XBOX
PS3 — DS
3
PSP — Wii

SPEC

Developer:
Bethesda
Publisher:
Various
Initial release:
*The Elder Scrolls:
Arena (1994), PC*

GAMEPLAY

*Traditional Dungeons
and Dragons-inspired
first-person role-playing
franchise peppered with
elements of action and
adventure games. Travel
long distances across
vast lands, and pick and
choose which quests
you wish to take on.*

Largest land-based game area The largest land-based game area ever is 163,492 km² (63,125 miles²), in *The Elder Scrolls II: Daggerfall*, released for the PC in August 1996. That's roughly the same size as two Great Britain's shoved together! Large land masses are important for giving players enough room to explore – but there's a careful balance to be struck. Pete Hines, the VP of public relations and marketing for Bethesda (the company behind the *Elder Scrolls* games) acknowledges that perhaps *Daggerfall* was too big: "I think the reason you've seen us go away from that and towards a smaller world, but still one that is enormous compared to pretty much any other game out there, is that we wanted to handcraft more things, and put more depth into characters."

Highest-rated PlayStation 3 game The highest-rated PlayStation 3 game is *The Elder Scrolls IV: Oblivion* **1**, with an average rating of 93% at both Gamerankings.com and Metacritic.com. Rankings are worked out by taking an average score from all the review scores a game has received across hundreds of different magazines and websites. *Oblivion* has also received numerous 2006 game of the year awards from sources including Gamespot, IGN, G4, IGN, Shacknews, Spike TV and GameSpy, not to mention the "Ultimate Game of the Year Award" at the 2006 Golden Joystick awards.

100 – the estimated number of "man years" it collectively took members of Bethesda to create *The Elder Scrolls III: Morrowind*

TRIVIA

➲ The Elder Scrolls themselves were rarely mentioned in the games until *Oblivion*, the fourth in the series. It was revealed that the scrolls were documents of prophecy – and that reading them could cause blindness. The final mission in the Thieves Guild story sees you attempting to steal one of the actual scrolls – although you cannot read it.

➲ *The Elder Scrolls IV: Oblivion* features some very famous actors providing voices for its characters. Patrick Stewart **3** (Captain Picard in *Star Trek: The Next Generation*) won an award for his role as the Emperor Uriel Septim VII. Sean Bean (*Goldeneye*) starred as Brother Martin, Terrence Stamp (*Superman*) as Mankar Camoran and Lynda Carter (*Wonder Woman*) played a selection of Orc females.

Largest number of NPCs in an RPG The largest amount of NPCs (non player characters) found in any role playing game is 750,000 in *The Elder Scrolls: Daggerfall*. Every single one of these characters can be talked to or interacted with. Every RPG features NPCs – they are essentially every character a player meets that cannot be controlled, ranging from shopkeepers or members of a crowd to the central villain. *Daggerfall* features over 15,000 unique locations populated with NPCs.

Fastest play-through for *The Elder Scrolls III: Morrowind* The fastest play-through for *The Elder Scrolls III: Morrowind* **2** is 7 min 30 sec, which was achieved by Russian Vladimir "Knu" Semenov on 19 July 2005 playing through the story as a barbarian Orc (birth sign "The Steed"). Vladimir's legendary achievement is all the more impressive when you consider that it is entirely non-tool assisted, and that most people take days to complete *Morrowind*.

FIGURES

During their adventures in *The Elder Scrolls IV: Oblivion*, the average gamer can expect to see **35,544** shrubs and bushes, **67,730** plants and mushrooms, **94,013** trees and fallen logs and **395,696** rocks.

HOT TIP

The mythical talking mudcrab merchant is in *The Elder Scrolls III: Morrowind*. He can be found on an island off the coast of Mzahnch, under the letter "h" of Mzahnch on your map. He will buy most items at full price, so don't kill him! Use a Mark spell to remember the location, and a Recall spell so you can warp back to sell more items.

BEST-SELLING MULTI-PLATFORM RPG

The best-selling RPG across multiple platforms (Xbox 360, PlayStation 3 and PC) is *The Elder Scrolls IV: Oblivion*, which has a total combined sales of over 3 million copies. Sales on Xbox 360 and PC reached 1.7 million in the first month alone.

POKÉMON

BEST-SELLING RPG ON THE NINTENDO DS

The best-selling role-playing game on the Nintendo DS is *Pokémon Diamond/Pearl* ❶, with combined sales of 12.1 million. The only game to have sold more copies on the DS is *Nintendogs* with 15 million sales.

PLATFORMS

PC
XBOX 360
XBOX
3DS
3
GAME BOY ADVANCE
Wii

SPEC

Developer:
Game Freak
Publisher:
Nintendo
Initial release:
Pocket Monsters (1996),
Game Boy

GAMEPLAY

The monster-trading craze that took the video game world by storm. As with the cartoon series, the concept is based around the challenge of collecting Pokémon species from around the world, training them up, defeating rival trainers and capturing the rarest creatures.

Most successful RPG series of all time The most successful RPG series of all time is Nintendo's *Pokémon* series, which has reached total sales of 155 million units. The only non-RPG series that is more popular is Nintendo's Mario franchise. This makes Nintendo the **most successful video game publisher** ever.

Most photosensitive epileptic seizures caused by a TV show An episode of the *Pokémon* TV series that aired on December 1997 triggered a record 635 photosensitive seizures. Strobing effects in the show caused the victims to convulse, and required hospital admission, even in cases where there was no previous history of photosensitivity.

First gaming series themepark *Pokémon* was the first gaming series to get its own themepark. The PokéPark ❷ was opened on 18 March 2005 in Nagoya, Japan. Attractions included the Pichu Brothers' Rascal Railway. It closed on 25 September 2005.

Highest score on *Pokémon Pinball: Ruby and Sapphire* The highest score on the Sapphire table of *Pokémon Pinball: Ruby and Sapphire* ❸, is 348,472,220, achieved by Terence O'Neill of the USA on 13 February 2006.

Fastest-selling *Pokémon* instalments Released in the USA on 22 April 2007, *Pokémon Diamond* ❶ and *Pearl* became the fastest-selling *Pokémon* instalments ever. Just eight days after launch, sales had reached the one million mark. Worldwide, the instalments have now sold 12.1 million copies since their initial release in Japan in September 2006.

Four – number of All Nippon Airways aircraft painted with *Pokémon* characters. Cabin crew also wore *Pokémon* aprons!

Youngest supermarket consultant

On 15 April 2000, supermarket chain Tesco announced that it had procured the services of seven-year-old Laurie Sleator from Hertfordshire, UK, to advise senior executives on the *Pokémon* craze sweeping the globe. His advice contributed to Tesco selling over £1 million ($1.55 million) worth of *Pokémon* goods **4** over the Easter weekend. Laurie was paid in the form of *Pokémon* products!

❝ Demons *are instructing the Nintendo and Hasbro companies on how to* **corrupt a child's innocence** *and create a future army of* **junior Satanists** *that will one day* **rule the world!** ❞

Christian Coalition on the *Pokémon* craze

TRIVIA

➲ The 2007 *Pokémon* Trading Card Game world champions are Jun Hasebe (Japan) in the Junior category, Jeremy Scharff-Kim (USA) in the Senior category and Tom Roos (Finland) in the Masters category. The 2007 finals took place in Hawaii.

➲ Previously owned by Wizards of the Coast, the *Pokémon* trading card game was taken over by Nintendo in 2003 – not a surprising move when you look at the company's roots. Nintendo was originally created to manufacture playing cards way back in 1889.

➲ The concept of the *Pokémon* saga stems from the hobby of insect collecting, a popular pastime in Japan, and one enjoyed by *Pokémon*'s creator Satoshi Tajiri.

➲ Pokémon never bleed or die in battle, only faint. This was a very touchy subject for Tajiri, as he didn't want to further fill the gaming world with "pointless violence".

FACTS

One of the most popular gimmicks of the *Pokémon* series is the ability to trade monsters with other players in order to fully complete the game. In the past this was achieved by linking Game Boys with a cable. The arrival of *Pokémon Diamond/ Pearl* on the Nintendo DS has now eliminated the need for wires – players can now trade with other players over Nintendo's Wi-Fi network. Since the game's launch, over 10 million trades have already taken place!

SPEED RUNS

source: speeddemosarchive.com

GAME	PLATFORM	COMPLETION TIME	PLAYER	DATE
Pokémon Red/Blue	Game Boy	2 hr 9 min	Ben Goldberg	12/04/07
Pokémon Yellow	Game Boy	2 hr 28 min	David Kim	14/07/05
Pokémon Gold/Silver	Game Boy	4 hr 15 min	James Bunkley	10/10/05

GAME SERIES WITH THE MOST SPIN-OFF MOVIES

The game series with the most spin-off movies is *Pokémon*, which has inspired 10 feature-length animated films. The first *Pokémon* movie is also the second most popular video game-inspired movie at the US box office (behind *Tomb Raider*), making $85,744,662 during its run. Its success was due, to some extent, to cinemas handing out rare *Pokémon* trading cards at the screenings.

RPG ROUND-UP

Step forward, step again.

BATTLE FACTS

Once in an RPG battle, there are certain statistics that are universally important:

Hit points – these are your basic health indicator. When the number reaches zero, the character will usually die or faint. When all members of your party are reduced to zero HP (known as a "party wipe") it will usually be game over.

Magic points – this secondary statistic refers to the amount of times a character can perform a special ability, such as a healing or attacking move. While it may not always be referred to as magic points, this ability is almost always present.

Experience points – a statistic driven by successful battling. Win a fight, and your XP bar will rise. Fill the bar and your character will go up a level, giving you better statistics and access to new moves.

Money – some form of gold or money is usually awarded after every battle. Money can be used to purchase more powerful weapons, items, armour and accessories.

Highest production budget

Game: *Shenmue*
Publisher: Sega

The game with the highest production budget was *Shenmue* ❶, which cost $70,000,000 to create. It took seven years to complete and first appeared on the Sega Dreamcast in Japan in December 1999. However, it may soon be beaten by the Silicon Knights game *Too Human* for Xbox 360, which sources claim has already cost over $80,000,000.

First role-playing computer game

Game: *dnd*
Publisher: N/A

The first role-playing game was *dnd*, which appeared on the PLATO computer system in 1975. Based on the table-top role-playing game *Dungeons and Dragons* *dnd* was a text-based adventure. Unfortunately, the PLATO system ❸ failed to become a commercially successful enterprise.

BEST-SELLING VIDEO GAME THEME SONG IN JAPAN

Game: *Kingdom Hearts* **Publisher:** Square Electronic Arts/Disney
"Hikari", the main theme from *Kingdom Hearts* by pop star Utada Hikaru ❺, exceeded sales of 598,000 copies – 270,370 of these were sold in its first week. In Japan, Utada is more famous than Madonna.

POPULAR RPG SPEEDRUNS

source: speeddemosarchive.com

GAME	PLATFORM	TIME	PLAYER	DATE
Icewind Dale	PC	58 min	Julien Langer	3 Sep 2005
Kingdom Hearts II 6	PS2	5 hr 6 min	Asa Tims	3 Oct 2006
Mario and Luigi: Superstar Sega	Nintendo	3 hr 26 min	Damien Moody	19 Jul 2006
Baldur's Gate	PC	30 min	Kevin Horst	27 Jan 2006
Star Wars: Knights of the Old Republic 2	PC	3 hr 14 min	Henrik Larsson	30 Jun 2006

Most valuable RPG game
Game: *Panzer Dragoon*
Publisher: Sega
Panzer Dragoon 4
for the Sega Saturn
has an estimated
value of $200.
Despite critical
acclaim, the game had an
extremely
limited print run of just 10,000 copies.

FASTEST-SELLING PC RPG

Game: *Diablo II* **Publisher:** Blizzard
The fastest-selling role-playing game on the PC was *Diablo II* 7, which sold more than 1 million copies within the first two weeks of being shipped in June 2000. By January 2001, it had sold an incredible 2.75 million copies worldwide.

BEST-SELLING RPGS

	GAME	PLATFORM	SALES
1	*Pokémon Red, Blue & Green*	Game Boy	29.7m
2	*Pokémon Gold & Silver*	Game Boy Color	21.2m
3	*Pokémon Ruby & Sapphire*	Game Boy Advance	14m
4	*Pokémon Yellow*	Game Boy	13.7m
5	*Pokémon Diamond & Pearl*	NintendoDS	12.1m
6	*Pokémon FireRed & LeafGreen*	Game Boy Advance	10.6m
7	*Final Fantasy VII*	PlayStation	9.8m
8	*Final Fantasy VIII*	PlayStation	7.8m
9	*Final Fantasy X*	PlayStation 2	7.7m
10	*Diablo II*	PC	7m

❝ *Combat in an RPG can be based on arcade-style reactions, but more often than not **it's a mathematician's delight, the computer rolling a hundred dice to decide who wins**.* **❞**

McCarthy, Curran & Byron
Game Development Art & Design

TOMMY TALLARICO

FIGURE

Tommy's SFX Kit features **19,655** sound effect files for use in video games. The library contains seven CDs of wav files in 110 categories, some of which can be heard at www.tallarico.com.

> **❝ Tommy Tallarico is the single most famous gaming soundtrack composer out there** – *his list of hit songs is astounding.* **❞**
>
> Gaming Enthusiast Online

HITTING ALL THE RIGHT NOTES WITH THE INDUSTRY'S MOST PROLIFIC MUSIC COMPOSER

Tommy Tallarico has worked on the soundtracks of more video games than any other person – an incredible 275 and counting. We talked to him about his life, his work and his Video Games Live project, and asked him how he got into writing music for video games.

I've been playing piano since I was three and composing music since I was a teenager. I grew up on video games, but never thought to put my two greatest loves together until I moved out to California when I turned 21. I got a job selling keyboards and the day I started, the first customer to walk in the store was a producer at a new video game company. We got talking and I went down to the studio and was hired the next day as their very first games tester! It was then that I decided what my career was going to be – I wanted to help change the way people thought and felt about video game music.

But isn't the music just a constantly repeating loop of blips and bleeps?
This is actually a huge misconception among people who haven't played a game in a while. The reality is that when I first got involved in the game industry over 18 years ago, a lot of the music was short repetitive bleeps and bloops. This was because the technology at the time didn't allow for real music and live musicians. In the mid 1990s DVDs became a viable storage medium for games. Once this happened, composers and musicians could use real instruments to create game music. It was an exciting time because no one had ever heard their video games make these kinds of sounds before.

What's a favourite composition that you've written?

I'd have to say that it's a toss up between *Earthworm Jim* and *Advent Rising*. *Earthworm Jim* because it was so much fun to work on, and to create such a unique character and gaming experience. The music was very whimsical and the goal was humour. In *Advent Rising*, the music was a more serious work where I wrote the score like an Italian opera. I used a 72-piece union orchestra in Hollywood and a 60-piece chorus in Salt Lake City.

Who's your favourite video game composer? And your favourite regular composer?

My favourite video game composer would be Nobuo Uematsu, who is the composer behind most of the *Final Fantasy* series of games. But my favourite composer of all time is Ludwig van Beethoven. I don't believe the world will ever have a person who could command and draw so much power and emotion from music.

What do you see happening next in the video game industry?

I think you'll see gaming continue to evolve into our culture. All of us who grew up on gaming are now having children… but we've never stopped playing games. It's taking time… but eventually everyone will understand how important gaming is to the fabric of our entertainment and culture.

When and why did you conceive Video Games Live?

Myself and fellow video game composer (and Video Games Live conductor) Jack Wall conceived Video Games Live because we wanted the world to know just how far video games and their music have come. It has been important for us to create a show with synchronized video, synchronized rock-n-roll lighting, stage show production, special effects, interactivity with the crowd, etc. The reception at the shows has been incredible all over the world. The orchestras and musicians we play with tell us that they have never received the kind of ovations and applause that they experience during our show. Our goal was to break that old, musty view of the symphony world and bring it into the 21st century for a generation of people who grew up on things like video games and using computers in their daily life. It's been quite a ride over the past five years and we still have many more goals to accomplish.

MMORPG

OUR EXPERT

Dave Hawksett was science and technology editor at Guinness World Records for five years and now acts as a consultant on topics ranging from computer games to astrophysics. His favourite games today are *Star Wars Galaxies*, where he fights dirty as a rebel spy, and *Armed Assault*.

OUTLINE

Players interact in online worlds in real time, co-operating in challenges or buying and selling in-game goods or skills. Gameplay is often self-determined and open-ended.

BE WHO YOU WANT TO BE IN A SPRAWLING ONLINE FANTASY WORLD. BATTLE, BEFRIEND OR DO BUSINESS WITH PLAYERS 24 HOURS A DAY IN NEVER-ENDING ADVENTURES OF YOUR OWN CREATION.

Massively Multiplayer Online Role-Playing Games (MMORPG) are the ultimate combination of computer games and the Internet. Players control a character within fictional worlds populated by computer-controlled characters and/or other online gamers engaged in a persistent online world.

In 1996, the **first commercial 3D MMORPG**, *Meridian 59* , was published by 3DO. A sword and sorcery, monster-battling adventure, *Meridian 59* was shut down by 3DO in August 2000 but was re-released by Near Death Studios Inc. in 2002, who eventually added a new graphics rendering engine in October 2004.

Ultima Online followed in 1997 and is widely regarded as the game that started the MMORPG revolution, and it is currently the **longest-running MMORPG** in the world. However, when *Everquest*  was released by Sony Online Entertainment in 1999 it became so popular and addictive it earned itself the nickname "Evercrack".

Since 1999 the online market has exploded dramatically, with more and more MMORPGs competing for the growing number of potential players around the world – each of whom usually pay a monthly subscription, typically of around £7.50 per month.

As millions of players began to subscribe to MMORPG, and the technical capabilities of the games improved, the events within these virtual worlds began to increasingly grab real world headlines.

In December 2001, Professor Edward Castronova , at Indiana University, USA, published a research paper titled *Virtual Worlds: A First-Hand Account of Market and Society on the Cyberian Frontier*, in which he provided evidence on how in-game markets compared to real life. He concluded that Norrath, the kingdom in Everquest ④, had a per capita Gross Domestic Product (GDP) of £1,317, meaning that every player, on average, was creating in-game

> **❚❚** There is no shortage of income-producing possibilities for the imaginative. **❚❚**
>
> Mark Wallace, *NY Times*, 29 May 2005

FIRST MMORPG PHOTOGRAPHIC EXHIBITION

The work of photo-journalist Robbie Cooper looks at online avatars and how they reflect a gamer's sense of identity and physical self, or how they compensate for realworld issues, such as illness or disability. Pictured here is Jason Rowe ⑥, who has Duchenne Muscular Dystrophy, next to his *Star Wars Galaxies* avatar. An exhibition of Robbie's work was held in London, England, in October 2004.

TRIVIA

➲ **Bugs** – Unlike other games, MMORPGs are constantly evolving while live. Patches, expansions and modifications are common. This inevitably leads to numerous bugs in games' software that are reported by the players and usually fixed in the next game patch.

➲ **Exploits** – The collective intelligence of hundreds of thousands of players will eventually find ways to cheat within MMORPG, often related to gaining free money and valuable items, or making a character much tougher than the game rules normally allow.

wealth worth that amount per year, and this figure was then compared to the GDP of real countries. Surprisingly, the kingdom of Norrath had a greater productivity of wealth than poor countries such as Namibia and, at the time, was the largest game economy in the world.

2001

2001: *Dark Age of Camelot* launches and soon becomes one of the most popular MMORPG in the USA

2003

2001: *Anarchy Online* is launched by Funcom

2003: MindArk releases *Project Entropia*, which allows the exchange of real money

2004

2003: LucasArts launch *Star Wars Galaxies*

2004: *City of Heroes* is published by NCSoft

2004: *EverQuest 2* is launched by Sony

2006

2004: Blizzard releases its first MMORPG, *World of Warcraft*

2006: WeMade's *Legends of Mir III* 7 launches to critical acclaim

2007

2007: *Lord of the Rings Online: The Shadows of Angmar* released.

WORLD OF WARCRAFT

World of
Warcraft

PLATFORMS

PC   XBOX 360

PS3   XBOX

PS2   DS

PSP   Wii

SPEC

Developer:
Blizzard Entertainment
Publisher:
Vivendi
Initial release:
*World of Warcraft
(2004), PC*

GAMEPLAY

*Currently the most
popular MMORPG, the
fantasy-themed* World
of Warcraft *allows
players to create a
character and explore
the fictional world
of Azeroth, taking
part in quests,
interacting with
other players and
advancing skills.*

> **"**You have to have the right group set up, and you obviously need a healer who keeps everyone in your group alive – *if you lose the healer, your group is toast*. **"**
>
> Sorath, Aerie Peak server

Most successful strategy expansion pack

The first official *WoW* expansion pack, and largest update, was *The Burning Crusade* ③. Launched in January 2007, the expansion included new playable races, high-level dungeons, and a brand new player-vs-player combat arena system with the Eye of the Storm battleground. The expansion was reported to have sold 2.7 million copies within the first 24 hours of release, making it the fastest-selling PC expansion pack. By the end of 2007, sales had reached over 3.5 million.

Most popular MMORPG

In November 2007, Blizzard announced that *World of Warcraft* had a total of over 9.3 million subscribers around the world ④. The future release of the second expansion pack, *Wrath of the Lich King*, will increase this player base.

Worst global video game epidemic

In September 2005, a new dungeon was added to *WoW* in which players encountered "Hakkar the Soulflayer", a new boss who gave the "Corrupted Blood" disease to nearby players. This could strip up to 300 points' worth of health every few seconds. The illness was supposed to remain confined within the dungeon but players were able to call pets and then store them once they caught the plague. This allowed the plague outside and into the main world. Thousands of player characters were affected for up to two days, causing social unrest and forcing many players to flee from populated areas in an attempt to avoid the disease. The problem was fixed by a restart of all game servers.

Most destructive exploit

World of Warcraft, like all MMORPG, contains unintended exploits that players can use to their advantage, against the rules and intentions of either the game or the developer. In August 2007, malicious players began using a newly-discovered exploit that allowed them to crash entire servers. This was the first – and most devastating – exploit of its type. The problem has thankfully since been fixed by Blizzard.

MOST ADDICTIVE GAME

World of Warcraft is renowned for its addictive nature. Blizzard founder Frank Pearce ⑤ is shown here accepting the award for "most addictive game" at the 2005 Spike TV awards. The developer also picked up, "best multiplayer", "best PC game" and "best RPG".

Largest instanced dungeon

Karazhan, an ancient abandoned tower, was released with *The Burning Crusade* expansion. A dungeon designed for a group of 10 players, this can take upwards of 20 hours to complete.

9 million – the number of *World of Warcraft* subscribers currently active in 2007, according to developer Blizzard Entertainment

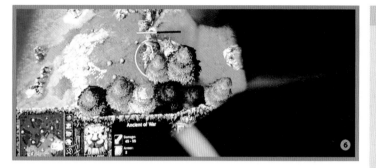

⑥

First cross-server battlefields

On 22 August 2006, patch 1.12 of *World of Warcraft* finally introduced battlegrounds that allow players to fight with players from other servers. Normally players in MMORPG can never interact with those on other servers.

Largest virtual beer festival

Once a year the warring factions of the Horde and the Alliance put down their arms and get together for "Brewfest", the virtual homage to the Bavarian Oktoberfest. Like the real-world festival, this lasts for a couple of weeks and features the best (virtual) beers.

TRIVIA

➲ A film based on *WoW* is due in 2009. Little is known, but it has been confirmed that it will be set one year before the game and features Orc Warlord "Thrall", who you can play in *Warcraft III: Reign Of Chaos* ①.

➲ With 9.3 million players, you've got to expect a few famous names. Rumoured regulars include Jessica Simpson, Robin Williams, Kevin Smith and Vin Diesel.

➲ Races in *World of Warcraft* are based on classic fantasy themes. There are 10 to choose from: Gnomes, Humans, Night Elves ②, Blood Elves, Dwarves ⑦, Orcs, Tauren, Trolls, Draenei and Undead. There are also nine character classes: Warrior, Hunter, Mage, Priest, Druid, Rogue, Paladin, Shaman, and Warlock.

FIGURES

1,129 – cards released in the *World of Warcraft* card game.

$435,000 – total prize figure at the 2005 World Cyber Games, in Singapore ⑥.

⑦

HOT TIP

New to *World of Warcraft*? Then do some research before you start! The last thing you want to do is jump in, only to realise that you don't like your own character. The official *World of Warcraft* website contains information on all the character races and classes as well as the professions and skills available to them. Choose your path before you walk it.

STAR WARS GALAXIES

SPEC

Developer:
Sony
Publisher:
Lucasarts
Initial release:
Star Wars Galaxies
(2003), PC

GAMEPLAY

Massive ground and space-based Star Wars-themed sci-fi roleplaying game that offers players a massive canvas of 12 planets and 13 space zones to explore.

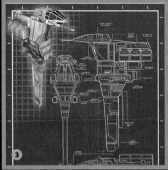

Largest creature Seen only as a sun-bleached skeleton in the *Star Wars* movies, the Grand Krayt Dragon ❶ inhabits a valley in eastern Tatooine. It measures some 80 m from its head to its tail.

First virtual memorial in a MMORPG The Moraj Memorial flag outside of Bestine on Tatooine is thought to be the first memorial in an MMORPG. It was placed by the Star Wars Galaxies (SWG) team in recognition of Nathan Larkins, one of the game's beta testers, who was killed in a car accident. The flag marks where beta testers entered the game.

First Jedi initiate in SWG In the first version of *SWG*, gamers who wished to be a Jedi had to unlock their force-sensitive character by completing tasks. The first person to do this was Monika T'Sarn on the Intrepid server. She unlocked her Jedi, Akinom T'Sarn ❷, on 8 November 2003.

Largest player ship The Y8 Mining Ship ❸ was introduced to the game in May 2005. It measures 129.7 x 40.64 x 160 m and needs a crew of eight players to operate at maximum efficiency.

Longest-lasting player corpse A quickly abandoned early feature of the game was that players who were killed had to return to their corpse to retrieve their items. One player, Icir, never bothered to return. His corpse was present at the Talus Imperial Base (Bloodfin server) for three years before being cleaned away by a gamesmaster.

❝ *Ultimately, everything we create for the world of SWG has to be approved through (George) Lucas.* ❞

John Donham, Senior Producer, SWG

First player cities
Although not the first game to allow players to own a house, *SWG* was the first that allowed groups of houses to formally be designated as coherent cities, run by player mayors with the ability to add better civic structures as a city increased in size and rank.

Largest Player v Player zone
In July 2006, the non-player character (NPC) city of Restuss on the moon Rori, was left in ruins in a massive live event across all servers. At the start of the battle, every player in the city became Player v Player (PvP) enabled and attackable by the opposite faction in the

Galactic Civil War between the Empire and the Rebel Alliance. After the battle ended, Restuss was left as a PvP zone, 800 m in diameter.

BOX EXPANSIONS

⊃ Jump to Lightspeed (27 October 2004) The introduction of a space zone for each of the 10 planets finally brought real-time twitch-based space combat to *Galaxies* – the first twitch-based combat system added to a traditional MMORPG.

Rage of the Wookiees (5 May 2005) The Wookiee homeworld of Kashyyyk was introduced to coincide with the cinema release of *Revenge of the Sith* (USA, 2005). The new planet was a departure from the layout of the 10 other planets, being split up into smaller areas rather than existing as one immense seamless playable surface.

Trials of Obi-Wan (1 November 2005). With content and quests aimed at higher-level players, Mustafar is lethal to the unprepared adventurer. As well as a series of new dungeons and content, there is a whole series of quests for the glowing ghost of Obi-Wan Kenobi, ending in a battle with the dark Jedi master Lord Vartonis.

INTERVIEW WITH... THOMAS BLAIR

Thomas Blair is a lead designer of *Star Wars Galaxies*. Guinness World Records asked him about what made the game so special...

I honestly think it's the sandbox environment. We gave people harvestors and said go mine something; here's a house, go make some cities! We provided them with the tools to go and live in that *Star Wars* universe. *SWG* has three spheres of gameplay: the combat, the entertainer and the trader. No other game has that variety of gameplay. We're about to introduce the "Collection System" – it'll give the design team a way to keep delivering even more game content based on feedback from our teams of players.

Were you a fan of the *Star Wars* films?
Yes! I was born in 1974 so I just about remember seeing the first movie at a drive-in theatre. I can just about remember seeing banthas – the big scary giant monsters with horns!

EVE ONLINE

PLATFORMS

PC | XBOX 360
| xbox
| DS
|
| Wii

SPEC

Developer:
CCP Games
Publisher:
CCP Games
Initial release:
EVE Online (2003), PC

GAMEPLAY

EVE Online is set in space, where players from one of four races pilot customised ships and travel between 5,000 solar systems. Progress can be made by establishing a reputation within the game, forming alliances, fighting battles and amassing currency in the form of the game's own Inter Stellar Kredits (ISK).

First Titan Titans are the largest possible ships in *EVE Online*. They can take months to construct. The first was called "Steve" and was constructed by the Ascendant Frontier (ASCN) player corporation. Launched on 25 September 2006, it was destroyed on 11 December 2006 by ships belonging to the Band of Brothers (BoB) corporation in the C9N-CC system.

OLDEST PLAYER CORPORATION

Mercurialis Inc. was established on 28 October 2002, prior to the game's release. As of September 2007 it had 51 members, with the player Isayo Arkindra ❸ acting as leader, or CEO. It is currently a member of the Interstellar Alcohol Conglomerate Alliance.

Largest player ship Titan-class ships are city-sized and are the only ship type that can create their own hyperspace jump portals. Currently the largest Titan is the *Minmatar Ragnarok* ❶, at 17.8 km (11 miles) from bow to stern.

Largest player corporation The Goonfleet corporation has 3,052 members, 2,515 of which were active as of September 2007.

Most hostile corporate takeover The Guiding Hand Social Club (GHSC) corporation perpetrated an ambitious corporate heist over a period of one year between 2004 and 2005. The target corporation was Ubiqua Seraph, which was infiltrated by a GHSC agent. Over 12 months, the agent gained the corporation members' trust before ultimately betraying them and assassinating their CEO in a grand heist that resulted in the loss of an estimated 30 billion ISK (about £8,000). This was one of the most controversial events in *EVE Online*'s history.

Most players logged in at once On 16 September 2007, *EVE Online*'s peak concurrent user (PCU) record stood at 35,783 players logged on simultaneously.

*The evolution of EVE Online continues in large part because of the **feedback we receive from subscribers** and the **direct involvement of our team with the community**.*

Hilmar Pétursson,
CEO CCP Games

TRIVIA

➲ None of the original development team had worked in the gaming industry before starting work on *EVE Online*.

➲ In 2002, the whole development team grew moustaches to protest at the slow progress of signing a publishing deal.

➲ Reynir Harðarsson, the Art Director on *EVE Online*, cites his key inspirations for the game as being *Elite* on the Commodore 64, Sid Meyer's *Civilization*, *Ultima Online* and *Magic: The Gathering*.

➲ Over 302,000 player ships were destroyed in *EVE Online* in September 2007, with a total of 2,790,919 ships destroyed between May 2005 and September 2007.

INTERVIEW WITH... HILMAR PÉTURSSON

We asked Hilmar Pétursson, CEO of CCP Games, about what he thinks attracts gamers to *EVE Online*.

It's definitely the open-ended gameplay. We built a world to be discovered by players but with a consistent setting. Also the game has a very harsh death penalty – there is real danger involved and so real reasons for players to be civil to each other. We do have rules but they are designed to facilitate emergent gameplay. I remember the first time players built a space station: they built a proper business plan and even issued an Initial Public Offering to sell stocks and shares in it to other players!

What's next for *EVE*?
We will have the ability to walk around space stations as human avatars for the first time. We have had countless requests for this but we'll release it when it is up to our standards.

What video games did you play as a child?
The first game I really played was *Atic Atac* for the ZX Spectrum. But the game I probably played the most was a multi-user dungeon game based on Terry Pratchett's popular *Discworld* series of books.

FIGURES

Building a Titan is no small undertaking. The following is a guide to the approximate amount of real time it takes to build one of these vast vessels.

550 – hours mining high-end materials ④

180 – hours spent transporting minerals to refineries ②

200 – hours spent hauling components to a capital construction yard

1,460 – estimated hours for building construction components

2,191 – estimated hours for finished build-time once all components are in place

ULTIMA ONLINE

PLATFORMS

PC · XBOX 360 · XBOX · PS2 · DS · PS3 · Wii

SPEC

Developer:
EA/Origin Systems
Publisher:
EA
Initial release:
Ultima Online
(1997), PC

GAMEPLAY

Massively multiplayer online role-playing game set in a classic fantasy world, played from an isometric view. Players can explore the world, take part in quests, design and sell items, hunt creatures and buy houses… while interacting with hundreds of players.

Longest-running MMORPG

Launched in 1997, the *Ultima Online* MMO franchise is not only one of the first MMORPGs but also the longest-running. Quite impressive considering *Ultima Online* has had no sequel. The existing world has instead been extended – both visually and physically – through the use of add-ons. Nine expansion packs are currently available, with more due in 2008.

First and only person to kill Lord British

The near-invincible Lord British ①, the ruler of Britannia, was killed during an early beta test. British was making a royal visit to the world, but, during a server reset, his invulnerability was switched off and a player named Rainz managed to kill him with a fire spell ②. Game creator Richard Garriott decided to ban Rainz from the beta soon after.

First player housing

Ultima Online was the first MMORPG to let players own their own houses ③, which could be decorated and even turned into shops with goods for other players to buy. An early problem with this system was players using rows of houses to wall off sections of the world for private use. This was eventually fixed and the housing system upgraded. From February 2003, players were able to custom design their houses as part of the *Age of Shadows* expansion.

Largest purpose-built player vs player (PvP) zone

In April 2000, the second expansion pack, *Ultima Online: Renaissance* ④, was released. It included the new worlds Trammel and Felucca – moons of the main game world of Britannia. The moons are nearly identical, but the darker Felucca was designed strictly as a PvP zone – an area where all players can attack and kill each other. The largest area of its kind, Felucca, is 25.1 million miles^2.

Largest networked MMORPG

With each of its 10 servers able to hold 2,500 players at the same time, *Ultima Online* is the largest massively multiplayer networked role-playing game in the world. At present, up to 14,000 players

HIGHEST BOVINE BONUS

Cows are a common sight in *Ultima*, but they're not just there for show. Cows can be tipped over by clicking on them and, if they are fed too much (9,999 times), they are renamed "Corey Johns". The game also includes its own version of mad cow disease, as every so often an aggressive "mad cow" ⑦ spawns instead of a standard bovine.

6,006,313 – lines of code in *Ultima Online*, totalling around 25,103,295 words. The novel *War and Peace* has "only" 552,896 words

INTERVIEW WITH... TIM COTTON

Tim Cotton is the lead content designer for *Ultima Online*. We asked him about his favourite games as a child.

The first games I really liked were *The Legend of Zelda* and the *Final Fantasy* games, and then I discovered *Ultima III*, one of the forerunners of *Ultima Online*.

What makes *Ultima* so special?
Back in 1997, it already had a real history to it with all the old *Ultima* games. *UO* was bringing that whole world to life. I remember before *UO* was released, talking in chat rooms with thousands of people all wondering what the game was going to be like and everyone was really excited. This was the early days of the internet, before even Google got big!

How was it received?
When *UO* was released the first thing everyone figured out was that it was not just a game but more about players interacting. There was some direction but you could be a bard, a warrior, an alchemist… You could even tame dragons as well as kill them – it just blew everyone's minds!

> ❚❚ *Ultima Online* is well established now, and we have so much lore and history to draw upon that **we can keep adding content to keep the game thriving.** ❚❚
>
> Tim Cotten, lead designer

take part each day, many of them staying online for up to four hours at a time. With 32,000 interacting "inhabitants", 15 major cities, nine sites of religious significance and at least seven dungeons, Britannia – the setting for *Ultima Online* – is the largest parallel universe on the internet. The game sold 100,000 copies in its first three months on the market.

First MMORPG to reach 100,000 players
Ultima Online achieved this historic milestone in December 1998, two months after the release of the first expansion pack, *The Second Age*. This pack also won the Interactive Achievement Award for "Best Role Playing Game" the following year.

TRIVIA

➲ In 2001, EA released a report of *Ultima Online* player "lifestyles", splitting players into two detailed male groups. For some reason, the report failed to survey female players, instead summarising their lifestyle choices simply as "varied and complicated"!

➲ After EA took over the original developer, Origin, sequels to *Ultima Online* ❻ went into development. Two were started (*Ultima Online 2* and *Ultima X: Odyssey*), but both were eventually cancelled over fears they might damage the existing user base.

➲ In October 2000, two players (Jelleke and Alexandre) became the first *Ultima Online* European players to get married… both in-game and in real life! Both weddings were attended by a Gamesmaster from the developer.

TOUGHEST NPC IN AN MMORPG

Lord British and his rival Lord Blackthorn ❺ are the main characters in *Ultima Online*. Both are considered indestructible by players due to the excessive number of hit points required to score a kill. Even experienced players with developed characters struggle to cause damage.

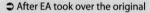

HOT TIP!
If you are new to *UO*, you should consider downloading the messaging system ICQ from www.icq.com. This online chat program will allow you to speak to other players in the game.

EVERQUEST II

FIRST IN-GAME PIZZA DELIVERY SYSTEM

In February 2005, *EverQuest II* added a pizza delivery system for its players. By typing /pizza players would be linked directly to the Pizza Hut ordering site **1**. This was the first time that an MMORPG could accept orders for real-world items.

PLATFORMS

PC · XBOX 360 · PS2 · XBOX · PS3 · DS · PS · GAMECUBE · Wii

SPEC

Developer:
Sony Online Entertainment
Publisher:
Sony
Initial release:
Everquest II (2004), PC

GAMEPLAY

Set on the world of Norrath, EverQuest II is a massive ground-based fantasy role-playing game where players can explore, complete quests for treasures and experience, kill monsters and socialise.

Largest player guild As of 1 November 2007, the largest *EverQuest II* **2** player guild is "Faith of Heroes" (Mistmoore server), with 1,459 members.

First official online game auction site Station Exchange **3** was launched by SOE in June 2005 and provided a legitimate means for players to buy and sell characters, items and money to other players, for real money, with SOE making a cut from the profits. As well as raising revenue for the company, Station Exchange provides players with a safe way of performing these transactions, without having to use third party websites such as eBay.

INTRODUCING STATION EXCHANGE.
THE OFFICIAL SECURE MARKETPLACE FOR EVERQUEST II PLAYERS

STATION EXCHANGE FOR
ENTER SITE

First MMORPG parallel universe *EverQuest II* is not really a sequel to the original *EverQuest* **4**, which launched in 1999. Instead, it is a parallel universe set in the same world of Norrath, but 500 years into the future in the Age of Destiny. The original *EverQuest* is still running online and still releasing new expansions. The 14th expansion, *Secrets of Faydwer*, is due for release in November 2007.

FIRST SPOKEN DIALOGUE

Upon its launch, *EverQuest II* established a major first for the MMORPG genre with the inclusion of actual spoken dialogue for non-playing characters. Some 59,233 lines of dialogue are in the game, adding up to around 500 hours of speech provided by actors, including British acting legend Christopher Lee **5**, who plays Lucan D'Lere **6**.

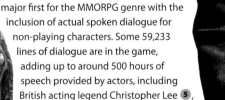

69,552 – items available in *EverQuest II*, such as armour, shields, weapons and magical trinkets. There are also 2,441 unique things to eat or drink

INTERVIEW WITH... SCOTT HARTSMAN

Scott Hartsman is a senior producer for *EverQuest II*. We asked him about the features that make the game so special...

EverQuest II is unique in that we've got so many different ways to experience the game world – you can choose to quest by yourself, join a group or a raid in some of the best dungeons in any MMO anywhere, advance yourself as a crafter, become a master of lore and legend by learning about each race of creature or just play the market on the broker. There's such a huge diversity of activity available.

What are your favourite aspects of the game?

Playing the game anonymously and seeing the kinds of tricks and gameplay that players come up with on their own. We call that "emergent gameplay" – when players make up fun on their own in this world that we've created.

What was the first computer game you ever remember playing or were a big fan of?

Wizardry! It opened my eyes to a whole new world where you could imagine being a part of the kinds of adventure stories that were only previously available in books.

> **❝ Subscriptions are growing and that makes me happy**. *We did it by releasing a quality game.* ❞
>
> Scott Hartsman

FIGURES

$1.87 million – total player transactions.

$37,435 – amount one seller earned from 351 auctions.

SECOND LIFE

PLATFORMS

PC

SPEC

Developer:
Linden Research Inc.
Publisher:
Linden Research Inc.
Initial release:
Second Life (2003), PC

GAMEPLAY

Second Life is not really a game, but more of an experimental virtual world with limitless options. People can make real money by selling virtual products and services for game currency (Linden dollars), which have a fluctuating exchange rate of 260–320 Linden dollars per real $1.

First professional *Second Life* art gallery
In August 2007, image library company Corbis, owned by Microsoft founder Bill Gates, announced that it was to open an art gallery ① sourced from its collection of more than 100 million images.

First Guinness World Record to extend into an MMORPG
The World's Biggest Coffee Morning is an annual fund-raising event for Macmillan Cancer Support. On 28 September 2007, residents of *Second Life* joined in the coffee morning, which also saw the opening of the Second Life Macmillan cancer information centre within the virtual world.

First *Second Life* millionaire
Anshe Chung ② (real name Ailin Graef ③) is an entrepreneur within *Second Life*. Her character was "born" on 26 March 2004 and is best known for being a virtual real estate broker. In November 2006 it was announced that she was the first person to achieve a net worth exceeding $1 million, a fact celebrated on the May 2006 cover of *BusinessWeek* magazine ④.

First *Second Life* lawsuit
In May 2006, *Second Life* player Marc Bragg filed a lawsuit against Linden Labs. His complaint was over Linden Lab's expulsion of his character after they discovered him using a loophole that allowed him to buy in-game property before other users could bid. The case was settled confidentially with Linden Labs in October 2007.

First portable avatar
In October 2007, IBM and Linden Labs announced that they had begun work on a project that would one day allow people to move their online avatars from one 3D world to another, including MMORPG and other 3D environments such as Google Earth. The project, which could take years to complete, could eventually lead to a next generation Internet, built from 3D worlds instead of today's 2D pages.

> ❝ *It's a 3D avatar having sex with another 3D avatar.* **What looks like a hot blonde babe could be a 60-year-old man in Milwaukee.** ❞
>
> Wagner James Au, author of *Second Life* blog *New World Notes*

PROFILE: ADAM REUTERS
Adam Reuters ⑤ is the *Second Life* avatar of Adam Pasick ⑥ – a real reporter for the Reuters news agency who works as a journalist within the game. He writes regular news reports on the happenings with the virtual world and, using its built-in audio streaming technology. He has conducted a number of interviews with famous people, recorded and broadcast within *Second Life*.

2.6 billion – amount of Linden dollars
invested by *Second Life*'s 8.3 million users, as of July 2007. This figure represented 9.6 million US dollars

First true virtual embassy
On 30 May 2007, Sweden opened a virtual copy of its Washington, DC, USA **7**, embassy in *Second Life*. The avatar of Minister for Foreign Affairs, Carl Bildt, performed the "cutting of the ribbon" for the virtual embassy **8**, which is intended to provide information to players about Sweden.

First FBI gambling investigation
In April 2007, it was reported that the FBI had visited in-game casinos in *Second Life*. It was legally unclear whether or not betting with Linden dollars, which can be exchanged for real world money, was in violation of US gambling laws. The three largest poker casinos reportedly were earning around $1,500 per month.

FIRST VIRTUAL WORLD MIND CONTROLLER
In October 2007, Japanese researchers announced a prototype mind-activated controller for *Second Life*. It consists of a headset containing electrodes that analyse brain waves **9**, translating them into the movement of an avatar within the game. The technology is hoped to help patients undergoing neuro-rehabilitation by stimulating brain activity.

TRIVIA
↪ *Second Life* has no levels for players, no points, no winners and no losers.

↪ In February 2007, the exchange rate was 270 Linden dollars for one US dollar.

↪ Aircraft in the game can fly up to a maximum "altitude" of 4,000 m. Characters also have the ability to fly, enabling quicker travel. However, this method (without the use of vehicle) limits flight altitude to 170 m above ground level.

↪ In July 2007, Linden Labs banned gambling in Second Life. Betting on some skill-based games is still allowed.

↪ Second Life is surprisingly popular with universities, such as Princeton (US) and the Open University (UK), which offer regular lectures.

FACTS
↪ Islands cost $1,675 for 65,536 m², with $295 monthly maintenance fees. There is a 50% discount for academic institutions and non-profit organisations.

↪ There are six basic island shapes to choose from, or you can create your own terrain map. Islands can be single, grouped or joined together.

↪ Many islands are bought and split up into smaller "lots" that the owner then sells on to other player avatars to build businesses or homes on.

MMORPG ROUND-UP

FACTS

➲ Wikipedia.com states that 8.7% of male players and 23.2% of female players have had an in-game wedding.

➲ Nick Yee's Daedalus Project has interviewed over 35,000 MMORPG players, looking at psychological and sociological aspects of their gameplay. View his findings at www.nickyee.com/daedalus.

➲ The Bartle Test of Gamer Psychology has, as of July 2007, interviewed over 300,000 players in an effort to determine their "Bartle Quotient". This is a player's gameplay preferences, which breaks down into degrees of behaviour – "Killer, Socializer, Achiever or Explorer". The Bartle Test is sometimes used by designers to make games more attractive to certain types of players. The survey, running between 1996 and 2006, can be found at www.guildcafe.com/bartle.php.

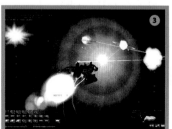

First networked 3D shooter

Game: *Maze War*
Publisher: Steve Colley/NASA
Maze War is the ancestor of many online gaming concepts. Its first version was written by Steve Colley at the NASA Ames Research Centre in 1973. It first ran on an Imlac PDS-1 computer. By connecting two Imlacs together using their serial ports, Colley and colleagues were able to play the game multiplayer – the first computer game in the world to accomplish this.

Largest free MMORPG runescape

Game: *RuneScape*
Publisher: Jagex Limited
RuneScape ❶, released in 2001, is an MMORPG that runs in a JAVA applet. It supports free subscription play as well as a paid membership option. More than 10 million free accounts have been created and more than one million who pay for added content, such as extra quests.

First console MMORPG

Game: *Phantasy Star Online*
Publisher: Sega
Phantasy Star Online ❷ was released for the Dreamcast console in 2000. It was real-time rather than turn-based and various versions were released for platforms including the PC, GameCube and Xbox. The first version of the game was finally shut down in 2003 following the commercial failure of the Dreamcast.

> **"***Out of 8 million people who play* WoW*… it never ceases to amaze me how I met the love of my life on the Gurubashi server at 3am PST. I'm the luckiest guy in the world.* **"**
>
> Anonymous *World of Warcraft* player

First space MMO

Game: *DarkSpace*
Publisher: Palestar
Released in 2001, *DarkSpace* ❸ is a massively multiplayer online RTS (real-time strategy) game. Described as having a "small but persistent" population, the game has survived well and is still open to new subscribers.

First cross-platform MMORPG

Game: *Final Fantasy XI*
Publisher: Sony Computer Entertainment (PS2)/ Square Enix (PC)
Final Fantasy XI was released for the PlayStation 2 in May 2002 in Japan. In November that year it was released for the PC, making it the first MMORPG where PC and console gamers could play together. In April 2006, *Final Fantasy XI* was released for the Xbox 360.

TYPES OF GAMEPLAY

There are a number of different types of massive multiplayer game:

MMORTS: Massively Multiplayer Online Real-Time Strategy, eg *Shattered Galaxy*
MMOR: Massively Multiplayer Online Racing, eg *Test Drive Unlimited* ❹
MMORPG: Massively Multiplayer Online Role-Playing Game, eg *World of Warcraft*
MMOFPS: Massively Multiplayer Online First Person Shooter, eg *PlanetSide* ❺
MMOMG: Massively Multiplayer Online Manager Game, eg *Hattrick*.

100,000 – number of people in China working as in-game "gold farmers" in December 2005, according to *New York Times* estimates

FIRST MMORPG FOR MOBILE PHONES

Game: *Tibia Micro Edition*
Publisher: CipSoft GmbH
Released in May 2003, *Tibia Micro Edition* **6** allows players on mobile phones to play together online as warriors or wizards. It was first available only to users of Nokia 3650 and 7650 phones subscribing to T-Mobile, but is now much more widely available.

via a web browser. Released in 1997, it now boasts around a million users, whose teams participate in roughly 1.2 million virtual football matches each week.

Largest online football manager game

Game: *Hattrick*
Publisher: Hattrick Limited
Hattrick is a management game in which the player runs a football team

Largest gold MMORPG currency seller

IGE (Internet Gaming Entertainment) is regarded as the largest and most profitable company that sells in-game currency to players. It reportedly uses cheap labour to acquire currency by farming gold and other currency in-game and selling it to gamers who want

short cuts around the usual necessary work in order to become rich in their virtual world of choice. IGE and its competitors are often criticised by gamers as they effectively allow other gamers to cheat.

FACT

On 30 March 2005, it was announced that Qiu Chengwei (China) stabbed friend Zhu Caoyuan to death over a virtual sword. Chengwei had loaned his rare weapon to Caoyuan in the popular Chinese MMORPG *Legend of Mir 3*, who promptly sold it in real life for 7,200 yuan.

LORD OF THE RINGS ONLINE

Publisher: Turbine, Inc.
Perhaps one of the most eagerly awaited online games in history, LotRO **7** was released in April 2007. It is the first MMORPG set in Tolkien's world and offers players a multitude of professions to play. It was launched to critical acclaim with some of the best reviews and scores ever seen by an MMORPG. As of November 2007, three free content updates have already been added to the game.

STRATEGY GAMES

OUR EXPERT

Dan Griliopoulos is Reviews Editor on *Xbox 360: The Official Xbox Magazine* and his freelance commissions have included *The Times, Edge, Eurogamer.net, PC Zone, PC Gamer, Official Playstation 2, Xbox World 360, Games Master, Official Nintendo, 101 PC Games* and *Game Boy Advance Magazine,* to name but a few.

OUTLINE

Strategy games are based on choice. Some let the players take turns playing, some are in real time, some let you lead entire armies; all put you in control of a large and complicated world where you have to deal with multiple variables simultaneously with the outcome dependent on the decisions you make.

STRATEGY GAME PLAYERS DON'T TRUST LUCK, THEY PLAY BY THE RULES. WHETHER IN CONTROL OF A SMALL ARMY OR A COMPLETE WORLD, THEY USE THE RULES TO THEIR ADVANTAGE.

Since the dawn of civilisation, people have played games that aren't chance-based but rule-based. The first of these "strategy" games were games similar to draughts or chess, and the earliest known game of this sort was *Senet,* an ancient Egyptian game regularly found in Predynastic burials of Egypt around 3500 BC.

The **first strategy game on a computer** was *OXO,* a version of noughts and crosses (known in the US as tic-tac-toe), which was recreated on the EDSAC (Electronic Delay Storage Automatic Calculator) by Alexander S. Douglas of the USA in 1952. *OXO* was ground-breaking in a number of ways, as it was also

the **first computer game** and the **first single-player game**.

Surprisingly, the next big development in strategy video games came nearly 30 years later in the early 1980s, where the genre diverged into now-familiar subgenres. The **first God game**, where you have control of the world but no direct troop control, was

Don Daglow's *Utopia,* released on the Intellivision. In the other direction, the **first real-time tactics game**, where you have no control over the world or which troops you have, but have complete control over the army's actions, was *Legionnaire* ① for the Atari 8-bit, released in 1982. Meanwhile, *Stonkers,* the **first real-time strategy (RTS)game**, where you control both your world or

LEGIONNAIRE

① COPYRIGHT 1982
THE AVALON HILL GAME COMPANY
HOW MANY LEGIONS FOR YOU? 5

SEGA MEGA DRIVE

DUNE II
BATTLE FOR ARRAKIS

Westwood
16-BIT CARTRIDGE

②

1952 – the year that *OXO*, the first strategy game on a computer, a game of noughts and crosses, was created

troops and their actions in battle, was created by John Gibson in 1983.

Dune II ② was a leap forward, pioneering the **first use of gathering, refining and spending resources** and the **first use of constructing bases and units**.

Meanwhile, 1993's *Xcom* series, from Microprose, created the **first multi-level strategy title**, with a global war that tied into local battles. *Warhammer: Shadow of the Horned Rat broke new ground* in 1995 when it introduced pausable real-time,

for the assessment of the battlefield and strategy, in a true rotatable 3D world.

These two titles inspired the *Total War* series ④, which began in 2000. This popular strategy series boasts a powerful games engine that has been used to graphically re-enact the full carnage of a wide range of historical battles for a variety of television shows.

TRIVIA

➲ The **first game to use 3D troops and a 3D environment** was *Total Annihilation*. The only series to use a fully 3D environment has been the *Homeworld* ⑤ series.

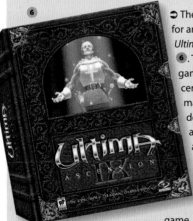

➲ The most comprehensive box set for an RPG/strategy game was for *Ultima 9: Ascension – Dragon Edition* ⑥. This contained all the previous games in the series, a music CD, certificates, a pendant, a cloth map, a poster, Tarot cards and a deluxe spellbook and journal. Oh, and the game itself, almost as an afterthought.

➲ The **longest game title** was for a Japanese game, *White Princess the Second – Yappari Itto ni Ittemo Soujyanakutemo OK-na Gotsugou Shugi Gakuen Renai Adventure*, or in English *White Princess the Second – Love Adventure in the School That Follows the Principle of Convenience, Where It's Okay to Stray From the Path or Stay on the Path*.

FACT

The most popular setting for a strategy game is World War II.

STARCRAFT

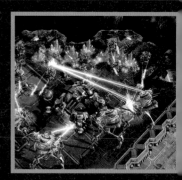

PLATFORMS

PC | XBOX 360
| XBOX
| DS
3 |
| Wii

SPEC

Developer:
Blizzard
Publisher:
Vivendi-Universal
Initial release:
StarCraft (1998), PC

GAMEPLAY

A real-time strategy game in which players control one of three distinct races. Players can either play through the campaign or play a multiplayer game with up to seven others. Players need to manage resources, defend bases and amass armies before marching into battle.

Largest audience for a game competition A total of 120,000 fans turned out to watch the final of the SKY proleague season 2005 in an arena in Busan, South Korea ❷. In terms of TV audiences, the South Korean OnGamerNet TV channel regularly attracts 3-4 million viewers in its peak viewing period of 6–10p.m. This places it in the top 20 Korean television shows.

Most successful *StarCraft* player Lim Yo-Hwan ❶ (SlayerS_'BoxeR') is the world's most successful competitive *StarCraft* player. He is the only player to win the World Cyber Games twice (2001, 2002), as well as the OnGameNet StarLeague twice. He has also been the KeSPA (Korea ESport Association) champion for an unprecedented 17 months.

Largest income in professional gaming Lim Yo-Hwan's ❶ income is the largest in professional gaming, exceeding $390,000 in a year, including $90,000 in sponsorship. He also has the **largest fan club in professional gaming**, reaching some 500,000 fans. His income is likely to drop in 2007, however, as he has been drafted into the Korean military for two-and-a-half years mandatory military service.

Best-selling PC strategy game *StarCraft* is the best-selling strategy game on PC, second only to the *Sims* in overall volume. Since its release, it has sold 9.5 million copies worldwide, with the next nearest game, *Cossacks: European Wars*, selling only 4 million copies, mostly in Germany. Indeed, *StarCraft* has sold 3.5 million copies in South Korea alone!

❝ *Blizzard stayed* **true to the product, true to the brand, true to the creative vision** *and never allowed anyone to get off that path.* **I've never seen them put out a bad game.** **❞**

Curt Schilling, pitcher for the Boston Red Sox and wannabe game developer

3.5 million – *StarCraft* sales in South Korea alone in 2006, equating to over a third of total worldwide sales

STARCRAFT RANKINGS AT THE 2006 WORLD CYBER GAMES

The annual World Cyber Games have featured team-based *StarCraft: Brood War* tournaments every year since 2001. They offer an impressive $25,000 purse for the Grand Final winner.

	COUNTRY	POINTS		COUNTRY	POINTS
1	South Korea	745.3	11	Spain	199.9
2	Germany	636	12	Italy	164
3	USA	451.4	13	Sweden	154.7
4	Russia	387.8	14	UK	130.5
5	Netherlands	375.6	15	Bulgaria	123.5
6	China	295.2	16	Poland	113.3
7	Canada	277.1	17	Kazakhstan	105.7
8	Brazil	259.5	18	Ukraine	102.2
9	France	257.8	19	Japan	97.9
10	Taiwan	214.3	20	Australia	95.5

TRIVIA

⮩ If a player clicks repeatedly on the units in *StarCraft*, they say different things, many of which are "Easter eggs". For example, the Terran Science Vessel impersonates Mr Burns from *The Simpsons* and quotes Spock in *Star Trek: The Wrath of Khan*: "Ship? Out of danger?"

⮩ The Terran Drop Ship responds entirely with quotes from the movie franchise *Aliens*, while one of the flamethrower-equipped Terrans is called Gui Montag, a reference to the fireman in Ray Bradbury's novel *Fahrenheit 451*, who is called Guy Montag.

⮩ The Zerg's facial structure ③ was derived from dental X-rays of human skulls.

⮩ *StarCraft* has contributed extensively to the vocabulary of computer gaming. "To zerg" is to rush an enemy headlong in the hope that your numbers will overwhelm them. Some even claim that "to be pwned", meaning "to be beaten", derives from a misspelling of "owned" when the game was first published.

FIGURES

800% – increase in traffic to Battle.net, the online gaming service, after *StarCraft*'s release

33% – percentage of South Koreans who have played video games online

CIVILIZATION

PLATFORMS

PC | XBOX 360
| XBOX
| DS
3 |
| Wii

SPEC

Developer:
Microprose/Firaxis
Publisher:
2K Games
Initial release:
Civilization *(PC),1991*

GAMEPLAY

Players use their strategic skills to take a nation from the dawn of time to the near future and conquer the world! On this journey, the player takes turns against the computer to develop his empire within a chosen historical civilization by, among other things, building and improving cities, signing treaties or declaring war.

Greetings from Grey Wolf of the Barbarians...
You have captured my favorite village.
This village is skilled in horsemanship,
but I have many others.

Ok

Most video game accolades
Sid Meier, founder of Microprose and creator of *Civilization*, has won more game awards than anyone else. He was also the second person (of nine) to be inducted into the Academy of Interactive Arts & Sciences Hall of Fame. *Civilization III* 1 was named the Game of the Year for 2001 by over 12 gaming critics, with *Civilization* and *Civilization II* picking up similar accolades in their respective time-frames. *Civilization IV* has continued this trend, picking up Strategy Game of the Year from

IGN, AIAS, Gamespy, Gamespot, 1UP, Gamerdad and others. In *CGW*'s 1996 Anniversary Edition, *Civilization* was chosen the #1 (of 150) Best Game of All Time. More awards are expected for the 2008 release, *Civilization Revolution* 2 .

Longest time period covered in a strategy game Starting from the year 4000BC, every game in the *Civilization* series has taken

THE NEW CULTURE NOVEL
IAIN M.
BANKS
MATTER

SHOOTING FOR THE STARS
Multi-million-selling author Iain Banks 3 missed his deadline for the first time in 2006 due to getting addicted to *Civilization*. The writer was quoted on *The Independent* newspaper website: "I played it for three months and then realised I hadn't done any work. In the end, I had to delete all the save files and smash the CD."

$22.3 million – the amount paid by Take-Two to Infogrames for the rights to the *Civilization* franchise in November 2004

TRIVIA

➲ It wasn't until *Sid Meier's Pirates* was released that the Meier name became attached to his games. This was because the publisher was worried about what people would make of *Pirates*. The game mixed a wide variety of genres and, as such, was a departure from previous offerings. The "*Sid Meier's*" tag was added to reassure fans.

➲ Firaxis had planned to release a "Dinosaurs and Cavemen" themed variation on classic *Civilization* gameplay, but this was cancelled after the developer realised that there just wasn't enough scope to make the idea fun to play.

➲ If you've played *Civilization*, the odds are high that you've seen Sid Meier. His likeness was used for the Science Advisor. He also appeared as Barbarian Leader in *Civilization IV* and provided the voice of new technology in the *Beyond the Sword* expansion pack.

FIGURES

34 – civilizations to choose from in *Civilization IV*; this includes **6** added in the *Warlord* pack and the **10** added in the *Beyond the Sword* pack.

8 million – the total number of *Civilization* games sold since the title's launch in 1991.

❝ *Our approach to making games is to find the fun first and then use the technology to enhance the fun*... Civilization *actually started as a real-time game. But it wasn't until we made it turn based that it started to make sense.* **❞**

Sid Meier, *Civilization* creator

the human race all the way to supposed interstellar exodus in the year 2100. *Alpha Centauri*, Sid Meier's only foray into science-fiction, is seemingly set after *Civilization* and deals with the colonists arrival on the new planet, stretching into the distant future.

Highest-rated strategy series
The average rating amongst games reviewers for the *Civilization* series has been higher than any other strategy game series. *Civilization II* scored an average of 94%, *Civilization III* hit 90% and *Civilization IV* scored 94%, based on metacritic.com figures.

Best *Civilization* player
The best *Civilization* player is "Moonsinger", who currently leads both the *Civilization III* and *Civilization IV* high score tables, according to www.civfanatics.com. In *Civilization III* he scored 88,553 points, beating his nearest rival by nearly 7,000 points. See below.

TOP 5 *CIVILIZATION III* HIGH SCORES
(Using Sid difficulty level and huge maps)

source: www.civfanatics.com

RANK	PLAYER	SCORE	DATE	CIVILIZATION
1	Moonsinger	88,553	2050 AD	Maya
2	Kuningas	81,609	2050 AD	Maya
3	Moonsinger	81,501	2050 AD	Maya
4	SirPleb	64,296	2050 AD	Iroquois
5	SpiffyKeen7744	31,072	1790 BC	Aztecs

CIVILIZATION
Build An Empire To Stand The Test Of Time

Sid Meier's

MICRO PROSE

COMMAND & CONQUER

PLATFORMS

PC · XBOX 360 · PS1 · XBOX · PS2 · DS · PS3 · GameCube · Wii

SPEC

Developer:
Westwood Studios/EA
Publisher:
Various
Initial release:
Command & Conquer
(1995), PC

GAMEPLAY

Players fight across a futuristic version of Earth devastated by a creeping, extremely valuable alien resource called Tiberium. Using infantry, vehicles, aircraft and fixed structures, players defeat AI enemies and follow a twisting, turning plot outlined through high-quality FMV cutscenes.

Most FMV used in a single franchise Almost every single game in the *Command & Conquer* series has used its trademark Full Motion Video (FMV) to convey mission objectives and to lay out the plot. Though the exact number of minutes is unclear, every mission of every game except *Command & Conquer: Generals* ❶ has featured an FMV scene.

First game to use SAGE The Strategy Action Game Engine (SAGE) was created by the Westwood development team as a way to introduce full 3D visuals to the *C&C* series. The first title to use it was *Command & Conquer: Generals*, and it has been used more recently on *Command & Conquer 3: Tiberium Wars* ❷, released in 2007, and *Command & Conquer 3: Kane's Wrath*, an eagerly-awaited game that is due for release at the end of 2008.

Longest-running actor in a video game role Joe Kucan ❸ has played the part of Kane, the villainous mastermind of the series, for 14 years, from the very first game, *Command & Conquer*, to the latest game, *Kane's Wrath*, which is based entirely around his character. He has only been absent from two of the 12 games in the series; *Command & Conquer: Generals* and *Command & Conquer: Red Alert 2* (for which he directed the cutscenes). By good fortune, his appearance has hardly changed over the years, making him a truly versatile character actor.

Most number of platforms for an RTS The *Command & Conquer* series has appeared on PC, Macintosh, N64, Playstation, Saturn and Xbox 360, making it the only strategy franchise so far to make the transition to console successfully. The franchise could move to PlayStation 3 in the future and possibly even to Wii.

First integrated game commentary system
Command & Conquer 3 on PC has the first built-in game commentary system. Called Battlecast, it's designed to make it one of the pre-eminent competitive games in the modern world.

WORLD CYBER GAMES

The World Cyber Games Champions 2007 Grand Final was held in Seattle, USA, on 3–7 October 2007. *Command & Conquer 3* was one of the eight PC games, and the results were: **1st** Shaun Clark ❹ ("Apollooo"), UK; **2nd** Leon Machens ❺ ("Xeon"), Germany; **3rd** Pascal Pfefferle ❻ ("Dackel"), Germany.

1

2

WCG 2007

28 – the number of available unit types in the original *Command & Conquer*; this was increased to 56 units by *Command & Conquer 3*

BIGGEST-SELLING RTS SERIES

Not just the longest running, the *Command & Conquer* **8** series is also the world's biggest-selling real-time strategy (RTS) series, having stacked up sales of over 25 million copies. There have been six full games and seven expansion packs released so far across a wide variety of formats. Indeed, it can be described as being the main reason for the success of the RTS genre.

8

Not only does it allow players to broadcast their games either live or as replays, but it also has its own show, "Battlecast Primetime", broadcast in high-definition at www.commandandconquertv.com. Moreover, selected viewers can provide commentary on the match for thousands of other players **7** and draw on the map using simple tools inspired by MS Paint and sports commentary.

" *My proudest moment on the project is when we brought in gamers to play some multiplayer and heard those magic words:* **'This feels like C&C! C&C is back!'** **"**

Mike Verdu, Executive Producer on Command & Conquer 3: Tiberium Wars

2

TRIVIA

➲ Tiberium, the fictional resource that the entire *C&C* story revolves around, is based on the 1958 movie about killer crystals called *The Monolith Monsters* **9**. In 2006, EA asked scientists at Massachusetts University to produce professional research documents detailing the biological and physical makeup of Tiberium to add depth to the story in *Command & Conquer: Tiberium Wars*.

9

➲ *Command & Conquer* has had its fair share of Hollywood talent, including James Earl Jones, Michael Ironside, Bille Dee Williams, Michael Biehn and Josh Holloway. Ironside also provides the voice for Sam Fisher in *Tom Clancy's Splinter Cell* series.

➲ Prequel *Red Alert* was originally planned as an expansion pack to the *Command & Conquer* timeline; it was only during development that Westwood Studios decided to expand it into a full game. Its success led to two *Red Alert* expansion packs and a sequel.

3

TOTAL WAR

PLATFORMS

PC

SPEC

Developer:
Creative Assembly
Publisher:
EA, Activision, Sega
Initial release:
*Shogun: Total War
(2000), PC*

GAMEPLAY

Total War *games are
dual-level; on the
main map you build
up cities, move armies
and manage finances,
in the style of* Risk *or*
Civilization. *When a
battle starts, focus is
switched over to the
battle maps where the
player wages war using
real-time tactics in 3D,
similar to* Command
& Conquer. *This gives
players the chance to
control not just one, but
several armies at the
same time.*

Most detailed in-game maps

The *Total War* maps ① cover the
whole of Europe and are generated
from the real terrain of the area,
giving it a working area
of around 10,000,000 km²
(400,000 miles²). Other games have
covered a larger area of the Earth
(e.g. *Civilization*), but not in such
detail. Every battle that takes place
in-game occurs on terrain that has
been modelled to match the land
and climate of the places where the
battles were actually fought.

Most realistic battles

The battle engine in the *Total War*
games is the most realistic around,
featuring individually-animated 3D
models drawn from each featured
nation ②. The user-made *Rome:
Total War Accuracy* modification
further increased the accuracy,
giving each soldier the appearance
and statistics that were the best
estimates of historical research.

First game used to relive historical battles on TV

The first video game to be used
to re-enact historical battles
on television was an upgraded
version of the *Rome: Total War*
③ engine. It was used in BBC2
and The History Channel's *Time
Commanders* production between
2003 and 2005. Both the presenters
and contestants were deliberately
selected for being
mostly ignorant
of video games,
with personnel on
hand to control
the armies, as
this was a test of
generalship not of
strategy game prowess.
Due to the BBC's rules against
product placement, no mention
was ever made of the game.

First real-time 3D sea battles

Empire: Total War ④ features
fully-functional 3D sea battles
using the same engine as the main
battles played on land. These are
also played in real-time. This allows
players to re-create historical sea
battles such as Trafalgar (1805) and
Lowestoft (1665).

Most in-game unit types

Medieval: Total War ⑤ can feature
over 10,000 individually animated
characters, more than any other
game. Although *Cossacks II:
Napoleonic Wars* can support far
more, up to 64,000 soldiers on-
screen, they are not dynamically
animated individual units. Instead
the soldiers in *Cossacks* move in
static fixed blocks.

> **" Much of the time, game
> development is not funny**.
> *It's like working in a Siberian
> salt mine, only without the
> nice décor, friendly guards,
> well-mannered colleagues,
> good food, nice weather and
> sense of achievement in a job
> well done. "*
>
> *Mike Brunton, designer and writer,*
> Rome: Total War

$30 million – price that game publisher Sega reportedly paid to acquire developers Creative Assembly in 2005

SHOGUN: TOTAL WAR MULTIPLAYER HIGH SCORES

	NAME	CLAN	WINS	LOSSES	BATTLES	HONOURS
1	Suda Daniel	Daniels Todesclan	190	2	111	170
2	So darealruler	E-TOWN	167	27	194	167
3	Tsuchiya Yoshikane	Clan Tsuchiya	140	25	165	167
4	Mizuno 1Unbeatable1	Mizuno Dominion	96	8	104	166
5	Akechi JoeMontana	HonorMeansNothing	31	0	31	163
6	Shimazu darealruler	E-TOWN	285	57	342	162
7	Shimazu drbninja	E-TOWN	239	63	302	161
8	Shiba TheDanesZandy	TheDanes	138	6	144	161
9	Yamamoto meekandmild	japanese women	57	2	59	161
10	Kosaka Nashwan	myclan <----	30	0	30	160

TRIVIA

➲ The publisher of *Total War* has changed three times – Electronic Arts, Activision and Sega have all released titles in the series.

➲ The latest addition, *Empire: Total War*, is also the most historically recent – players can access the technologies of the industrial revolution.

➲ In 2005, Creative Assembly released *Spartan: Total Warrior*, a spin-off from the franchise. In something of a departure for the company, the game took the form of an action-adventure game, rather than a large-scale strategy.

STRATEGY GAMES ROUND-UP

> ❚❚ *What I want to achieve in my career is very simple.* **I want to create a truly great landmark game**, *a game that people would put in their all-time top 10.* ❚❚
>
> Peter Molyneux, creator of *Black & White*

First real-time strategy game
Game: *Stonkers*
Publisher: Imagine Software
Designed by D. H. Lawson and John Gibson in 1983, *Stonkers* was an RTS for the ZX Spectrum. Set in a theatre of war, players moved troops, weapons and supplies around a battlefield in an attempt to win. It won the "Best Wargame" award from *Crash* magazine in 1984.

Most actions per minute
Game: *Starcraft*
Publisher: Blizzard
Players of *Starcraft* and similar games have developed several different programs to track in-game statistics. Key to success in these games is the number of actions per minute a player can manage. A new player of *Starcraft*, after about a week's play, can manage perhaps 20 actions-per-minute (APM). A pro-gamer will be looking to maintain around 180 APM, though they can reach peaks of over 1,000 APM during battles in-game. This is the equivalent of clicking a mouse or pushing a button up to 17 times every second!

First 3D strategy game
Game: *Warhammer: Shadow of the Horned Rat*
Publisher: Mindscape
Warhammer: Shadow of the Horned Rat (1995) featured true 3D terrain, although *Total Annihilation* (Cavedog Entertainment, 1997) was the first game to feature both fully 3D terrain and 3D units. More impressively, however, *Homeworld* ❶ (1999) featured a full 3D space simulation in which you could control your ships, allowing you to establish proper 3D formations and allowing for tactics employing the full breadth (it took the *Cataclysm* expansion pack to make it fully playable though).

18 million – the number of copies sold of the award-winning Ensemble Studios real-time strategy series *Age Of Empires*

LONGEST TITLE FOR A STRATEGY GAME

Game: *Lord of the Rings…*
Publisher: EA Games
The Lord of the Rings: The Battle for Middle-Earth II – The Rise of the Witch-King [2] (2006) is conceivably the longest name for a strategy game. Indeed, it is believed to be the longest title in the English language for any game.

BEST-SELLING STRATEGY GAMES

TITLE	DEVELOPER	UNITS SOLD
StarCraft	Blizzard	9.5 million
Warcraft: Orcs and Humans	Blizzard	8 million
Populous	Bullfrog	4 million
Cossacks: European Wars	GSC Gameworld	4 million
Warcraft III	Blizzard	4 million
Civilization III	Firaxis	4 million
Age of Empires	Ensemble Studios	3 million
Command & Conquer: Red Alert	Westwood Studios	3 million
Anno 1602	Max Design	2.5 million
Black & White [3]	Lionhead	2 million
Age of Empires III	Ensemble Studios	2 million
Command & Conquer: Tiberium Sun	Westwood Studios	1.5 million

HIGHEST SCORING STRATEGY GAME

Game: *Company of Heroes* **Publisher:** Relic Entertainment
Company of Heroes [4] (2005) scored an average of 93% from 55 media scores aggregated on www.metacritic.com, which brings together all the mainstream scores. The game is a standard real-time tactics title that brings simple elements of RTS resource-gathering into the equation. This, combined with an exceptionally balanced multiplayer and the overworn-but-somehow-still appealing World War II setting, became a clear winning formula.

TRIVIA

➲ If there was an award for weirdest strategy it would go to *Perimeter* [5], in which an exiled humanity is travelling along an incomprehensible Psychosphere pathway in floating cities. The aim is to gather energy to power your "perimeter" by deforming the terrain and using autonomous morphing troops to fight off creatures. And it's a lot weirder than that makes it sound!

➲ Sadly the MMO/strategy hybrid hasn't really taken off. Despite the release of *Mankind* (1998) and *Shattered Galaxy* (2001), no major publisher since has chosen to tackle the combination of an always-on universe and resource-gathering. Games like *Dreamlords* [6] have been released, but have achieved little success.

➲ The genre-defining *Populous*, created by Peter Molyneux, featured terrain that could be altered by the players. Peter later revealed that this was because he was too lazy to create hundreds of maps with fixed terrain.

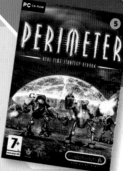

SIMULATION GAMES

OUR EXPERT

Adam Phillips was hooked by arcade games in the early 80s: *Zaxxon*, *Phoenix* and *Galaxian* being the main culprits. He has worked on various computer titles including *Amiga Computing* and *Atari ST User in the past*, and for *Official Dreamcast Magazine* and *PC Zone* more recently. He is currently addicted to *SimCity 3000*.

OUTLINE

Simulation games give the player the opportunity to replicate the experience of a variety of real-life activities in a realistic way, whether it be nurturing a family, building a city, looking after a pet dog, creating a beautiful garden or controlling a railroad company.

WE ALL HAVE URGES TO TRY THINGS THAT WE CAN'T DO IN REAL LIFE. AS THE HISTORY OF SIMS SHOWS, THE ALLURE OF BEING ABLE TO WALK IN SOMEONE ELSE'S SHOES CAN BE IRRESISTIBLE...

While simulation video games, or sims, embrace many different themes, the most enduring and successful have been those based around creating worlds, cities and homes, either for vast populations or a single virtual family. The two sims credited as being the most influential in the genre are *Utopia* **6** and *M.U.L.E.* **8**

Designed by Don Daglow and released in 1981 for the Intellivision games console, *Utopia* is recognised as the **first simulation game.** Its object is to manage an island, its people, food and natural disasters while fending off aggressors. Such a premise was evolved further by *M.U.L.E.* in 1983, where up to four players try to make their mark on the planet Irata (Atari spelt backwards) as robotics entrepreneurs.

In 1985, gaming saw the arrival of *Little Computer People (LCP)*, the **first "people" simulator**, where players took care of a man and his dog living in a three-storey house. The most innovative aspect of *LCP* was that every disk featured a serial number, which was typed in before the game first started; the result was a little computer person with a unique appearance and personality.

The person responsible for bringing such diverse life and society-building simulator ideas together into

the mainstream was Will Wright. His creation, *SimCity*, released in 1989, was the **first city-building simulator** and heralded an era of simulation games that appealed to the mass market. The huge success of *SimCity* enabled Wright to develop his most successful simulation game, *The Sims*, in 2000, which is now the **best-selling game on the PC**.

While Wright brought life simulators to the masses, other sims makers during the 1980s and 90s focused on big business. In 1990, Sid Meier's

TIMELINE

1981

1981: *Utopia* released by Intellivision

1982: *Flight Simulator 1.00* debuts for PC

1983: *M.U.L.E.* released for Atari 800

1984

1984: *Gato* is published for PC

1985: *Southern Belle* released for ZX Spectrum

1985

1985: *Little Computer People* released for various formats

1985: Activision unleash *Alter Ego* onto the world

1989

1989: *SimCity* makes its debut for PC

1990: *Railroad Tycoon* released for PC

1994: *Transport Tycoon* comes to PC

TRIVIA

➲ The now-deceased designer of *M.U.L.E.*, Dani Bunten Berry, claimed that she had been considering converting the board game *Civilization* into a video game but was dissuaded by Sid Meier – who went on to create his own best-selling sim, also called *Civilization*.

➲ First published in 1986, *Alter Ego* had two versions – one for males and one for females. Given the male-driven video game market at the time, it is perhaps unsurprising that the female version sold fewer copies and is harder to find today.

FIGURES

6 – number of nominations for awards for *Viva Piñata* by the Academy of Interactive Arts and Sciences in 2006.

Railroad Tycoon ③ enraptured train nerds the world over and was the **first Tycoon game**, triggering a multitude of business simulators such as Chris Sawyer's *Transport Tycoon* ② in 1994. However, it took the release of *Theme Park* in 1994 for business sims to really take off.

Some simulators, though, remain as hardcore as the day they were born – the **first plane sim**, *Flight Simulator 1* for the Apple II, was created by SubLogic in 1980. In 1982, Microsoft released the PC version ④, which went on to spawn a vast franchise that has spanned 25 years.

Many other forms of transport and craft have inevitably been simulated – submarines made their first appearance in *Gato* ⑤, in 1984, and *Southern Belle* released in 1985, was the **first 3D train simulator for a home computer**.

The leap in graphical quality over the past decade has meant the creation of more and more realistic environments for the player to control, with developers creating wholly believable and, most importantly, accessible worlds for player to indulge themselves in.

From pitch-perfect hacking in *Uplink*, and *Animal Crossing* ⑩, the **most successful sim on the Nintendo GameCube**, both released in 2001, through to 2005's *Nintendogs,* the **best-selling game on the Nintendo DS** ①, and the beautiful, but slightly surreal gardening sim *Viva Piñata* ⑦, the sims scene remains an influential cornerstone of video gaming.

1994		2000	2004	2006
1994: *Theme Park* released for PC	**1996:** *Harvest Moon* hits the SNES	**2000:** *The Sims* unleashed for PC	**2004:** *The Sims 2* released for PC	**2006:** *Viva Piñata* released for Xbox 360
1995: *Capitalism* unleashed on PC	**1997:** *Theme Hospital* released for PC	**2001:** *Uplink* released for PC	**2005:** *Nintendogs* debuts on Nintendo DS	**2006:** *Flight Simulator X* arrives for PC
1995: *Flight Unlimited* released for PC	**1999:** *Rollercoaster Tycoon* comes out for PC	**2001:** *Animal Crossing* released for GameCube	**2005:** *The Movies* released for PC	**2006:** *Kudos* released for PC

SIMCITY

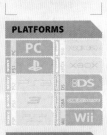

PLATFORMS

PC
XBOX360
PS3
XBOX
DS
3
GAMEBOY
Wii

SPEC

Developer:
Maxis
Publisher:
Maxis
Initial release:
SimCity (1989), Mac/
Amiga

GAMEPLAY

Starting from the ground up, create and maintain a city, keeping the populace happy and safe from crime and disasters. Although the game does not technically end, a wide variety of expansion packs allow you to focus and customise your gameplay.

Best-selling game in the SimCity series

According to VGChartz, the comprehensive online videogame chart, the PC version of *SimCity 2000* is the best-selling *SimCity* title with 2.14 million copies sold. The next best is the SNES's *SimCity*, which sold 1.98 million copies.

*" He showed me SimCity, and I died. **It was what I was looking for**. "*

Jeff Braun **2**, Maxis co-founder

First city-building game

The original *SimCity* **1** was the world's first fully fledged city-building game. While *Utopia* (1981) allowed players to create cities on the game's two islands and therefore could arguably be described as the first city-building game, the technology was not advanced enough at the time to actually show the city, whereas *SimCity* could.

Most dedicated player New York resident Elliot Hanson has been constructing the Big Apple in *SimCity 4* **3** for nearly four years, "one pixel at a time". He has even reconstructed tributes to major events, such as the Macy's Thanksgiving Parade and 9/11. In his downtime, Elliot is working on recreating San Francisco, Chicago, Washington DC and Boston.

Most controversial Sim-based Easter Egg One of *SimCity*'s many spin-offs, *SimCopter* **4**, featured a secret Easter Egg coded by Jacques Servin, where, on particular days, male citizens of the city would walk around in swimming trunks kissing each other and everyone they met. The Easter Egg was discovered after 78,000 copies of the game had been sold and Servin lost his job for inserting the code without permission.

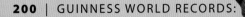

£11.5 million – the amount the *SimCity* series has earned Maxis, its developer, since its launch in 1989 through to the end of 2006

Greatest set of accolades for Sim series

On 8 March 2007, *SimCity* was included in a list of top games created to preserve titles that are seen as particularly culturally important to the world of gaming. Ten games were chosen by a selection of videogaming luminaries – *SimCity* was included because the game is "one of the most important artworks of the 20th century. It completely reinvented the whole notion of games. And then it transcended the game world to become a cultural phenomenon." Other games featured on the list include *Doom* and *Tetris*.

Will Wright **5**, the game's creator, was awarded a Lifetime Achievement Award at the 2001 Game Developers Choice Awards, the Ivan Allen Jr Prize for Progress and Service in 2005 for exemplary contributions and a coveted BAFTA fellowship in 2007 for his game designs, in recognition of the impact they have had on films and pop culture.

TRIVIA

➲ Veteran video game critic Stuart Campbell **6** gave one of the shortest ever game reviews with his comment on the budget version of *SimCity* in issue 37 of the UK magazine *Amiga Power*. He simply stated: "Look, I'm not reviewing *SimCity* again. No way. Forget it." And in the summary box, declared: "It's *SimCity*, all right? 90%."

➲ Maxis has stated that the game has been used in over 10,000 classrooms as a teaching aid, and that the company was approached by the CIA and the Defense Department about exploiting its "potential".

➲ In the PC version of the game, your city can be destroyed by a huge red lizard; in the SNES release, however, Bowser from the Mario games makes a guest appearance as the monster!

➲ In the late 1980s, *Newsweek* magazine printed a one-page feature on *SimCity* that prompted a few players to try it. They were soon completely addicted, and sales rocketed as the word-of-mouth enthusiasm spread.

THE SIMS

SIM SINGERS

The official language of *The Sims* is Simlish, a made-up language that has elements of Ukrainian and Tagalog. Many popstars have re-recorded their greatest hits in Simlish, including: Lily Allen – "Smile" (*Seasons Pack*); The Flaming Lips – "Free Radicals" (*Pets Pack*) and The Pussycat Dolls ❶ – "Don't Cha" (*Pets Pack*).

Best-selling PC game of all time
The original *The Sims* ❷ is the best-selling PC game of all time, with 16 million units sold since its launch in 2000. It has outsold the likes of *Diablo II* by almost two to one. Electronic Arts' original projections for sales of the game were estimated at just 160,000 units.

Largest *Sims* object
The largest object ever created for *The Sims 2* ❸ series is the pirate ship featured in the expansion pack, *Bon Voyage*, released in September 2007.

World's biggest-selling simulation franchise
With over 90 million units sold, *The Sims* franchise is the best-selling series in the simulation genre. In terms of all genres, *The Sims* is only beaten by the *Pokémon* series (more than 155 million units sold) and *Mario* (more than 193 million units sold).

Biggest *Sims* controversy
The biggest controversy to surround the *Sims* franchise was Florida attorney Jack Thompson's accusation in July 2005 that Sims characters could be seen fully nude with rude bits showing by using a patch or a cheat. The game's publisher, Electronic Arts, swiftly rebutted this allegation by stating: "This is nonsense… Players never see a nude Sim. If someone with an extreme amount of expertise and time were to remove the pixels, they would see that the Sims… appear like Ken and Barbie."

Most popular *Sims* video
The most viewed video on YouTube created using *The Sims* in-game movie software is *Male Restroom Etiquette* by Zarathustra Studios. This tongue-in-cheek guide to "the simple rules of 'evacuation' etiquette" was posted on 1 September 2006, and had been viewed 4,278,196 times as of 1 October 2007. Its nearest rival is the pop video created by Jaydee to accompany Avril Lavigne's song "Sk8er Boi", which had been viewed 4,221,555 times since 6 June 2006.

SILVER SCREEN *SIMS*?

In May 2007, 20th Century Fox acquired the rights to make *The Sims* into a live action movie. *Sims* studio head Rod Humble ❹ told *Variety* magazine: "*The Sims* has done an interactive version of an old story, which is what it's like to have infinite power and how do you deal with it. Given that that's an old story, you can imagine how easily that would translate to traditional story-telling."

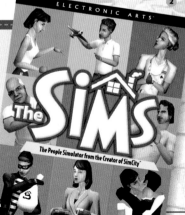

ELECTRONIC ARTS

The **SIMS**

The People Simulator from the Creator of SimCity

22 million – worldwide sales of *The Sims* series of games during the financial year 2007.

> **Working on The Sims has completely transformed my relationship with normal, everyday objects.** You haven't lived until you've attended an hour long meeting discussing toilets.
>
> Joe Maris, *Sims* Software Engineer

TRIVIA

⊃ *The Sims* creator, Will Wright **5**, is a huge fan and one-time champion of *Robot Wars*, the TV show where competitors pit their robot creations against each other. Wright and his daughter have appeared in many series of the show in the US and have built a total of nearly 40 robots.

⊃ Will Wright has said that *The Sims* came about because of his house burning down during the 1991 fires in Oakland, USA. Having lost most of their possessions, Wright and his wife set about rebuilding their household layer by layer – from new underwear and toothbrushes through to a new car – and the process inspired him to create *The Sims*.

FACTS

⊃ A Sim cannot kill another Sim, however much they may fight.

⊃ *The Sims* is available in 17 different languages.

FLIGHT SIMULATOR

Flight Simulator

PLATFORMS

PC · XBOX360 · PS · XBOX · PS2 · DS · PS3 · Wii

SPEC

Developer:
Microsoft
Publisher:
Microsoft
Initial release:
FS-1 (1980), Apple II

GAMEPLAY

Fly a wide variety of civilian, military and commercial aircraft across an accurate virtual recreation of Earth. Renowned for its high level of realism, Microsoft's Flight Simulator is one of the most demanding simulation games ever created; this is the closest you'll ever get to flying a real plane.

Longest-running flight sim franchise The *Flight Simulator* series began life on the Apple II ②, courtesy of subLOGIC, back in 1980. Microsoft published the PC version in 1982. Since then, the franchise has continued for 26 years – making the *Flight Simulator* series the longest running sim franchise.

Best-selling *Flight Simulator* The best-selling version of *Flight Simulator* remains the PC-based original released back in 1982. It has sold 4.69 million units and has outsold blockbusters such as *Tomb Raider*.

Most successful flight simulator Microsoft's *Flight Simulator* series has sold over 20 million units since its launch in 1982.

Largest real-world sim playing area *Flight Simulator* is the only real-world simulator game to offer you the entire planet and its skies to explore.

Most-used virtual training tool Its depth and realism has placed *Flight Simulator* at the forefront of virtual training. Flight schools, private pilots and the military are all known to use the game to train.

Longest Flight Simulator session On 4 November 2007, a Boeing 777 took off from Sydney, Australia. 39,848 miles and seven days of flying later it landed back in Australia. The whole journey, organised to raise money for Cancer Research UK, took place on *Flight Simulator* with a team of 17 (including Iron Maiden's Bruce Dickinson!) working in shifts.

*" Flight Simulator pushed hardware to the limit. PC designers **used Flight Simulator as a benchmark** for PC compatibility. "*

Bruce Artwick, creator of *Flight Simulator*

LITERARY INSPIRATION

Microsoft founder Bill Gates ① wanted to take on the *Flight Simulator* series after reading French aviator and writer Antoine de Saint-Exupéry's passionate book *The Night Flight* (published in 1931), which fired Gate's imagination.

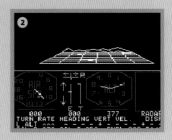

MOST EXPENSIVE HOME FLIGHT SIMULATOR COCKPIT

Australian trucking tycoon Matthew Sheil has spent the last eight years constructing a flight simulator cockpit based round the 747-400. The project to date has cost $300,000 Australian dollars (£132,000) and features 12 computers controlling motion, audio and the *Flight Simulator* game itself. The motion is provided by a hydraulic system fitted to the cockpit, and visuals are provided by a projector for the front view and two LCD monitors for the side views.

FIGURES

7,500 – types of ground textures in *Flight Simulator X*.

49 – planes that have appeared in the *Flight Simulator* series so far. This doesn't include the hundreds of fan-made additions that can be downloaded.

137,000 – players (either pilots or air traffic controllers) registered on the virtual air traffic system known as "VATSIM".

TRIVIA

➲ In *Flight Simulator X* ❹, players are rewarded with all manner of goodies for flying and completing missions. For example, postcards can be earned if you spot the Caspian 'sea monster', Ekranoplan, in the Aleutian Cargo Run mission or spot the 'ghost ship' in the Lost in the Triangle mission.

➲ The *Flight Simulator* franchise has a surprising new competitor – Google Earth 4.2, released in August 2007, contains an Easter Egg flight simulator that can be activated by pressing Ctrl + Alt + A on a PC or Command/Open Apple Key + Option + A on the Mac. Using either an F-16 jet fighter or a Cirrus SR22 propeller aircraft, users can set off from a selection of airports and explore the planet from the air.

FLYING INTO TROUBLE WITH THE LAW

Massachusetts-based USAF Reserves pilot Julie Olearcek had a surprise visit from the police in 2004, the evening after she went to her local Staples store to try to buy a copy of *Flight Simulator* for her 10-year-old son. A Staples employee had called the police because he thought it was illegal to ask how to fly planes after the events of 9/11. Olearcek was then visited by the cops, who were only convinced of her 'innocence' after she showed her military ID. The Shelburn Falls State Police stated at the time: "Those programs are quite common for entertainment and training, but [we] felt it was suspicious enough to warrant a call."

SIMS ROUND-UP

Best-selling simulator on Nintendo DS
Game: *Nintendogs*
Publisher: Nintendo
The dog sim *Nintendogs* has sold nearly 15 million copies since its release in Japan on 21 April 2005. Its nearest rival is *New Super Mario Bros*, which has sold 10.7 million copies since its release in North America on 15 May 2006.

Highest score attained in *Utopia*
Game: *Utopia*
Publisher: Intellivision
The highest points score ever achieved in the genre-defining and hugely influential sim *Utopia* is 2,171 by Mike Morrow of Denton, Texas, USA, on 2 March 2002.

First dog simulator
Game: *Dogz*
Publisher: PF Magic
While *Nintendogs* has been a runaway success, Nintendo was actually 10 years too late to create the world's first dog simulator – PF Magic released *Dogz* ② on the PC back in 1995. The main difference (other than graphics and how you interact with the canine) was that in *Dogz*, the puppy actually grew up into a dog over time. *Dogz* was followed by *Catz* in 1996.

MOST INNOVATIVE USE OF WII CONTROLLER IN A SIMULATOR
Game: *G1 Jockey* **Publisher:** KOEI
Described in reviews as a truly innovative way to use the Wii controller, the horse-racing sim *G1 Jockey* ③ lets you 'hold' the horse's reins by motioning with the nunchuk, while whipping is controlled by flicking the Wii controller from side to side.

TRIVIA

➲ *Rollercoaster Tycoon* and *Transport Tycoon* creator Chris Sawyer ④ became famous for making his best-selling games almost by himself. He stated in an interview with Pontbuzz.com: "Because I'm responsible for all the programming, design and management of the project, I always know exactly what's happening, and I can keep very tight control of how the project forms and evolves."

➲ The Japanese market is obsessed with pet games; in 2000, Sega released *Walk the Dog* where players take a virtual dog for a walk using a treadmill and a lead, to steer the pup with. More recently came Sega's *Together With Doggy* ⑤, a strange children's arcade ride: the child sits in a card-dispensing, vibrating car while petting a virtual dog on screen.

➲ Soccer sim *Football Manager 2005* was banned in China because it features Hong Kong, Macau and Tibet as individual nations, not Chinese territories.

> **❝** *There have been so many 'Tycoon' games that **it's almost become a cliché.* **❞**

Sid Meier, creator of *Railroad Tycoon*

Most dollars earned in Oil Tycoon

Game: *Oil Tycoon*
Publisher: Global Star
The greatest number of dollars amassed in the classic business simulator *Oil Tycoon* ⑥ is a whopping $1,556,862,714,127,530, achieved by Louis Martin of Longmont, Colorado, USA, on 15 February 2004. His closest rival, Kristopher Knox of Warren, Michigan, USA, only managed to amass $132,256,590,371 six months later.

MOST BONES BROKEN BY A SIM GAME

Game: *Arm Spirit* **Distributor:** Atlus
Three players broke their arms on the arcade simulator *Arm Spirit* ⑦ while testing their strength against the game's mechanised arm. The game's distributor, Atlus, recalled all 150 machines for inspection in August 2007, as a precautionary measure. They stated: "We think that maybe some players get overexcited and twist their arms in an unnatural way."

MUSIC GAMES

OUR EXPERT

Ellie Gibson's first job in the games industry was with Sony Computer Entertainment, writing manuals for PlayStation titles. She then worked for a variety of gaming magazines before joining Eurogamer Network. Following a stint as editor of GamesIndustry.biz she is now Content Editor for Eurogamer.net.

OUTLINE

Music games provide a variety of different entertaining gameplay options: you can dance your way to success, drum out a rhythm to score points, learn to play guitar like a rock god or sing along to karaoke classics. Some games even let you and your friends combine your talents to form a band.

WANT TO MAKE BEAUTIFUL MUSIC, BUT CAN'T PLAY A NOTE? NO PROBLEM, THERE'S A MUSIC GAME OUT THERE THAT WILL TURN YOU INTO A DISCO DIVA OR GUITAR HERO IN AN AFTERNOON.

Music games are a relatively new development in the gaming world. The **first rhythm action game**, *PaRappa the Rapper* ④, was released in 1996. It saw players taking on the role of a cartoon dog, pressing the right button at the right time to make him perform raps.

The game's creator, Masaya Matsuura, went on to enjoy further success with other music titles. These included *Vib Ribbon* (1999) ③, which allowed you to input CD tracks to play along to – making it the **first rhythm action game to let players choose their own music**.

Also in 1999, Sega released *Space Channel 5* ⑦ for the Dreamcast. It starred intergalactic TV presenter Ulala, who defeated alien hordes using the power of dance.

Tetsuya Mizuguchi, who created *Space Channel 5*, later developed *Rez* (2001). The game involved creating sounds by shooting targets,

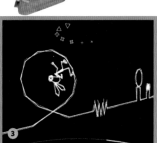

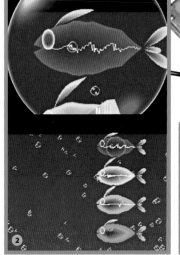

making it the **first music game to let players choose the rhythm of the music**. Mizuguchi also created *Lumines* in 2004, which also allowed gamers to alter the soundtrack according to how they played.

Electroplankton ②, released the next year, was the **first game to allow players to compose music**. Some have suggested it isn't a game at all, but a composing tool.

The **first game designed for use with a controller shaped like a musical instrument** was *MTV Drumscape*, released in 1997.

Players used a pair of drumsticks hooked up to an arcade cabinet and a set of drum pads to play along in time to the beat. *Donkey Konga*, released in 2003, was the **first console game to come with a drum controller**.

Konami's *GuitarFreaks*, which appeared in arcades in 1998, was the **first game playable with a guitar controller**. Harmonix's *Guitar Hero*, which came bundled with a guitar, proved to be a surprise global hit on launch in 2005, spawning three sequels.

Perhaps taking the idea to its rock 'n' roll limits, the new Harmonix title *Rock Band* is playable not only with a drum kit and guitar, but also a microphone, enabling gamers to form their own bands.

650,000 – number of *Guitar Hero II* song packs downloaded through Xbox Live Marketplace in just five months

Other musical controllers have included the turntable for 1997's *Beatmania*, which allowed players to scratch records, and the maracas for *Samba de Amigo* ❶, which became a cult hit following its limited release on Dreamcast.

TRIVIA

➲ Music games are sometimes referred to as Bemani games. Bemani was originally used as the shortened form of Beatmania in Japan. Although Konami has never officially released games under the Bemani label, the term is often used with reference to the publisher's music titles, such as *Dance Dance Revolution*.

➲ *Space Channel 5* ❼ had a cameo from Michael Jackson, making it the first music game to feature a pop star as a main character. He went on to play an even bigger role in the sequel.

The **first successful dance mat game**, *Dance Dance Revolution*, was a huge success when it appeared in Japanese arcades in October 1998. Since then, more than 100 iterations have been released worldwide

It wasn't until 1987 that Bandai's *Karaoke Studio*, the **first karaoke game**, was released. Karaoke games, such as Konami's *Karaoke Revolution* ❽ and Sony's *SingStar* ❻, remain popular today, and many instalments in these series have followed.

NOT SO DEEE-LITEFUL

In 2003, the lead singer of Deee-Lite, best known for their 1990 chart hit *Groove is in the Heart*, filed a lawsuit for "misappropriation of likeness" against Sega. Lady Miss Kier (real name Kierin Kirby ❾) alleged *Space Channel 5* character Ulala ❼ was modelled on her without permission. The judge rejected her claims and she was ordered to pay Sega $608,000 in legal costs.

TIMELINE

1996: *PaRappa the Rapper*

1997: *MTV Drumscape, Beatmania*

1998: *Bust-A-Groove, GuitarFreaks, Dance Dance Revolution*

1999: *Vib Ribbon, Space Channel 5, Beatmania IIDX, DrumMania, Samba de Amigo, Pump it Up, Dance Dance Revolution Solo*

2000: *Beatmania III, Taiko Drum Master* ❺, *Disney's Jungle Book Groove Party*

2001: *FreQuency, Rez and Gitaroo Man*

2003: *Amplitude, Donkey Konga, EyeToy: Groove, Dance: UK, Karaoke Revolution*

2004: *In the Groove, SingStar*

2005: *Lumines, Electroplankton, Guitar Hero, StepMania*

2006: *Elite Beat Agents, Guitar Hero II, Dance Factory*

2007: *Guitar Hero III, Rock Band*

1996 · 1998 · 1999 · 2000 · 2003 · 2005 · 2008

DANCE DANCE REVOLUTION

PLATFORMS

PC · XBOX 360 · XBOX · 3DS · Wii

SPEC

Developer:
Konami
Publisher:
Konami
Initial release:
Dance Dance Revolution
(1998), Arcade

GAMEPLAY

Players perform a series of dancing steps on a special mat in time with the music and on-screen arrows. Dance Dance Revolution, or Dancing Stage as it's known in Europe, is also available for home consoles, where it can be played using a conventional controller.

First video game recognised as an official sport

Dance Dance Revolution (or DDR)  became the first video game in the world to be given the status of an official sport when, in Oslo, Norway, on 9 December 2003, it was registered under the term "machine dancing". New York-based *Dance Dance Revolution* league Maximum Overdrive has since begun an online petition to have the game recognised as a sport in the US, and has collected more than 700 signatures.

Most widely used video game in schools

In January 2006, West Virginia's education authority announced plans to make *DDR* part of the curriculum in all of the state's 765 schools. Other parts of the USA followed suit, and *DDR* is now played in several hundred schools across at least 10 states. It is estimated that *DDR* will be part of the curriculum in more than 1,500 schools by the end of the decade.

Most calories burned using a video game

Most *Dance Dance Revolution* games feature a Workout Mode which calculates the number of calories you burn as you play. According to GetUpMove.com, a person weighing around 68 kg (150 lb) will use an average of 16 calories per song, or 640 calories per hour – compared with 501 calories burned during an hour of jogging. Playing a video game sitting down burns around 100 calories per hour, while playing *Wii Sports* uses up approximately 560 calories per hour. That makes *DDR* the most effective game for burning calories. *See pp.30–31 for more on the health benefits of video gaming!*

10 million – the number of copies of *Dance Dance Revolution* sold worldwide since its initial launch in 2001

DANCE DANCE REVOLUTION: COMPLETIONS

VARIATION	SCORE	POINTS	PLAYER	VERIFIED
DDR Extreme: 3 songs	100%	487,065,870	Sterling C. Franklin	24 Oct 2007
DDR Extreme: 3 songs (doubles)	100%	223,403,725	Luke C. Weibe	14 Jan 06
DDR Extreme: 5 songs	100%	680,808,465	Jason T. Gilleece	16 Nov 05
DDR Max 2: 3 songs	100%	166,794,050	Kelly R. Flewin	28 Feb 06
DDR Max 2: 5 songs	100%	652,095,760	Takeo Ueki	8 May 06

Longest Dance Dance Revolution marathon On 3 September 2006, Airy Peterson of Campbellsport, Wisconsin, USA, danced on a *Dance Dance Revolution: Extreme* (aka *8th Mix*) arcade machine for a bone-shattering 13 hr 9 min 40 sec.

The record was organised and verified under Twin Galaxies' strict supervision. Participants earn a five minute break for every hour of play and can save these breaks up to a limit of two hours. For the first five hours, the machine is set to "light difficulty"; between five and 10 hours, difficulty increases to "standard"; and beyond 10 hours, it is upped again to "heavy"!

TRIVIA

➲ It appears that even dance games aren't immune from the movie remake… According to the Internet Movie Database, a film version of *Dance Dance Revolution* is currently in development. The plot is set to revolve around an underdog slacker who enters the world of competitive dancing.

HOT TIP

Don't get stuck in the middle! Lots of beginner *DDR* players instinctively move their feet back to the centre of the mat after stepping on each arrow. This isn't necessary – you can keep your feet stationary on arrows without being penalised – this saves you time as well as extra effort!

*"Activity-promoting **video games have the potential to increase energy expenditure in children** to a degree similar to that of traditional playtime."*

Lorraine Lanningham-Foster,
Mayo Clinic obesity researcher

SMALLEST VIDEO-GAME DANCE MAT

The Venom Mini Dance Mat lets gamers play *Dance Dance Revolution* using their fingers instead of their feet. It measures 10 cm (4 in) wide by 11.5 cm (4.5 in) long and weighs just 20 g (0.7 oz), and is the world's first hand-held dance mat.

ACTUAL SIZE

GUITAR HERO

PLATFORMS

PC
XBOX 360
XBOX
PS2
DS
3
Wii

SPEC

Developer:
Harmonix (GHI and II),
Neversoft (GHIII)
Publisher:
Activision
Initial release:
Guitar Hero (2005),
PlayStation 2

GAMEPLAY

Players use a special guitar-shaped controller to play notes as they appear on the screen. Hitting the coloured buttons at the top of the neck replicates the action of fretting the strings on a real guitar, while the strum bar is used to get the rhythm right. The main mode of play is Career Mode, where players travel between various venues playing sets of four or five songs. If they put on a good show, they move on to a bigger, better venue.

Largest audience for a video game performance
The largest public performance of a video game took place at the Download Festival in Donington, UK, between 7–10 June 2007. Each night of the festival, players took to the stage to perform tracks from *Guitar Hero II*, to an audience of 3,000 people!

Hardest song on Guitar Hero
The hardest song in the *Guitar Hero* series so far is "Through the Fire and Flames" by Dragonforce, which appears in *Guitar Hero III* ➊. In Expert mode, this contains 3,722 notes. The song lasts for 7 min 24 sec, that's 8.38 notes every second! The previous hardest song was *Guitar Hero II*'s "Freebird".

BIGGEST FUNERAL FOR A FICTIONAL OBJECT
On 23 November 2006, to mark the launch of *Guitar Hero II*, a funeral for the air guitar was held in London, UK. More than 80 mourners were in attendance, making it the biggest ever funeral for a fictional object.

Highest percentage score in "Knights of Cydonia" track on Guitar Hero III (first play)
The highest percentage of correct notes hit in "Knights of Cydonia" (first play, on Hard level) was 86% by Luke Albiges of the UK. Luke achieved his score at the 2007 Games Media Awards held at the Soho Revue Bar, London, UK, on 11 October 2007. The score was verified by Guinness World Records' Editor-in-Chief Craig Glenday, who presented Luke with a certificate confirming his axe-wielding efforts ➋.

Best-selling guitar-based game
Launched in 2005, *Guitar Hero*, with its unique guitar controller, has become the best-selling guitar-based game in the world. By November 2007, combined sales of the *Guitar Hero* games have totalled in excess of six million copies.

Highest-scoring Guitar Hero II player in a public competition
On 11 April 2007, five of the top-scoring *Guitar Hero II* ➌ players entered a jam off in New York City to decide who was the best player in the world. Top scorer and new world champion was J. W. McNay of the USA, who got to jam with Gene Simmons from KISS.

$115 million – amount that *Guitar Hero III* grossed on its first week on sale in the USA

First BAFTA award-winning music-based video game
In 2006, the PlayStation 2 version of *Guitar Hero* picked up a BAFTA game award for the "Best Soundtrack", making it the first music game to win the award. Nominees beaten were *SingStar Rocks*, *Reservoir Dogs* and *B-Boy*.

Fastest-selling guitar-based game
In November 2007, *Guitar Hero III* became the fastest-selling guitar-based game in the world, shifting over 1.4 million copies in the first week. By comparison, *Guitar Hero* took an entire year to hit one million.

Best Guitar Hero III player
The highest-scoring player on *Guitar Hero III* is the guitarhero.com regular "WPI09" (USA) who, by the end of 2007, had amassed an impressive career score of 308,650,726 points on the Wii version – beating his nearest rival by over 80,000,000!

*"The first demo was **basically a black screen with three coloured lines** that scrolled down the screen. Even so, people were queuing up to play."*

Kai Huang, co-founder of RedOctane, publisher of *Guitar Hero*

TRIVIA
➲ All of the guitars from the *Guitar Hero* series are scaled-down versions of real world Gibson guitars. The Gibson SG **5** features in the original game and *Guitar Hero II* on the PlayStation 2, while the Xbox 360 version of *Guitar Hero II* includes the Gibson X-Plorer. *Guitar Hero III* features the Gibson Les Paul on all versions, except the PlayStation 2 which offers the Gibson Kramer.

The *Guitar Hero III* online community, at guitarhero.com, features virtual rock groupies. Players registered with the site amass "groupies" based on the amount they play. In November 2007, the individual player with the highest number of fans was "SilentShadow9" with 7,459 groupies. The tour group with the highest number was "Xbox 360 Heroes" with an impressive 3,648,478.

➲ Fancy yourself as a record-breaking guitar hero? Then find five pals and have a go at the Guinness World Record for the ***Guitar Hero III* multiplayer high score**. Each person in your team takes responsibility for a single note on the guitar, while the sixth person strums – the aim is then to secure the highest score on an Expert level song.

FACT
In 2007, *Guitar Hero* publisher Activision and *Halo* developer Bungie joined forces to give *Guitar Hero III* Xbox 360 players a treat; the *Halo 2* theme as played by Steve Vai! The free download was part of a thanksgiving reward for loyal fans.

FIRST VIDEO GAME BUSKING SESSION
On 6 April 2006, Luke Albiges **4** of the UK gave the first ever public performance of a video game on the London Underground. He played *Guitar Hero* for two hours at Leicester Square tube station, thrashing his way through all 30 songs featured in the game. The money Luke raised was given to charity.

FIGURES
253 – songs that you can play in the *Guitar Hero* series. This excludes downloadable tracks.

21,887 – notes to hit to get 100% across all **30** songs on *Guitar Hero: Rock the 80's*, at Expert difficulty.

650,000 – downloads of extra tracks for the Xbox 360 version of *Guitar Hero II*.

MUSIC GAMES ROUND-UP

Had a heart of glass
Seemed like the real thing

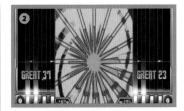

Most successful singing game series

Game: *SingStar*
Publisher: Sony

The first *SingStar* game was published for PS2 in May 2004. Since then more than a dozen instalments have followed, including *SingStar Rocks*, *SingStar 80s* ❶ and *SingStar Bollywood*. More than 10 million *SingStar* titles have been shipped around the globe and the games are available in over 67 countries worldwide.

Highest score for *Beatmania*

Game: *Beatmania*
Publisher: Konami

Justin Goeres of Iowa, USA, holds the record for the highest score on *Beatmania* ❷, a DJ simulation game which features a controller shaped like a record deck. Goeres achieved a score of 3,461.67, with no errors, on 22 August 2004. He was playing the arcade version of the game, using Twin Galaxies Tournament Settings, and his record was verified by a Twin Galaxies referee.

First customisable soundtrack in a singing game

Game: *SingStar*
Publisher: Sony

Released in December 2007, *SingStar* was the first singing game to let players create their own soundtrack. The game disc features 30 songs but extra ones can be downloaded from the SingStore. *SingStar* was also the **first music game to let players record their performances and share them online**.

INTERVIEW WITH... PAULINA BOZEK

Paulina Bozek ❹ joined Sony in 2003 where she has since overseen all the instalments in the hit karaoke series *SingStar*. We asked her where the idea for *SingStar* originally came from...

We were looking for a new way to interact with the game world and decided to experiment with voice as an input device. The next step was to develop the pitch detection technology which would become the fundamental judging mechanic. Once this was in place, the game experience started to take shape.

Can you explain how the game is able to tell how well you're singing?

It analyses the sound frequencies of your voice to determine the pitch you are singing. Your performance is compared with the pattern of the original vocal recording and you are given a score for how close you are to the original.

Why is *SingStar* so popular?

Almost everyone likes to sing, even those that aren't so good – the game brings out the exhibitionist in everyone! This, combined with the competitive scoring system, the original music, expansive track lists and the *SingStar* microphones makes a product that is highly addictive and endless fun.

Which is your favourite instalment in the series?

It's so hard to choose! *SingStar Legends* was a favourite of mine for a while, full of classic and timeless tracks from Black Sabbath to Aretha. And then in 2007, *SingStar 90s* came around with MC Hammer's "U Can't Touch This"... Classic!

3,500 – the number of songs considered for inclusion in *Rock Band* by the game's development team at Harmonix

5

TRIVIA

➲ Music game creator Tetsuya Mizuguchi says he gets his ideas from a wide variety of sources, including rave music and the dance troupe Stomp. One of his most famous games, *Rez* **3**, was inspired by the paintings of Russian artist Wassily Kandinsky.

➲ The Trance Vibrator **6** is a special peripheral for use with musical shooter *Rez*. It's designed to be placed next to the player's body, where it vibrates in time with the music, much more powerfully than the Dual Shock controller. The Trance Vibrator was only released in Japan.

6

7

Most master recordings in a music game
Game: *Rock Band*
Publisher: EA
Of the 58 tracks included in the initial release of *Rock Band* **5**, an impressive 51 are based on the original masters of the recordings, more than in any other music game. Featured tracks include The Rolling Stones'"Gimme Shelter", The Hives' "Main Offender" and Radiohead's "Creep". Among the tracks available as downloads is The Who's "Who's Next" album in its entirety, making it the **first video game to offer digitally distributed game levels based on full-length albums**.

❞ We've seen the future of awesome, and its name is **Rock Band.** *❞*

Game review, worthplaying.com

FACT

Dance Factory was the first dance mat game that enabled players to personally choose the music tracks they wanted to dance to from their own CD collection, which meant dance gaming was not limited to titles with pre-set track lists or music genres.

ADDING ANARCHY TO *GUITAR HERO III*
British punk band the Sex Pistols **7** re-recorded their hits, "Anarchy in the UK" and "Pretty Vacant", specially for *Guitar Hero III*. "Anarchy" is on the featured tracklist, while "Pretty Vacant" is set to be released as a download. It was the first time the band had been in a recording studio together for 30 years. "A bit of anarchy in a video game is all right by me," said lead singer John Lydon (right).

PUZZLE & MAZE GAMES

OUR EXPERT

Martyn Carroll's first article on retro gaming was published in 1997 and since then he has contributed classic gaming features to numerous magazines including *GamesTM*, *PC Utilities* and *Micro Mart*. In 2003, Martyn launched *Retro Gamer* magazine, editing the first 20 issues; he still contributes regularly to the publication.

THERE'S A GENERAL RULE FOR A SUCCESSFUL PUZZLE OR MAZE GAME: IT'S EASY TO PICK UP BUT DIFFICULT TO PUT DOWN, AND SIMPLE TO GRASP BUT DIFFICULT TO MASTER.

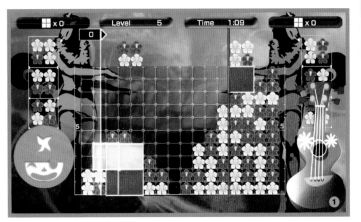

OUTLINE

The puzzle genre traditionally includes games where the player engages the old grey matter to solve logical problems, but modern puzzle games often rely as much on quick reflexes as cerebral skill. Maze games are a popular spin-off of the puzzle genre and see the player trying to escape from a maze or outwitting enemies within a maze.

Although Alexander S. Douglas's 1952 Cambridge University project *OXO*, a version of noughts and crosses, could claim to be the first computer puzzle game, it wasn't until 1973 that these games became available to a wider audience, when a number of puzzle-style games were packaged together for the PDP-11 mini-computer. Included in this package was a title called *Cube*, which is the earliest known precursor of

Minesweeper 6, the puzzle game that just about everyone is familiar with thanks to its inclusion in all home versions of *Microsoft Windows* from 1992 onwards.

Along with *Cube*, 1973 also saw the release of *Gotcha* 4, the **first arcade maze game**. *Gotcha* was developed by Atari and was a departure from the popular bat 'n' ball games on which the company was founded. Sports games and shoot-'em-ups were popular throughout the 1970s, but it was another maze game that dominated the market at the turn of the decade. Namco's *PAC-Man* was a

huge hit, particularly in the United States where it was the **highest earning arcade game of 1981**. *PAC-Man* effectively established the maze-chase sub-genre; he also introduced the concept of video game characters and spawned numerous clones, both on home consoles and in the arcades.

Throughout the 1980s, hardware advances allowed developers to

TIMELINE

1973

1973: *Cube* and *Gotcha*, the first arcade maze game, released

1979: *PAC-Man*, the genre-defining maze game, released

1982

1982: *Sokoban* released

1984: *Bomberman* 2 and *Boulder Dash* 7 released

1985: *Tetris* has a small local release in Moscow

1987

1987: *Solomon's Key* released, defining the puzzle-strategy genre

1988: *Tetris* released for all home computers and becomes a massive hit

1989

1989: *Columns* and *Klax* 3 released

1990: *Dr Mario* released

1991: *Puyo Pop* released

1996: *Tetris Attack* released

1998

1998: *Devil Dice* released

1999: *Mr Driller* released

1999: *ChuChu Rocket!* released

2001: *Bejeweled* released

2,900,600 – the highest number of points reached on *Bust-A-Move 2* on the default setting, achieved by Californian Paul Luu

and commercial success. With so many versions of the game, both official and unofficial, it's impossible to put a figure on the huge number of *Tetris* copies sold, although sales of the Nintendo Game Boy version alone stand at 32 million, making it the **best-selling Game Boy game ever**.

Popular *Tetris* derivatives including *Columns*, *Puyo Pop*, and more recently, *Meteos* and *Lumines* ❶, have continued to fly the flag for the puzzle genre on handheld consoles, in a market

build more complex games with advanced graphics, but it was the relatively simple puzzle game *Tetris* that gained worldwide attention. Developed in 1985, but on mainstream release from 1988, *Tetris* achieved great critical

that is dominated by increasingly realistic action, shooting and role-playing games.

❹
ATARI

TRIVIA

➲ *Bomberman* ❷ debuted in Europe on the Sinclair Spectrum in 1984 under the title *Eric and the Floaters*.

➲ *Minesweeper* ❻ made its debut bundled in Microsoft Windows 3.1, replacing *Reversi*, which had been included in previous versions of the operating system.

➲ *PAC-Man* may be the longest running maze franchise, but two *PAC-Man*-inspired games, *Bomberman* and *Boulder Dash* (aka *Rockford*) ❼, have gone on to become long-running series' in their own right.

➲ The **first iPod game** was *Brick*, in which a paddle is used to bat a ball into a wall of bricks, eliminating each brick touched by the ball. It was originally hidden in the iPod as an "Easter egg" or hidden feature.

FACTS

Puzzle and maze games have now made it on to the iPod (see TRIVIA, left). On 12 September 2006, games became available for the first time on iTunes (the **largest online music store**) with the release of *Bejeweled*, *Cubis 2*, *Mahjong*, *Mini Golf*, *PAC-Man*, *Tetris* ❺, *Texas Hold 'Em*, *Vortex* and *Zuma*.

TRAIN YOUR BRAIN

The arrival of easy-to-use handheld consoles in recent years has led to a renaissance in puzzle gaming. This rise in puzzle popularity has not been in the youthful gamer's market, however, but among older non-gamers. The reason for this surge in interest is a new wave of "brain training" games, which claim to help stave off dementia. Foremost among these is *Dr Kawashima's Brain Training* for the Nintendo DS: the series has sold over 14 million copies since its initial release.

2005

2004: *Lumines* released

2005: *Meteos* released

2005: *Dr Kawashima's Brain Training* released, attracting an older generation of gamers

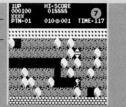

❺

TETRIS

PLATFORMS

PC | XBOX 360
PS1 | XBOX
PS2 | DS
3 | GAME BOY ADVANCE
PSP | Wii

SPEC

Developer:
Alexey Pajitnov
Publishers:
Various
Initial release:
Tetris (1985),
Electronika 60

GAMEPLAY

Inspired by Roman "pentomino" puzzles, Tetris sees the player arranging falling pieces (of four blocks each) to create horizontal lines. Once a line is complete, it vanishes, and the rows above drop down. The rate at which the pieces fall increases as more lines are eliminated. The game ends when the playfield becomes full.

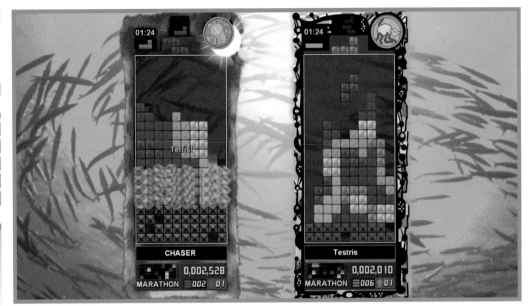

01:24 CHASER 0,002,528 MARATHON 002 01

01:24 Testris 0,002,010 MARATHON 006 01

Most ported video game

Tetris, created by Alexey Pajitnov in 1985, has been translated (or "ported") to more than 55 different computer game platforms, including mobile phones.

Game with the most official and unofficial variants

Tetris has more official (and unofficial) variants than any other computer game. So far, 55 variants – 36 of which are licensed and official – have been logged.

Smallest game of *Tetris*

With the aid of a microscope, a game of *Tetris* was played at the Physics of Complex Systems Department at Vrije University,

Amsterdam, the Netherlands, in November 2002 using tetraminoes made of tiny glass spheres. Each block measured just one micrometre (1/1000th of a millimetre) across.

First wireless *Tetris* game

Tetris DS, launched in March 2006, was the first incarnation of the game to go wireless. It can support up to 10 players locally or four online via wi-fi connection. At a Twin Galaxies-refereed event on 16 September 2006, Ginger Stowe registered the **most points scored in a *Tetris* DS standard marathon**, with an incredible 58,707 points.

Most sought-after version of *Tetris*

Fewer than 10 copies of the Sega Megadrive version of *Tetris* are currently known to exist, making it one of the most sought-after video games of all time. One complete example was recently sold to a private bidder for almost £4,000 ($8,130). The Megadrive version of *Tetris* is so scarce because the original release was quickly withdrawn after the game became involved in a legal battle in which the rights were eventually awarded to Nintendo.

LONGEST PRISON SENTENCE FOR PLAYING A VIDEO GAME

In September 2002, the UK's Faiz Chopdat ① was jailed for four months for playing *Tetris* on his mobile phone while on a flight home, "endangering the safety of an aircraft". Cabin staff warned Chopdat twice to turn off the game and he was arrested on touching down in Manchester, UK.

70 million – the total number of units of *Tetris* sold worldwide up to February 2007, according to THQ, one of the game's publishers

LARGEST GAME OF *TETRIS* EVER

In November 1995, students at the Delft University of Technology, the Netherlands, created the world's largest game of *Tetris* on the side of the institution's 15-storey-high faculty of electrical engineering **2**. A similar feat was achieved in April 2000 at Brown University, Rhode Island, USA, but a smaller 10-storey building was used.

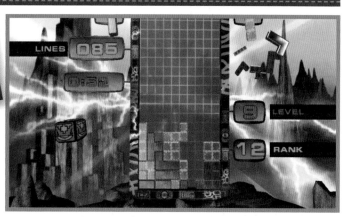

2

First video game to be proven to improve brain functioning and efficiency

In 1991, American Richard Haier of the University of California at Irvine's Department of Psychiatry and Human Behaviour began scanning the brains of *Tetris* players. Inspired by the buzz that gamers get after long-term *Tetris* sessions, Haier monitored cerebral glucose metabolic rates (GMR). He discovered that, with first-time players, the GMR levels soared; after daily playing for four to eight weeks, brain functioning and efficiency was significantly improved – and success rates at the game rose sevenfold!

> *Playing games is a very specific **rhythmic and visual pleasure**. For me, Tetris is a song which you sing and sing inside yourself and **can't stop!***
>
> Alexey Pajitnov,
> *Tetris* creator

CREATOR

Alexey Pajitnov **3**, a Russian computer scientist at the Soviet Academy of Science, developed *Tetris* in 1985. He created the name *Tetris* by joining the words "tetramino" and "tennis". ("Tetramino" itself was a made-up word based on the Greek "pentominoes", referring to the five-block shapes or tiles used in mathematics.)

As a result of a series of ugly copyright wrangles and patent infringements, Pajitnov made very little money from his game. Only in 1996 did he form The Tetris Company LLC, which has helped him claim royalties for his addictive invention.

Highest number of lines (Game Boy Color version)

With an amazing line tally of 4,988, and the highest possible score of 9,999,999, American gamer Harry Hong was crowned "*Tetris DX* Marathon Champion" on 13 September 2007. His feat was recorded at his home in Artesia, California, USA and was later verified by Twin Galaxies.

TRIVIA

➲ There is an online Church of Tetris. The church is founded on the belief that "all people should receive the glory of Tetris", and that those who oppose the game shall be "crushed in a rain of blocks from on high"!

➲ In October 2000, a team of Harvard Medical School scientists monitored the dreams of 27 *Tetris* players. They found that 17 of the those tested dreamt of falling blocks.

➲ The catchy theme music most closely associated with the game is called "Korobeiniki" ("Peddlars"), and is a famous Russian folksong.

3

PAC-MAN

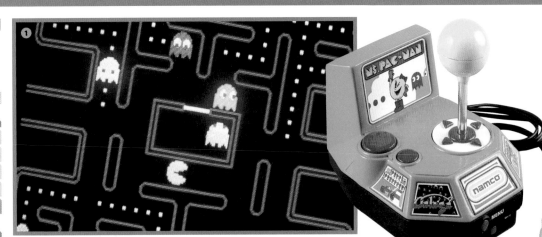

PLATFORMS

PC · XBOX 360 · PS3 · XBOX · PS2 · DS · PS3 · PSP · Wii

SPEC

Developer:
Namco
Publisher:
Namco/Midway
Initial release:
*Puckman (1979),
Arcade*

GAMEPLAY

*The player guides
PAC-Man around
mazes, eating all the
dots while avoiding
the four ghosts. There
is a power-pill (or
"energizer") in each
corner which, once
swallowed, makes the
ghosts vulnerable for a
few seconds. During
this time PAC-Man can
eat the ghosts for extra
bonus points.*

First perfect PAC-Man game

The first person to max-out *PAC-Man* ❶ by scoring the **highest possible score** of 3,333,360 points was the USA's Billy Mitchell on 3 July 1999. His total play time was 5 hr 30 min 00 sec, but since then several challengers have bettered his time. The current holder of the **fastest perfect game** record is Chris Ayra, also from the USA, who completed a game of *PAC-Man* in 3 hr 42 min 04 sec on 16 February 2000.

Highest PAC-Mania score

Tongki Linderman (USA) holds the *PAC-Mania* record with a score of 2,172,250. Linderman's score – nearly six times that of the score in second place – was verified by Twin Galaxies' Walter Day (USA) on 11 August 2003.

Xbox 360 PAC-Man World Champion

Mexico's Carlos Borrego was named PAC-Man World Champion on 5 June 2007 at an event in New York City, USA. Carlos was one of the elite players on the Xbox Live version of *PAC-Man* and along with nine other high scorers he was invited to compete for the title of World Champion. He triumphed with a score of 459,330 and was presented with a plaque by *PAC-Man* creator Toru Iwatani (Japan).

Longest-standing PAC-Man record

On 21 November 1983, Shannon Ryan (USA) scored 3,213,900 on *PAC-Man Plus*, the fourth instalment of the *PAC-Man* franchise. To date, Ryan's score has not been beaten.

Most popular *PAC-Man* song

"PAC-Man Fever", a *PAC-Man* inspired pop song by US group Buckner & Garcia that featured original sound effects from the game, sold more than 2.5 million copies when released in 1982. The single, which appeared on an album of the same name, reached No.9 on the US Billboard Hot 100 chart in March 1982.

HIGHEST MS. PAC-MAN SCORE

Abdner Ashman ❷ of the USA marks his record Ms. PAC-Man score of 933,580 – set on 6 April 2006 at Apollo Amusements in Pompano Beach, Florida, USA – at a special presentation hosted by Twin Galaxies' founder Walter Day.

3,333,360 – the highest possible score in *PAC-Man*, achieved over the maximum of 256 screens; only five people have managed this

MOST SUCCESSFUL COIN-OPERATED GAME

From 1981 until 1987, a total of 293,822 *PAC-Man* arcade machines ③ were installed around the world. Designed by Toru Iwatani (Japan) of Namco, the original game took eight people 15 months to complete. It is estimated that *PAC-Man* has been played more than 10 billion times in its 20-year history.

PAC-MAN RECORDS

TwinGalaxies

GAME	SCORE	RECORD	PLAYER	DATE
PAC-Man	100%	3 hr 42 min 04 sec	Chris Ayra	16 Feb 00
Ms. PAC-Man	100%	933,580 pts	Abdner Ashman	6 Apr 06
Jr. PAC-Man	100%	3,330,950 pts	Abdner Ashman	5 Dec 05
PAC-Man Plus	100%	3,213,900 pts	Shannon Ryan	21 Nov 83
PAC-Mania	100%	2,172,250 pts	Tongki Linderman	11 Aug 03
Professor PAC-Man	100%	999,990	Greg Gunter	11 Jun 04
PAC-Man Turbo	100%	1,321,020	Ron Corcoran	22 Jul 01
Ms. PAC-Man Turbo	100%	922,810	Victor Kunisada	9 Nov 01

PACMANHATTAN

1UP 31060   HIGH SCORE 31060

ANNOUNCED !

WASHINGTON SQUARE PARK

MASTERING PACMAN
KEN USTON

FACTS

➲ *Ms. PAC-Man* was an unofficial hack of the original *PAC-Man* that started life as an upgrade kit for *Crazy Otto*. It became so popular that Midway stepped in and released it as an official *PAC-Man* sequel.

➲ The game's popularity resulted in a number of guides on how to predict the ghost's movement patterns and earn high scores. The first of these was *Mastering PAC-Man* ⑤, written in 1981 by Ken Uston and published in 1982.

LARGEST *PAC-MAN* GAME

In 2004, students from New York University created PAC-Manhattan ④, a "real-life" re-enactment of the game in which people, dressed as PAC-Man and the four ghosts, chased each other around Manhattan city blocks. Each player was teamed with a controller who communicated the player's positions using mobile phones.

BRAIN TRAINING

BRAIN TRAINING
How Old Is Your Brain?

PLATFORMS

PC · XBOX 360
· XBOX
PS2 · DS
PS3 ·
PSP · Wii

SPEC

Developer:
Nintendo
Publisher:
Nintendo
Initial release:
*Dr Kawashima's Brain
Training: How Old is
Your Brain? (2005),
Nintendo DS*

GAMEPLAY

*Treat your brain to a
workout with number,
word and shape
puzzles inspired by the
research of Japanese
neuroscientist Dr Ryuta
Kawashima. The aim of
the game is to reduce
your personal brain age
through daily training.*

BEST-SELLING BRAIN-TRAINER [1]

Brain Age: Train Your Brain in Minutes a Day! (aka *Dr Kawashima's Brain Training: How Old is Your Brain?* in Europe) [1] has sold 8.61 million copies to date, and is the 20th best-selling video game of all time. Its sequel, *Brain Age 2: More Training in Minutes a Day* (aka *More Brain Training: How Old is Your Brain?* in Europe), has achieved sales of over 5.3 million to date. The more simplified *Big Brain Academy* [4] has managed 3.73 million. However, the Wii version of *Big Brain Academy* has yet to reach the million mark.

Largest driver of DS hardware sales According to figures from Nintendo, as many as six out of ten people who purchased the Nintendo DS [1] also picked up a copy of *Dr Kawashima's Brain Training*, indicating that consumers are buying the hardware primarily in order to play the game.

First vertically oriented game on the DS *Dr Kawashima's Brain Training* [1] was the first major game to utilise the Nintendo DS on its side, making the experience of playing the game more akin to that of reading a book. By opening the DS vertically, the game instantly feels more "worthy".

Best "consumer product of choice, 2006" (Japan) Dentsu, Japan's largest advertising agency, announced that the 2006 "consumer product of choice" – chosen by the Japanese public from the vast spectrum of products available – was some form of brain-training software or literature.

First brain game to be banned Ubisoft opted voluntarily to have its brain development game *Mind Quiz* [5] removed from the shelves of UK games stores when it was revealed that players scoring poorly were categorised as

MENTAL GURU

In 2003, Dr Ryuta Kawashima [2], a professor of neuroscience at Tohoku University, Japan, launched the first of his best-selling *No o Kotaeru* (Brain Training) books. Kawashima had spent years studying the benefits to the brain of solving simple mathematical problems and picture puzzles, and spawned countless books, TV shows and board games in Japan. Nintendo, on the look out for a solution to the problem of the ever-shrinking teenage market, snapped up the rights, selling 3.3 million units in the first year alone – largely to the over-50 market, now termed "grey gamers", on the basis that the games help stave off brain deterioration in old age. Dr Kawashima can be seen as an on-screen tutor in his games [3].

Measure your brain age

Oh, dear… Your brain is very tired. But don't lose heart!

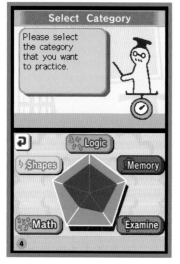

BRAIN TRAINING FASTEST SCORES

source: www.cyberscore.net

GAME	TIME	PLAYER	DATE
Calculations x20	7 sec	Alexandre "Doraki" Viel (France)	8 Oct 2006
		Alexandre "Starkiller" Barbieux (Germany)	21 Jul 2007
Calculations x100	45 sec	Viktor "Vikke" Strauss (Germany)	6 Sept 2007
Connect maze	8 sec	PJ "TheQuiff" Stapleton (Ireland)	21 May 2007
Number cruncher	34 sec	Diego Arturo "DiegoAvp11" cubic player (Mexico)	21 Aug 2007
Stroop test	40 sec	Barron "tetriseffect" Ng (USA)	8 Jul 2006
		Alexandre "Starkiller" Barbieux (Germany)	16 Aug 2006
Time lapse	9 sec	Diego Arturo "DiegoAvp11" cubic player (Mexico)	2 Oct 2006
Triangle maths	8 sec	Diego Arturo "DiegoAvp11" cubic player (Mexico)	6 Sept 2006
Voice calculation	38 sec	Alexandre "Starkiller" Barbieux (Gemany)	27 Jul 2006

"super spastic". The game was developed in Japan, where the word was overlooked during quality assurance testing.

Fastest time to complete 20 calculations (*Brain Training*)

Using the original *Dr Kawashima's Brain Training* game, YouTube poster hirokiti55nanakusado from Japan submitted a time of just 7 seconds to complete the "20 calculations" component. This effectively means solving three (simple) maths problems every second!

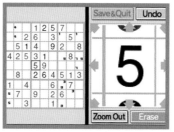

" I wanted to **make a contribution to society** through my findings. **"**

Dr Ryuta Kawashima

FIRST VIDEO GAME ADVERTISED IN *SAGA* MAGAZINE

The original *Dr Kawashima's Brain Training* game was the first video game to be advertised in *Saga* magazine. It was also the first video game to be written about in a *Saga* feature. Aimed solely at the over-50s and senior-citizen market, *Saga* is usually associated with holiday destinations, health and finances.

PUZZLE & MAZE ROUND-UP

FACTS

➲ When Sega launched the Game Gear handheld console internationally in 1991, it chose the graphically rich *Tetris*-clone *Columns* as the bundled game, following in the footsteps of Nintendo, which bundled *Tetris* with the original Game Boy.

➲ Released in 1984, *Marble Madness* was the first game to appear on the Atari System I arcade platform. A sequel was playtested in 1991, but never released.

Fastest completion of *Marble Madness*

Game: *Marble Madness*
Publisher: Atari Games
America's Elliott Feiertag completed the NES version of *Marble Madness* **1** in a fastest-ever time of 3 min 13 sec on 31 August 2005. This speed run saw Feiertag finish all six levels without losing any of his marbles – quite literally!

First arcade game to feature a stereo sound chip and soundtrack

Game: *Marble Madness*
Publisher: Atari Games
Marble Madness **1** was the first arcade machine to feature true stereo sound. The game also featured a specially commissioned movie-style soundtrack, which took full advantage of the arcade machine's stereo capabilities.

Highest score for *Bust-A-Move*

Game: *Bust-A-Move*
Publisher: Taito
Arcade puzzle expert Stephen Krogman of the USA tops the high-score table for the original *Bust-A-Move* **2** arcade game with 13,874,390 points, achieved on 1 September 1996. On 1 May 1997, Krogman posted a world record score of 75,275,450 for the arcade sequel *Bust-A-Move II*, known as *Bust-A-Move Again* in the USA.

Highest score for *Columns* (arcade version)

Game: *Columns*
Publisher: Sega
April Simmonds of Canada holds the highest score on the arcade version of Sega's *Columns* **3** with 267,350, playing according to Twin Galaxies Tournament rules on 13 November 2006.

HIGHEST SCORE FOR *BERZERK*

Game: *Berzerk*   **Publisher:** Stern Electronics
The highest-ever score for the arcade version of *Berzerk* was 304,570, achieved by Phil Younger of the USA on 12 August 2007. This score smashed the previous record of 178,500, achieved by Ron Bailey of the USA on 30 August 1982. Bailey's record lasted an incredible 25 years before it was finally beaten.

> **"** Most *Tetris* players experience complete escapism, which is why **many corporations... loathe its existence**. **"**

IGN's Top 100 Games

100 – the number of levels in the NES version of Gauntlet. Other versions had no set ending and allowed the player to continue indefinitely

HIGHEST SCORE FOR *WIZARD OF WOR*

Game: *Wizard of Wor*   **Publisher:** Midway

David Yuen achieved a highest score of 384,200 for *Wizard of Wor* ⑤ on 1 January 2005, playing the single player/three lives variation of the game. The quest to secure the highest score on *Wizard of Wor* is fiercely contested, with 23 players ranked on the Twin Galaxies leaderboard.

Fastest time to complete *Gauntlet* (NES version)

Game: *Gauntlet*
Publisher: Atari Games

On 21 April 2005, American gamer Tom Votava completed all 100 dungeons of the Nintendo NES version of *Gauntlet* ④ in 20 min 17 sec. Votava achieved this time playing as Questor the Elf, the quickest of the game's four playable characters. *Gauntlet* is credited as one of the first graphical "dungeon crawl" games.

Highest score for *Klax*

Game: *Klax*
Publisher: Atari Games

Playing on the Atari 2600 version of *Klax* under competition rules (Game 1, Difficulty B), Nathan Page of the UK recorded a high score of 89,090 on 11 June 2004. Twin Galaxies' referee Kelly R. Flewin is ranked second with 55,765.

Highest score for *Solomon's Key* (Commodore 64)

Game: *Solomon's Key*
Publisher: Tecmo

Norway's Stig Remnes recorded a high score of 127,000 for puzzle game *Solomon's Key on* 4 June 2003.

Highest score for *Mouse Trap* (arcade)

Game: *Mouse Trap*
Publisher: Exidy

Bill Bradham scored a record high of 61,366,060 on Exidy's arcade maze game *Mouse Trap*. He achieved his high score haul on 24 July 1983.

Highest score for *Boulder Dash* (Commodore 64)

Game: *Boulder Dash*
Publisher: First Star Software

The highest score achieved on the Commodore 64 version of *Boulder Dash* ⑥ is 4,423 by Terence O'Neill on 18 January 2007. ⑥

FASTEST COMPLETION: *KATAMARI DAMACY*

Game: *Katamari Damacy*   **Publisher:** Namco

The fastest completion time for a single section of *Katamari Damacy* is 30 min 26 sec by Tom "slowbro" Batchelor on 3 August 2006. According to speeddemosarchive.com, Batchelor also holds the single section record for *We Love Katamari* ⑦ with a time of 1 hour 5 min 31 sec.

FACTS

➲ When UK magazine *Amiga Power* asked various famous programmers which game they wished they had written, the most common answer was the manic puzzle *Lemmings* ⑧, published by *Psygnosis* and developed by DMA Design.

➲ Released in 1992, the Atari 2600 version of the puzzle game *Acid Drop* was the last commercial game to be published for the console.

JONATHAN SMITH

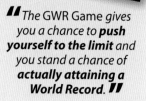

FIGURE

120 – the number of different playable characters included in *LEGO Star Wars: The Complete Saga*.

1

2

3

TT GAMES' HEAD OF PRODUCTION TELLS US ABOUT THE SUCCESS OF *LEGO STAR WARS* AND MAKING THE *GUINNESS WORLD RECORDS GAME*.

FIGURE

42 million – the number of games sold by TT Games since it started video game development in 1989. The company, which employs over 200 people, was sold to Warner Bros. in a deal announced in November 2007.

So, what does the Head of Production at a video games developer actually do?
We have a close-knit team at TT Games, incorporating an immensely talented group at Traveller's Tales; and everything you see in our games is the result of joint efforts. But my primary responsibility is to ensure we're making the right games, in the right way, and to ensure that everyone knows exactly what we're setting out to achieve.

You were part of the team responsible for *LEGO Star Wars* 1 , how did the plastic characters make the transition to the virtual world?
LEGO Company has always reached in to new areas of technology and media where the LEGO experience can be relevant; so games were a natural step for them. I was part of a team briefed to find a match between the qualities that made LEGO so special, and elements of good gameplay. After some initial experiments, we set our sights on LEGO Star Wars, to match some of the systematic ideas we'd been working on, with the emotional hook and credibility of the world's favourite entertainment property.

What do you think is the secret of its success?
The LEGO figures are beautifully designed and naturally fun to play with; the Star Wars settings and characters are intrinsically exciting and cool. From

> **"** The GWR Game gives you a chance to **push yourself to the limit** and you stand a chance of *actually attaining a World Record*. **"**
>
> Jonathan Smith, TT Games

a game design point of view, we're unusually player-friendly – we're very careful to prevent you from getting frustrated or bored, so there are always good reasons to continue playing.

What are you and TT working on at the moment?
We're thrilled to be working on the brand new *Guinness World Records Game* 5 , currently in development at Traveller's Tales. It's based on an idea we've been working on for a few years now: to put yourself in to the world of Guinness World Records, full of the

YOUR SECRET BONUS GAME CODE!

DOWNLOAD THE *GWR GAME* ON YOUR MOBILE PHONE NOW!

The *Guinness World Records Game* on mobile phone 4 features five record-breaking game challenges, plus one secret game – which you can unlock

using the special code below – AND the opportunity to break the real text-messaging speed record. The games feature classic GWR records, such as tearing the most

phone books and completing the longest tightrope walk. Download the game at **www. guinnessworldrecords.com/ thegame**

How to unlock your secret bonus game:
You can unlock a bonus game on the *Guinness World Records Game* for mobile phone using the following code: **816285**. See **www.guinnessworldrecords.com/thegame** for details.

4

13,978 – the number of polygons used to make the Millenium Falcon, the largest model in *LEGO Star Wars: The Complete Saga*

LEGO Indiana Jones ③. They are both amazing, and each is different from *LEGO Star Wars* in many fun ways.

So how does the *GWR Game* work?
The idea is very simple: to give players the opportunity to break World Records. We've all read about amazing people doing incredible things in the Guinness World Records book; the game gives you the chance to do those things for yourself. Push yourself to the limit and you stand a chance of actually attaining a World Record, and getting your name in the Guinness World Records book!

Once you've got an idea like that, how do you set about making the actual game?
We spent a long time learning exactly which elements of gameplay are best suited to record-breaking attempts. The best way to learn, we always find, is to try things out – so while we did a lot of thinking and planning in documentation, the team at Traveller's Tales was simultaneously building some initial "prototypes". We knew we'd nailed the "fun factor" on

most incredible challenges imaginable, and become a real record-breaker on your games console. We're also working on two new LEGO games: *LEGO Batman* ② and

those early demos when we had people queuing up to play the game in the office.

What versions of the game are you working on?
It very quickly became obvious that the types of gameplay we were working on would be well suited to play on mobile phones: games you can get into quickly, that don't last too long, but can be played again and again. So we made mobile phones our initial focus for the *Guinness World Records Game*, and we're absolutely delighted with that first title, which you can download and play now.

How about on other platforms?
We're creating lots of new games for other consoles, adding new features like the ability to create your own "avatar" to put yourself right in the game, and to offer "co-operative" challenges, where you'll need to work as part of a record-breaking team!

GAMES

Each of the five games that feature in the *Guinness World Records Game* for the mobile phone capture the record-breaking spirit of GWR perfectly:
➲ Most telephone directories torn with bare hands
➲ Longest tightrope walk
➲ Fastest sheep shearing
➲ Most melons smashed with the head in one minute
➲ Fastest 100m on a pogo stick
And remember, there's a secret bonus game for readers of this book.

TOP 100 ARCADE GAMES

CONTENTS

A high score to aim for

Since 3 July 1999 when Billy Mitchell (USA) achieved the first "perfect" score of 3,333,360 points on the arcade version of *PAC-Man*, only four other players – Chris Ayra, Rick Fothergill, Tim Balderramos and Donald Hayes – have been officially credited with equaling this feat. Twin Galaxies adjudicator Walter Day (USA) described the achievement as "one of the most sought-after accomplishments in the gaming world", likening it to running a four-minute mile.

THOUSANDS OF ARCADE GAMES HAVE BEEN RELEASED IN THE LAST 30 YEARS, SO CHOOSING A TOP 100 WASN'T EASY. THE NAMES ON THE LIST HAVE BEEN RANKED ON THEIR TECHNICAL, CREATIVE AND CULTURAL IMPACT; BUT AT HEART IT'S A CELEBRATION OF GREAT GAMES.

100 TWIN COBRA Date: 1987 Publisher: Taito/Romstar • Shoot-'em-up where you controlled heavily armed helicopters. **99 JUMP BUG** Date: 1981 Publisher: Rock-Ola • Bounce your tiny car along a series of lively levels, shooting enemies and collecting treasure. **98 TAPPER** Date: 1983 Publisher: Midway • Unique game that saw you serving up beers to a bar full of thirsty punters. **97 HARD DRIVIN'** Date: 1988 Publisher: Atari • Driving simulator that featured a deluxe sit-down cabinet. **96 QIX** Date: 1981 Publisher: Taito • Simple puzzle game where the player had to claim as much screen space as possible. **95 STRIDER** Date: 1989 Publisher: Capcom • Platform game where you took control of the ninja Hiryu on a mission to save the Earth. **94 MOON PATROL** Date: 1982 Publisher: Irem/Williams • Guide a buggy along a lunar landscape, jumping craters and shooting alien ships. **93 METRO-CROSS** [1] Date: 1985 Publisher: Namco • Run, jump and skateboard your way through 32 hazard-filled levels. **92 VIRTUA RACING** Date: 1992 Publisher: Sega • F1 racing game that developed the idea of letting the player switch between different driving views. **91 HOUSE OF THE DEAD** [2] Date: 1986 Publisher: Sega • On-rails light-gun battle against an army of zombies.

> **Fastest *Time Crisis* completion**
> On 20 November 2004, Charlie Weatherbee (USA) completed the three stages of the *Time Crisis* [3] story mode in 11 min 1 sec. This speed-run was completed at the Funspot arcade in New Hampshire.

90 I, ROBOT Date: 1983 Publisher: Atari • Innovative 3D game where you played a robot trying to avoid Big Brother's omnipresent gaze. **89 MILLIPEDE** Date: 1982 Publisher: Atari • Manic update of Centipede that introduced new enemies and an increased challenge. **88 STAR CASTLE** Date: 1980 Publisher: Cinematronics • Vector graphics game in which the aim was to destroy the cannon in the centre of the screen. **87 TIME CRISIS** Date: 1996 Publisher: Namco • The first in the light-gun series where, as a lone enforcer, you could shield yourself behind objects. **86 GHOULS 'N GHOSTS** Date: 1988 Publisher: Capcom • Sequel to *Ghosts 'n Goblins* following the further escapades of the fearless knight Arthur. **85 METAL SLUG** Date: 1996 Publisher: SNK • Frantic run-and-gun game that featured excellent hand-drawn graphics and grandiose boss battles. **84 SOLOMON'S KEY** Date: 1986 Publisher: Tecmo • Collect the key and escape through the locked door in this frantic puzzler set over many levels. **83 SPLATTERHOUSE** [4] Date: 1988 Publisher: Namco • Gore-drenched action game where you punched, kicked and sliced your way through a nightmarish mansion. **82 ROBOCOP** Date: 1988 Publisher: Data East • Suitably violent on-foot shooter based on the 1987 movie. Included bonus round set in a shooting range. **81 SUPER SPRINT** Date: 1986 Publisher: Atari • Simple top-down racing game.

187,880 – Stan Szczepanski's (USA) record high score on the arcade version of *Marble Madness*, which was achieved in June 1985

80 RAIDEN Date: 1990 **Publisher:** Seibu Kaihatsu Inc. • Vertical shoot-'em-up that featured explosive power-ups and huge end-of-level bosses. **79 MARBLE MADNESS Date:** 1984 **Publisher:** Atari • Much imitated 3D game in which you used a tracker-ball to roll a sphere to safety. **78 ALIENS Date:** 1990 **Publisher:** Konami • Multi-stage shooter based on the hit movie where two players teamed up to take on the alien menace. **77 XEVIOUS Date:** 1982 **Publisher:** Atari • Early vertical shooter in which you controlled a small ship laden with missiles and bombs. **76 PENGO Date:** 1982 **Publisher:** Sega • Cute puzzle game starring Pengo the penguin. **75 SINISTAR Date:** 1982 **Publisher:** Williams • Atmospheric space game where you had to collect crystals to make bombs. **74 ZAXXON Date:** 1982 **Publisher:** Sega • Shoot-'em-up that was the first arcade game to view the action from an isometric perspective. **73 AFTER BURNER Date:** 1987 **Publisher:** Sega • Shoot down the enemies' aircraft in this game that's best remembered for its large cabinet that simulated a fighter pilot's cockpit. **72 SHINOBI Date:** 1987 **Publisher:** Sega • The first in the Shinobi series that saw ninja Joe Musashi wage war on an evil clan of kidnappers. **71 BOMB JACK Date:** 1984 **Publisher:** Tecmo • As caped hero Jack, you had to collect all of the bombs on screen while avoiding enemies.

70 BERZERK Date: 1980 **Publisher:** Stern Electronics • Maze game that pits you against an army of laser-firing robots. **69 JOUST Date:** 1982 **Publisher:** Williams • Bizarre action game where you attempt to lance winged enemies. **68 CRYSTAL CASTLES Date:** 1983 **Publisher:** Atari • An isometric 3D take on PAC-Man. **67 RALLY-X Date:** 1980 **Publisher:** Midway/Namco • Top-down maze game where you had to collect the flags while steering clear of the dastardly red racers. **66 WIZARD OF WOR Date:** 1980 **Publisher:** Midway • Simple shooter in which two players teamed up to rid a maze of enemies. **65 ROLLING THUNDER Date:** 1986 **Publisher:** Atari/Namco • Action game where you had to run-and-gun through criminal hideouts. **64 GORF Date:** 1981 **Publisher:** Midway • A "greatest hits" package that borrowed bits and pieces from other shoot-'em-ups. **63 COMMANDO 5 Date:** 1985 **Publisher:** Capcom • Shooter in which a lone soldier takes on an entire enemy army. **62 RASTAN SAGA Date:** 1987 **Publisher:** Taito • Platform adventure featuring a sword-wielding warrior. **61 GOLDEN TEE GOLF 6 Date:** 1989 **Publisher:** Incredible Technologies • The first in a series of arcade golf sims.

60 VIRTUA COP Date: 1994 **Publisher:** Sega • Blast baddies while avoiding innocents caught in the crossfire. **59 RIP OFF Date:** 1980 **Publisher:** Cinematronics • Shooter in which players prevent enemies from ripping off fuel canisters **58 FROGGER Date:** 1981 **Publisher:** Sega • Guide frogs across the busy road and the fast-flowing river. **57 1942 Date:** 1984 **Publisher:** Capcom • WWII-set shooter involving 32 waves of airborne enemies. **56 TETRIS Date:** 1988 **Publisher:** Atari • Two-player port of classic puzzle game. **55 RAMPART Date:** 1990 **Publisher:** Atari • Multi-phase game mixing puzzle, shoot-'em-up and strategy. **54 ARKANOID Date:** 1986 **Publisher:** Taito • Reworking of Atari's *Breakout*. **53 OPERATION WOLF Date:** 1987 **Publisher:** Taito • First-person gun game controlled using a replica Uzi. **52 GHOSTS 'N GOBLINS Date:** 1985 **Publisher:** Capcom • A brave knight ventures to rescue a princess. **51 DRAGON'S LAIR Date:** 1983 **Publisher:** Cinematronics • Guide Dirk the Daring through a number of cartoon scenes.

Highest *GORF* score

Todd Rogers of the USA has held the record *GORF* 7 score for over 25 years. His score of 653,990 (set on "three ship" rules) was achieved on 24 November 1982. No competitor has managed to reach even half that total.

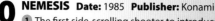
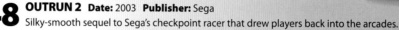

50 NEMESIS Date: 1985 Publisher: Konami
 The first side-scrolling shooter to introduce a weapon upgrade system.

49 SMASH TV Date: 1990 Publisher: Williams
Violent semi-sequel to *Robotron: 2084* with similar plot to *The Running Man*.

48 OUTRUN 2 Date: 2003 Publisher: Sega
Silky-smooth sequel to Sega's checkpoint racer that drew players back into the arcades.

47 CHASE H.Q. Date: 1988 Publisher: Taito
Fast 3D race game that saw the player chasing and apprehending criminals in an unmarked police car.

46 MARIO BROS. Date: 1983 Publisher: Nintendo
Two-player spin-off from *Donkey Kong* that starred Mario and his brother Luigi.

45 BREAKOUT Date: 1976 Publisher: Atari
A single-player variation on *Pong* where players batted a ball against a wall, smashing the bricks one by one.

44 PANG Date: 1989 Publisher: Capcom
A two-player arcade game in which players had to destroy bouncing balls with their trusty pop-guns.

43 DONKEY KONG JUNIOR Date: 1982 Publisher: Nintendo
DK's young son sets out to rescue his father from Mario's prison in this sequel to the smash-hit original.

42 SPY HUNTER Date: 1983 Publisher: Midway
 Top-down racer loosely based on the *James Bond* films.

Highest score for *Spy Hunter*
On 28 June 1985, Paul Dean (USA) set a new highest score of 9,512,590 on *Spy Hunter*. Incredibly, his total was a massive 12 times greater that the previous high score of 794,495 and earned Dean a place in the 1986 *Guinness World Records* book. More than 20 years on and his world record score still stands.

41 MORTAL KOMBAT Date: 1992 Publisher: Midway
One-on-one fighter that mixed classic martial arts with magical abilities.

40 POLE POSITION Date: 1982 Publisher: Namco/Atari
Early 3D racing simulation featuring just a single circuit (Fuji) and two modes – qualification and race.

39 CONTRA Date: 1987 Publisher: Konami
Run-and-gun platform game in which players were tasked with destroying an invading alien race.

38 PAPERBOY Date: 1984 Publisher: Atari
Unique arcade game where you controlled a kid on a bike delivering newspapers to a lively neighbourhood.

37 DAYTONA USA Date: 1994 Publisher: Sega
Multiplayer racing game that married gorgeous-looking visuals with realistic handling and physics.

36 TEKKEN Date: 1994 Publisher: Namco
A 3D brawler that introduced the idea of having a control button for each of the fighters' limbs.

FACT

Nemesis (also known as *Gradius*) is part of a series of shoot-'em-ups that began with 1981's *Scramble*. Arcade sequels and home conversions followed. The most recent game in the series is 2004's *Gradius V* for the PlayStation 2.

FACT

Contra has appeared under several different titles. The original arcade game was released worldwide as *Contra*, but renamed *Gryzor* and *Probotector* for the European home computer and console markets respectively.

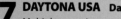

35 **DANCE DANCE REVOLUTION** **Date:** 1998 **Publisher:** Konami
The first in a series of dance games where the players had to move their feet to the beat.

34 **TRACK & FIELD** **Date:** 1983 **Publisher:** Konami
A popular button-basher in which players competed in a series of decathlon-style events.

33 **CENTIPEDE** **Date:** 1980 **Publisher:** Atari
③ Shooter that pits the player against the eponymous leggy creature and other nasties.

32 **VIRTUA FIGHTER** **Date:** 1993 **Publisher:** Sega
Seminal one-on-one fighting game that was the first to use a full 3D fighting engine.

31 **GOLDEN AXE** **Date:** 1989 **Publisher:** Sega
A trio of warriors take on the ominous Death Adder in this slick beat-'em-up.

30 **WARLORDS** **Date:** 1980 **Publisher:** Atari
Bat-and-ball-style game in which up to four players set out to destroy each others' forts.

29 **SPACE HARRIER** **Date:** 1985 **Publisher:** Sega
A fast 3D shooter that featured a custom cabinet that lurched about as you controlled the game.

28 **SCRAMBLE** **Date:** 1981 **Publisher:** Konami
Early side-scrolling shooter that paved the way for *Gradius* and a multitude of clones.

27 **RAINBOW ISLANDS** **Date:** 1987 **Publisher:** Taito
Cute sequel to *Bubble Bobble* that saw Bub and Bob defeat enemies using magic rainbow power!

26 **FINAL FIGHT** **Date:** 1989 **Publisher:** Capcom
Beat-'em-up where two players worked together to rescue the Mayor's daughter from a local gang.

25 **R-TYPE** **Date:** 1987 **Publisher:** Irem/Nintendo
A space shooter in which the player single-handedly took on the mighty Bydo empire.

24 **GALAXIAN** **Date:** 1979 **Publisher:** Namco
④ Classic *Space Invaders*-inspired player vs. alien hordes shoot-'em-up.

FACT

Rainbow Islands includes several stages that are based entirely around other Taito arcade games: Doh Island is based on *Arkanoid*, Magical Island is based on *Fairyland Story*, Darius Island is based on *Darius* and Bubble Island harks back to the original *Bubble Bobble*.

Highest score for *Galaxian*

The UK's Gary Whelan made headlines when he claimed the *Galaxian* high score record with 399,490 points in August 2005. But even after beating Perry Rodgers' long-standing high score of 389,770, Whelan continued to challenge his own record. On 10 September 2006, he posted a new personal best of 1,114,550 points.

23 **BATTLEZONE** **Date:** 1980 **Publisher:** Atari
Combat simulation that used monochrome vector graphics to display a first-person tank battle.

22 **TRON** **Date:** 1982 **Publisher:** Midway
A series of mini-games based on scenes from the Disney movie released the same year.

21 **MS. PAC-MAN** **Date:** 1981 **Publisher:** Midway
Slight update to the classic original saw PAC-Man's partner chased around a new set of mazes.

20 RIDGE RACER

Date: 1993 **Publisher:** Namco
3D *Ridge Racer* incorporated many driving elements not previously seen in racing games, including a six position gear stick, three active pedals and a force-feedback steering wheel.

16 DIG DUG

Date: 1982 **Publisher:** Namco/Atari
One of the more obscure games of 1982, *Dig Dug* 1 involved tunnelling underground to reach enemy characters, then attempting to inflate them with a pump until they popped!

15 MISSILE COMMAND

Date: 1980 **Publisher:** Atari
Players took command of three anti-missile batteries and attempted to prevent a constant bombardment of ballistic bombs from destroying their six cities.

Highest Missile Command score (TGTS)

On 9 March 2006, Tony Temple (UK) scored 1,967,830 on *Missile Command* under Twin Galaxies Tournament Settings. This has caused much controversy; previous record-holder Roy Shildt (USA) scored 1,695,265 in 1985 using a harder setting that decreases cursor speed.

19 DOUBLE DRAGON

Date: 1987 **Publisher:** Taito
As the first fighting game to feature two-player, co-operative gameplay, *Double Dragon* 2 had a great impact on the fighting genre. Many different moves were possible using the punch, kick and jump buttons.

18 PUZZLE BOBBLE (a.k.a. Bust-a-Move)

Date: 1994 **Publisher:** Taito
Operating a bubble-firing cannon, players had to aim randomly at coloured bubbles to connect three or more of the same colour at the top of the screen. Once three bubbles were matched, they dropped off the play area.

17 Q*BERT

Date: 1982 **Publisher:** Gottlieb
The player moves Q*bert around an isometric pyramid-like structure of tri-coloured cubes. Q*bert hops from cube to cube with the aim of changing every square to a specific colour.

14 BUBBLE BOBBLE

Date: 1986 **Publisher:** Taito
Taking control of bubble-blowing dragons, *Bubble Bobble* required players to trap enemies within a bubble and then burst it before they broke free. Two people could work together in simultaneous gameplay.

13 STAR WARS

Date: 1983 **Publisher:** Atari
Atari's vector-based *Star Wars* 3 game put players directly in control of Luke Skywalker's X-Wing Fighter as it attacked the Death Star. The game featured several audio samples from the film, while accurately depicting the vehicles and locations with vector graphics.

4,401,169 – the highest single-player score for *Gauntlet*, achieved by Charles Nagle of the USA on 28 March 2003

12 TEMPEST
Date: 1980 **Publisher:** Atari

Tempest featured an impressive pseudo-3D effect using Atari's Color-QuadraScan vector system. Players controlled a ship as it moved around the circumference of a tube-like playing field, shooting at enemy ships.

9 OUTRUN
Date: 1986 **Publisher:** Sega

Classified as a "driving" game, and not a "racing" game, *OutRun* is remembered as much for its astonishing music as it is for gameplay. With its impressive, hydraulic-seated cabinet, the game became an instant classic.

8 GAUNTLET
Date: 1985 **Publisher:** Atari

One of the first titles to bring the popular Dungeons & Dragons concept to video games, *Gauntlet*'s **4** huge, imposing cabinet and stylistic gameplay made a significant impact on arcade culture.

7 GALAGA
Date: 1981 **Publisher:** Namco

Galaga provided a colourful and dynamic variation on the Space Invaders theme. This *Galaxian* sequel saw players controlling a spaceship across a horizontal plane, while fending off formations of insect-like enemies.

FACT

Gauntlet supported four simultaneous players. Gamers could choose from Warrior, Valkyrie, Wizard or Elf to traverse an endless number of dungeons and mazes. Packed with a huge number of exciting gameplay aspects that enticed gamers into the arcades, such as hordes of enemy characters, digitised speech and a feature that allowed players to buy extra health for their characters, *Gauntlet* was well known for bringing in substantial amounts of revenue.

11 ROBOTRON: 2084
Date: 1982 **Publisher:** Williams

One of the first games to incorporate a background story, *Robotron: 2084* players were called upon to rescue the last human family from attacking robots using one joystick for movement and another for directional fire.

Highest Galaga score (TGTS)

Richard Marsh of the USA scored 1,557,580 points on arcade classic *Galaga* using Twin Galaxies Tournament Settings (player starts with five ships, no bonus ships awarded). He achieved the feat on 31 July 2004 under the watchful eye of a Twin Galaxies referee.

10 PONG
Date: 1972 **Publisher:** Atari

The simple bat and ball gameplay of Pong was largely responsible for the first wave of arcade game popularity. Just two white lines hitting a white dot across the screen, the game was groundbreaking in its day.

6 DEFENDER
Date: 1980 **Publisher:** Williams

Generally considered to be one of the hardest classic games, *Defender* **5** was slow to gain the massive popularity it ultimately achieved. Players navigated a scrolling, mountainous landscape defending small humanoids from the aliens who attempted to abduct them. The game's difficulty was mainly due to its overly complex control system, which consisted of a joystick for vertical movement and separate buttons for reverse, thrust, fire, bomb and hyperspace.

Highest Defender score (TGTS)

Under Twin Galaxies Tournament Settings, where the player begins the game with five ships and no bonus ships are awarded, Gino Yoo of the USA scored an unrivalled 230,125 points on *Defender* on 30 June 1985.

5 ASTEROIDS

Date: 1979 **Publisher:** Atari

Loosely based on *Computer Space*, the first ever coin-operated game, *Asteroids*  used vector graphics to make superb use of simulated inertia in deep space. The developers also added a high-score table to the game where players could enter their initials, making Asteroids the first game with this feature.

GAMEPLAY: Navigating by thrust and direction, players travel through space shooting asteroids. When an asteroid is hit, it separates into two smaller pieces. These smaller rocks separate again and again when shot until finally being destroyed. Colliding with an asteroid costs a life.

Highest Asteroids score

The highest score ever achieved on the *Asteroids* arcade machine is 41,336,440 by Scott Safran of the USA on 13 November 1982. Various competitors have come close to beating this score since, but Safran has stood firm at the top of the Asteroids league for more than 25 years.

4 STREET FIGHTER II

Date: 1991 **Publisher:** Capcom

Causing the kind of arcade mania not seen since *PAC-Man*, 1991's *Street Fighter* sequel redefined the one-on-one tournament fighting genre. The use of six attack buttons, defensive capabilities and a host of powerful hidden fighting moves made *Street Fighter II* unique and massively popular.

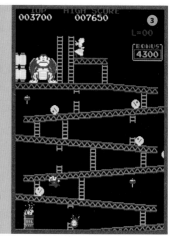

GAMEPLAY: While Ryu and Ken from the original *Street Fighter* were available, for the first time players could choose any of eight selectable characters to compete against as they travelled the world in a bare knuckle competition.

3 DONKEY KONG

Date: 1981 **Publisher:** Nintendo

Game design legend Shigeru Miyamoto created *Donkey Kong*  in an attempt to help Nintendo break into the American market. His game was a massive success, and saved the almost bankrupt Nintendo of America overnight.

GAMEPLAY: Jumpman (an early version of Mario) attempts to scale the steel beams of a building site to rescue his heroine from the giant ape Donkey Kong. Barrels are thrown by the gorilla in an attempt to stop him, which Jumpman can either avoid using the ladders, jump over or bash with a mallet.

54,450 – points scored on *PAC-Man* by Fazli Kandemir, the winner at the 2005 Pan European *PAC-Man* Tournament

2 PAC-MAN

Date: 1980 **Publisher:** Namco

The first coin-op designed specifically to appeal to female players, game designer Toru Iwatani single-handedly broke the profuse arcade trend for space-based shooters. Originally named Puck-Man due to the main character's disk-like shape, the title was changed outside of Japan to *PAC-Man* **4** to avoid creative graffiti on the game cabinets. Many sequels have followed, both by Namco in Japan and Midway in the US, with the most recent being the 2007 release of *PAC-Man Championship Edition* for Xbox Live Arcade.

GAMEPLAY: Players guide *PAC-Man* around a maze, eating dots while avoiding four coloured ghosts who are out to kill him. When *PAC-Man* eats a larger dot, he can protect himself and earn points by eating the ghosts. Bonus items appear twice per level near the ghost's den, and clearing the maze of dots begins the game again, only with faster moving ghosts.

❚❚ The success of PAC-Man stems from its fun gameplay and host of characters that have been enjoyed by families for generations. ❚❚

Toru Iwatani **5**, creator of *PAC-Man*.

1 SPACE INVADERS

Date: 1978 **Publisher:** Midway

Released by Taito in Japan, *Space Invaders* **6**, which the game's designer Tomohiro Nishikado based on his own interpretations of H.G. Wells' *War of the Worlds* novel, spearheaded a new and prolific era for the worldwide video game industry. Now seen as the most influential arcade game of all time, *Space Invaders* has been revamped, repackaged and released on almost every platform.

TOP RATED

GAMEPLAY: Five rows of aliens move across and down the screen in a relentless march. The player controls a laser cannon, which he moves from side to side shooting the invaders while avoiding return fire. Four shields offer the player's cannon protection, but these are gradually destroyed by laser fire. As more invaders are hit, the faster the remainder descend. If they reach the bottom of the screen the earth is invaded and the game finishes.

Longest game of Space Invaders

Eric Furrer of Canada holds the record for the longest *Space Invaders* marathon session after playing the game for 38 hr 30 min between 29 August and 2 September 1980. The machine on which 12-year-old Furrer played was fitted with a special button that he used to pause the game for bathroom breaks.

FACT

The iconic *Space Invaders* image is of rows of different coloured aliens advancing across the screen, but when the game was first launched the graphics were black and white. As the game gained popularity, a new upright version was released where plastic strips were stuck onto the monochrome monitor to provide colour. The monitor was also reflected against a mirror with an image printed on it to give the game its lunar landscape background.

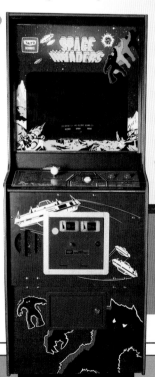

CONTENTS

***Pure Pinball* high score**

On 15 April 2005, Troy Whelan of the USA set three Guinness World Record high scores on the Xbox version of *Pure Pinball*. He achieved 59,526,200 playing the Excessive Speed table; 92,552,400 playing the Hyperspace table; and 99,269,000 on the World War table. *Pure Pinball* was released in August 2004; it features a multiball-enabled physics engine that can calculate ball movement 1,500 times per second.

HIGH SCORES

NOTES

➲ All records shown here are based on points won, unless otherwise stated in the "NOTES" column.

➲ All consoles and arcade machines are set at their default mode unless specified in the "NOTES" column.

➲ TGTS = Twin Galaxies Tournament Settings.

FACT

Asteroids [1] was a huge commercial success following its release by Atari Inc. in 1979, and contributed to making video games the enduring entertainment media that we know today. The arcade classic was followed by *Asteroids Deluxe* (1980), *Space Duel* (1982) and *Blasteroids* (1987).

1

WELCOME TO THE A–Z OF VIDEO GAME HIGH SCORES, AS OFFICIALLY RATIFIED BY THE EAGLE-EYED JOYSTICK JUDGES AT TWIN GALAXIES. CAN YOU BEAT ANY OF THESE GAMING GODS? IF SO, FIND OUT HOW TO REGISTER YOUR SCORE ON PAGE 8...

GAME	PLATFORM	RECORD	PLAYER	DATE	NOTES
Alleyway	GB/GBC	26,817	Tom Duncan (USA)	21 Mar 2005	
Animal Crossing	GameCube	212,800	Steve Pierson (USA)	29 Jun 2003	Donkey Kong
Area-51	Arcade	324,700	Frank Bryan (USA)	11 Jun 2004	
Arkanoid	Arcade	1,658,110	Zachary B. Hample (USA)	13 Mar 2000	
Arkanoid	Arcade	554,300	Jason Wilson (USA)	1 Sep 1997	TGTS
Arkanoid Returns	Arcade	1,589,770	Zachary B. Hample (USA)	5 Jun 2000	
Arkanoid II: Revenge of Doh	Arcade	3,120,570	Zachary B. Hample (USA)	31 Dec 2002	
Asteroids ①	Arcade	41,336,440	Scott Safran (USA)	13 Nov 1982	
Atari Anniversary Advance	GBA	17,181	Troy Whelan (USA)	2 Jun 2004	Atari Trivia Challenge
Atari Anniversary Advance	GBA	28,000	Troy Whelan (USA)	2 Jun 2004	Battlezone
Battletoads in Ragnarok's World	GB/GBC	483,300	Tom Duncan (USA)	4 Apr 2005	
Battlezone	Arcade	23,000,000	David Palmer (USA)	30 Aug 1985	
Big Brain Academy	Nintendo DS	1,186 grams	Matthew Wroblewski (USA)	16 Sep 2006	Biggest Brain; Test
Biohazard: Gun Survivor	PlayStation 2	38 min 29 sec	Shin Sato (Japan)	1 Apr 2004	Normal Difficulty; Fastest Completion
Black Widow	Arcade	930,100	James Vollandt (USA)	1 May 1984	
Blasteroids	Arcade	2,773,840	Mark Twitty (USA)	11 Jun 2004	TGTS
Bo Jackson: Hit & Run	GB/GBC	74	Tom Duncan (USA)	21 Mar 2005	Football; Biggest Blowout
Burai Fighter Deluxe	GB/GBC	10,101,050	Tom Duncan (USA)	9 Nov 2005	
Burgertime	Arcade	9,000,000	Bryan L. Wagner (USA)	9 Jul 2006	
Burgertime Deluxe	GB/GBC	224,600	Tom Duncan (USA)	5 Nov 2006	
Bushido Blade	PlayStation 2	9 min 58.5 sec	Glenn Cravens (USA)	2 Apr 2004	Fastest 100 Kills; Fastest Completion; TGTS
Capcom vs SNK 2	PlayStation 2	10	Aaron C. Collins (USA)	15 Sep 2002	Extreme Dan Challenge; Most Wins; TGTS
Captain America & The Avengers	Arcade	496,801	Josh Bycer (USA)	11 Jun 2004	
Carnevil	Arcade	2,083,180	Jeff Matza (USA)	19 Feb 2000	
Centipede	Arcade	16,389,547	Jim Schneider (USA)	11 Jun 2004	Marathon
Centipede	Arcade	7,111,111	Donald Hayes (USA)	4 May 2001	TGTS
Centipede	Arcade	59,106	Donald Hayes (USA)	19 Nov 2006	TGTS; 3 Minute Time Limit Board
Chase H.Q.	GB/GBC	580,323	Tom Duncan (USA)	26 Dec 2005	
Children of Mana	Nintendo DS	2,871	William Willemstyn III (USA)	12 Jan 2007	High Score; Mana Tower
Children of Mana	Nintendo DS	3,594	William Willemstyn III (USA)	12 Jan 2007	High Score; Star Lake
Choplifter	Arcade	1,781,000	Charles Collins (USA)	11 Jun 2004	
The Chronicles of Riddick	Xbox	1 min 50.13 sec	Mike K. Morrow (USA)	10 Apr 2005	Escape from Butcher Bay
Conflict: Desert Storm	Xbox	1 hr 4 min 57.00sec	Joseph Baiocchi (USA)/ Salvatore DiBenedetto (USA)	9 Apr 2005	2 Player Speed Completion; Hard

CAN'T FIND YOUR FAVOURITE GAME? PERHAPS NO-ONE'S SET A WORLD RECORD YET. FIND OUT HOW TO REGISTER YOUR SCORE ON P.8

11,691,623,007,326,677,330 points
– **the most points ever scored** by a gamer
(J. C. Padilla [USA] playing *GigaWings2*)

GAME	PLATFORM	RECORD	PLAYER	DATE	NOTES
Conflict: Desert Storm	Xbox	1 hr 28 sec	Joseph Baiocchi (USA)/ Salvatore DiBenedetto (USA)/ Chris Bartella (USA)	9 Apr 2005 15 Apr 2005	3 Player Speed Completion; Hard
Conflict: Desert Storm 2	Xbox	1 hr 2 min	Joseph Baiocchi (USA)/ Salvatore DiBenedetto (USA)	9 Apr 2005	2 Player Speed Completion; Hard
Conflict: Desert Storm 2	Xbox	55 min 54 sec	Joseph Baiocchi (USA)/ Salvatore DiBenedetto (USA)/ Chris Bartella (USA)	15 Apr 2005	3 Player Speed Completion; Hard
Crash Boom Bang **2**	Nintendo DS	18	William Willemstyn III (USA)	12 Jan 2007	Free Throws
Crash Boom Bang	Nintendo DS	7	William Willemstyn III (USA)	12 Jan 2007	Pizza Shop
Crazy Rally	Arcade	280,250	Stefano Muffolini (Italy)	20 Apr 1985	
Daedalian Opus	GB/GBC	36	Tom Duncan (USA)	23 Nov 2005	Most Levels Cleared
Dance Dance Revolution: Extreme (8th Mix)	Arcade	341,833,530	Luke C. Wiebe (Canada)	14 Jan 2006	3 Songs; Factory Settings
Dance Dance Revolution: Extreme (8th Mix)	Arcade	223,403,725	Luke C. Wiebe (Canada)	14 Jan 2006	3 Songs; Factory Settings; Doubles Mode
Dance Dance Revolution: Extreme (8th Mix)	Arcade	680,808,465	Jason T. Gilleece (USA)	16 Nov 2005	5 Songs; TGTS
Dance Dance Revolution: Extreme (8th Mix)	Arcade	13 hr 9 min 40 sec	Airy Peterson (USA)	1 Jan 2007	Marathon
Darius Gaiden	PlayStation 2	9,159,160	Matt Schulz (USA)	1 Jun 2001	
Daytona USA	Arcade	2 min 55.79 sec	Jason DeHeras (USA)	11 Jun 2004	Advanced; Fastest Race; With Traffic
Daytona USA	Arcade	18.2 sec	Kelly R. Flewin (Canada)	14 Jan 2006	Beginner; Fastest Lap; Time Attack Mode
Daytona USA	Arcade	18.95 sec	Kelly R. Flewin (Canada)	14 Jan 2006	Beginner; Fastest Lap; With Traffic
Daytona USA	Arcade	2 min 29.93 sec	Kelly R. Flewin (Canada)	14 Jan 2006	Beginner; Fastest Race; Time Attack Mode
Daytona USA	Arcade	2 min 15.9 sec	Jason DeHeras (USA)	11 Jun 2004	Beginner; Fastest Race; With Traffic
Daytona USA	Arcade	3 min 21.14 sec	Jorge Abreu (USA)	9 Sep 1998	Expert; Fastest Race; With Traffic
Daytona USA 2: Battle on the Edge	Arcade	3 min 7.14 sec	Greg Profetta (USA)	18 Aug 1999	Advanced
Daytona USA 2: Battle on the Edge	Arcade	2 min 15.68 sec	Greg Profetta (USA)	18 Aug 1999	Beginner
Daytona USA 2: Battle on the Edge	Arcade	17 min 59.2 sec	John T. Nguyen (USA)	29 Aug 1998	Fastest Lap
Daytona USA 2: Battle on the Edge	Arcade	2 min 15.64 sec	Danny Rodriguez (USA)	11 Jun 2004	Power Edition
DDR Max 2 **3** *(Dance Dance Revolution: 7th Mix)*	Arcade	166,794,050	Kelly R. Flewin (Canada)	28 Feb 2006	3 Songs
DDR Max 2 (Dance Dance Revolution: 7th Mix)	Arcade	652,095,760	Takeo Ueki (Japan)	8 May 2003	5 Songs; TGTS
Defender	Arcade	79,976,975	Chris Hoffman (USA)	1 Jan 1984	Marathon
Defender	Arcade	230,125	Gino Yoo (USA)	30 Jun 1985	TGTS
Deluxe Asteroids	Arcade	167,790	Donavan H Stepp (USA)	22 Aug 2004	TGTS
Dig Dug	Arcade	4,388,520	Donald Hayes (USA)	12 Dec 2003	Marathon

FACT

Dance Dance Revolution Max 2 **3** features an exhausting "Endless Mode", which allows players to dance to every song in the game as one continuous mix.

HIGH SCORES

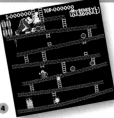

4

FACT

Released on the PlayStation 2 in March 2003, *Dynasty Warriors 4* **6** managed to sell over 1 million copies in Japan in the nine days after it went on sale. The tactical action series has sold over 5 million copies worldwide since the first *Dynasty Warriors* was released in 1997.

6

GAME	PLATFORM	RECORD	PLAYER	DATE	NOTES
Dig Dug	GB/GBC	999,990	Tom Duncan (USA)	11 Mar 2005	Dig Dug
Dig Dug	GB/GBC	96,440	Tom Duncan (USA)	11 Mar 2005	New Dig Dug
Dig Dug Arranged	Arcade	771,960	Robert Johnson (USA)	20 Apr 1997	Dig Dug Arranged
Donkey Kong **4**	Arcade	1,050,200	Billy L. Mitchell (USA)	26 Jul 2007	Hammer Allowed; TGTS
Donkey Kong	Arcade	317,000	Shawn Cram (USA)	5 May 2006	No Hammer Challenge; TGTS
Donkey Kong	GB/GBC	3 hr 1 min 42 sec	Tom Duncan (USA)	5 Apr 2005	Fastest Completion
Donkey Kong	GB/GBC	1,344,500	Tom Duncan (USA)	5 Apr 2005	
Donkey Kong Junior	Arcade	957,300	Billy L. Mitchell (USA)	11 Jun 2004	
Donkey Kong 3	Arcade	2,544,400	Shawn Cram (USA)	3 Aug 2003	Marathon
Donkey Kong 3	Arcade	473,400	Dwayne Richard (Canada)	22 Oct 2005	TGTS
Double Donkey Kong Junior	Arcade	1,004,000	Steve J. Wiebe (USA)	10 Sep 2002	Double Donkey Kong; Kit
Double Dragon	Arcade	151,210	Jason Wilson (USA)	24 Jul 1999	Singleplayer
Double Dragon 2 The Revenge (World)	Arcade	7,700	Kelly R. Flewin (Canada)	19 Nov 2005	TGTS
Double Dribble: 5 on 5	GB/GBC	156	Rudy J. Ferretti (USA)	3 Mar 2006	Biggest Blowout
Downhill Domination	PlayStation 2	20,081	Mike K. Morrow (USA)	20 Jul 2005	Stoppie
Dr Mario **5**	GB/GBC	522,000	Nik Meeks (USA)	4 Nov 2007	
Dragon's Lair	Arcade	374,954	Greg Sakundiak (Canada)	11 Jun 2004	Factory 3 Men
Dragon's Lair	Arcade	558,724	Judd Boone (USA)	31 Oct 1983	Factory 5 Men
Duck Tales	GB/GBC	$16,524,000.00	Nolan Martinez (USA)	11 Jun 2004	Most Money
Dynasty Warriors 2	PlayStation 2	3 min 44 sec	Matt O'Rourke (USA)	2 Dec 2004	Yellow Turban Rebellion; Fastest Completion
Dynasty Warriors 2	PlayStation 2	1,218	Matt O'Rourke (USA)	2 Dec 2004	Yellow Turban Rebellion; Most KO's
Dynasty Warriors 2	PlayStation 2	11,897	Matt O'Rourke (USA)	2 Dec 2004	Yellow Turban Rebellion
Dynasty Warriors 4 **6**	Xbox	2 min 54.7 sec	Mike K. Morrow (USA)	10 Apr 2005	Yellow Turban Fortress; Time
Dynasty Warriors 4	Xbox	2 min 38.56 sec	Mike K. Morrow (USA)	10 Apr 2005	Yellow Turban Rebellion; Time
Eagle	Arcade	108,640	Sam Blackburn (USA)	14 Nov 1983	
18 Wheeler: American Pro Trucker	Arcade	$46,600.00	Erik Backhaus (USA)	22 May 2000	Most Money Earned; Normal Difficulty; TGTS
Elevator Action	Arcade	84,200	Cameron Feltner (USA)	2 Jun 2002	Hard; Difficulty 4
Elevator Action	Arcade	143,450	G. Ben Carter Jr (USA)	11 Jun 2004	Normal; Difficulty 3; TGTS
Elevator Action	GB/GBC	999,990	Tom Votava (USA)	3 Apr 2003	
Fantavision	PlayStation 2	20,443,000	Jared Bottorff (USA)	30 Sep 2005	Hard Difficulty
Fantavision	PlayStation 2	18,167,500	Jared Bottorff (USA)	30 Sep 2005	Normal Difficulty
The Flintstones: Burgertime in Bedrock	GB/GBC	44,300	Tom Duncan (USA)	5 Dec 2006	
Frogger	Arcade	589,350	Donald Hayes (USA)	2 Apr 2005	TGTS
Frogger	GB/GBC	19,060	Tom Duncan (USA)	14 Apr 2005	
Galaga	Arcade	15,999,990	Stephen Krogman (USA)	1 Jun 1989	Marathon

5

512 – the number of additional dungeons added in the *Gauntlet* expansion pack, *The Deeper Dungeons*, released in 1987

GAME	PLATFORM	RECORD	PLAYER	DATE	NOTES
Galaga	Arcade	205,690	Jerry Dixon (USA)	10 Jul 1999	Rapid Fire
Galaga	Arcade	1,557,580	Richard W. Marsh (USA)	31 Jul 2004	TGTS
Galaga '88	Arcade	1,575,490	Stephen Krogman (USA)	12 Feb 1989	
Galaga 3/Gaplus	Arcade	1,393,200	Dennis Gori (USA)	20 Aug 1985	
Galaxian	Arcade	1,114,550	Gary S. Whelan (UK)	25 Sep 2006	
Galaxian 3	Arcade	15,410	Alan Ngo (USA)	29 Aug 1998	
Game & Watch Gallery 2	GB/GBC	1,140	Tom Duncan (USA)	15 Dec 2006	Helmet
The Game of Harmony	GB/GBC	18,300	Tee Jester (USA)	15 Jan 2007	
Gauntlet ⑦	Arcade	4,401,169	Charles Nagle (USA)	28 Mar 2003	Single Player
Gauntlet: Dark Legacy	Arcade	3,090,778	Dino G. Duet (USA)	26 Aug 2000	Experience Gained
Gauntlet II	Arcade	104,398	Ron Corcoran (USA)	19 May 2003	Single Player
The Getaway	GB/GBC	149,138,030	Tom Duncan (USA)	24 Feb 2006	
Ghosts 'N' Goblins	Arcade	1,000,100	David Nelson (USA)	15 Nov 2007	
Go! Go! Tank	GB/GBC	31,800	Tom Duncan (USA)	11 Mar 2005	
Golf	GB/GBC	73	Tom Duncan (USA)	21 Mar 2005	Total Number of Strokes
Gorf	Arcade	653,990	Todd Rogers (USA)	24 Nov 1982	3 Ships
Gorf	Arcade	487,470	Todd Rogers (USA)	3 Jun 2006	6 Ships; TGTS
Grand Theft Auto: Vice City ⑧	Xbox	1 min 13 sec	Mike K. Morrow (USA)	10 Apr 2005	Alloy Wheels of Steel
Grand Theft Auto: Vice City	Xbox	2 min 8 sec	Mike K. Morrow (USA)	10 Apr 2005	RC Baron Race
Grand Theft Auto: Vice City	Xbox	3,437 ft	Mike K. Morrow (USA)	10 Apr 2005	Stoppie Distance
Gyruss	Arcade	47,024,400	Michael Bangs (USA)	5 Jul 1987	Marathon
Gyruss	Arcade	1,306,100	Richard W. Marsh (USA)	2 Jun 2004	TGTS
Halloween Racer	GB/GBC	29,309	Tom Duncan (USA)	19 Jul 2006	Rookie
Hardcore Pinball	GBA	412,021,000	Tom Duncan (USA)	15 Dec 2006	Retro
Hardcore Pinball	GBA	18,637,000	Tom Duncan (USA)	15 Dec 2006	Robomech
Hardcore Pinball	GBA	153,105,000	Troy Whelan (USA)	2 Jun 2004	Soccer
Hardcore Pinball	GBA	48,827,000	Tom Duncan (USA)	15 Dec 2006	Station
Hatris	GB/GBC	74,259	Gary A. Hatt (USA)	26 Feb 2007	
The House of the Dead	Arcade	107,300	Ottis Pittman (USA)	11 Jun 2004	Single Player
The House of the Dead 2	Arcade	89,950	Derick Kim (USA)	26 Jun 2000	Single Player

FACT

In June 2003, Devin Moore was charged with the murder of two policemen and a police worker in Alabama, USA. At his arrest Moore was claimed to have said "life is a video game, everybody has to die sometime", and during his trial he claimed his violent act was caused by exposure to virtual violence in *GTA: Vice City* ⑧ as a child. Despite lengthy legal arguments in court, Moore's defense was rejected and he was sentenced to death on 9 October 2005.

9

FACT

Kengo 9 was released in Japan on 14 December 2000. Gameplay involves perfecting your sword skills to develop your Samurai, and, bizarrely, also features Zen meditation whereby your character has to sit perfectly straight to gain insight points.

GAME	PLATFORM	RECORD	PLAYER	DATE	NOTES
The House of the Dead 3	Arcade	149,974	J. C. Padilla (USA)	17 Mar 2003	Single Player
Ikaruga	GameCube	1,023,040	William Willemstyn III (USA)	6 Oct 2006	Easy; High Score
Ikaruga	GameCube	1,006,290	William Willemstyn III (USA)	6 Oct 2006	Normal; High Score
Indiana Jones & The Temple of Doom	Arcade	1,260,570	Darren Harris (USA)	5 Jun 2006	Hard Path; 3 Lives
Indiana Jones & The Temple of Doom	Arcade	1,471,710	Darren Harris (USA)	3 Jun 2007	Hard Path; 7 Lives
Indiana Jones & The Temple of Doom	Arcade	848,910	Brian Kuh (USA)	31 May 2007	Medium Path; 3 Lives
Joust	Arcade	107,216,700	James Vollandt (USA)	7 Aug 1985	Marathon
Joust	Arcade	600,750	Steve Sanders (USA)/ Donald Hayes (USA)	3 Jun 2006	TGTS; Doubles
Joust	Arcade	1,008,500	Donald Hayes (USA)	30 May 2006	TGTS
Joust 2: Survival of the Fittest	Arcade	13,012,450	Robert Griffin (USA)	2 Jun 2006	Marathon
Joust 2: Survival of the Fittest	Arcade	572,800	Robert Griffin (USA)	3 Jun 2006	TGTS
Jungle King/Hunt	Arcade	1,510,220	Michael Torcello (USA)	16 Dec 1983	Original Settings
Jungle King/Hunt	Arcade	364,480	Mark Kohler (USA)	18 May 1983	TGTS
Junior PAC-Man	Arcade	3,330,950	Abdner Ashman (USA)	5 Dec 2005	
Kengo 9	PlayStation 2	9 hr 24.93 sec	Wolff K. Morrow (USA)	18 Feb 2003	Survival Mode; Tournament; Fastest Completion
The Legend of Zelda: Link's Awakening	GB/GBC	1 hr 22 min 57 sec	Rodrigo Lopes (Brazil)	9 Jul 2006	Fastest Completion; TGTS
The Legend of Zelda: Link's Awakening DX	GB/GBC	1 hr 36 min 11 sec	Rodrigo Lopes (Brazil)	20 Aug 2006	Fastest Completion; TGTS
The Legend of Zelda: The Minish Cap 10	GBA	2 hr 46 min 32 sec	Michael B. Damiani (USA)	7 May 2005	Fastest Completion; TGTS
The Legend of Zelda: The Wind Waker	GameCube	9 hr 36 min 13 sec	Ryan M. Williamson (Canada)	9 Apr 2005	Fastest Completion
The Legend of Zelda: The Wind Waker 11	GameCube	36	Pierre Barthod (France)	1 Mar 2005	Letter Sorting
Lethal Enforcers	Arcade	706	Kelly R. Flewin (Canada)	11 May 2005	TGTS
Lethal Enforcers II: Gun Fighters	Arcade	858	Willie Stotts (USA)	20 Apr 1997	TGTS
Lock N' Chase	GB/GBC	$84,670.00	Tom Duncan (USA)	15 Sep 2005	
Lock N' Chase	GB/GBC	$96,210.00	Tom Duncan (USA)	15 Sep 2005	
Looney Tunes: Back in Action	GameCube	361	Tom Votava (USA)	2 Jun 2007	Traffic Attack; Wile E. Coyote's Rocket Ride
Looney Tunes Hotel	Atari 5200	29,200	David B. Yancey (USA)	19 Jun 2005	Default Setting
Lunar Lander	Arcade	1,525	David Nelson (USA)	7 Jun 2003	
Lunar Pool	GBA	58,220	Tom Duncan (USA)	27 Apr 2006	
Major Havoc (rev 3)	Arcade	1,940,078	Ettore Ciaffi (USA)	11 Jun 2004	Marathon
Marble Madness	GB/GBC	1,010,100	Tom Duncan (USA)	15 Sep 2005	Game A
Mario Bros.	GBA	999,990	Terence O'Neill (USA)	17 Feb 2006	Super Mario Advance Series

6.6 million – the number of copies of the original *Metal Gear Solid* that have been sold, according to Konami in 2007

GAME	PLATFORM	RECORD	PLAYER	DATE	NOTES
Mario Bros.	Wii Virtual Console	1,016,380	Michael Frankovich (USA)	6 Sep 2007	NES
Metal Gear Solid	PlayStation 2	1 min 55.15 sec	Shin Sato (Japan)	21 Mar 2004	VR Mission; Fastest Completion
Metroid Prime	GameCube	2 hr 19 min	Henru Wang (USA)	10 May 2003	Fastest 100% Completion
Metroid Prime	GameCube	1 hr 46 min	Henru Wang (USA)	5 Apr 2003	Fastest Completion Any %; Normal Difficulty
Metroid Prime	GameCube	4 min 20.67 sec	Henru Wang (USA)	10 May 2003	Frigate Escape; Normal Difficulty
Metroid Prime Pinball	Nintendo DS	12,538,070	William Willemstyn III (USA)	6 Oct 2006	High Score; Multi Mission; Normal Difficulty
Metroid II: Return of Samus	GB/GBC	1 hr 15 min 11 sec	Jonathan Fields (USA)	11 May 2004	Fastest 100% Completion
Microsoft Pinball Arcade	GB/GBC	7,120	Tom Duncan (USA)	30 Sep 2006	Baffle Ball
Microsoft Pinball Arcade	GB/GBC	558,440	Tom Duncan (USA)	30 Sep 2006	Haunted House
Microsoft Pinball Arcade	GB/GBC	6,090,000	Tom Duncan (USA)	30 Sep 2006	Knock Out
Microsoft Pinball Arcade	GB/GBC	2,366	Tom Duncan (USA)	14 Dec 2006	Slick Chick
Microsoft Pinball Arcade	GB/GBC	99,990	Tom Duncan (USA)	30 Sep 2006	Spirit of 76
Midway Arcade Treasures 3 [13]	GameCube	165,815	Richard W. Marsh (USA)	19 Nov 2005	S.T.U.N. Runner
Midway Arcade Hits: Moon Patrol/Spy Hunter	GB/GBC	65,000	Tom Duncan (USA)	14 Feb 2006	Moon Patrol
Miner 2049'er	GB/GBC	15,970	Tom Duncan (USA)	16 Sep 2005	
Missile Command	Arcade	80,364,995	Victor Ali (USA)	23 Dec 1982	Marathon
Missile Command	Arcade	1,967,830	Tony Temple (UK)	30 Mar 2006	Tournament
Monopoly	GB/GBC	14 min 39 sec	Rudy J. Ferretti (USA)	20 Sep 2006	Fastest Bankruptcy of the PC
Moon Patrol	Arcade	740,070	Eric Ginner (USA)	25 Nov 1982	
Mortal Kombat	Arcade	7,691,000	David Nelson (USA)	28 Jan 2006	TGTS
Mouse Trap	Arcade	61,366,060	Bill Bradham (USA)	24 Jul 1983	
Mr Do!	GB/GBC	270,700	Tom Duncan (USA)	14 Apr 2005	Skill 1
Mr Do!	GB/GBC	203,000	Tom Duncan (USA)	5 May 2005	Skill 2
Mr Do!	GB/GBC	168,250	Tom Duncan (USA)	5 May 2005	Skill 3
Ms. PAC-Man [12]	Arcade	933,580	Abdner Ashman (USA)	6 Apr 2006	
Ms. PAC-Man Turbo	Arcade	922,810	Victor Kunisada (USA)	9 Nov 2001	
Nail 'N Scale	GB/GBC	11	Tom Duncan (USA)	21 Mar 2005	Easy; Levels Cleared
Nail 'N Scale	GB/GBC	7	Tom Duncan (USA)	27 Sep 2005	Hard; Levels Cleared
Namco Museum	GBA	137,120	Tee Jester (USA)	1 Nov 2006	Galaga
Namco Museum	GBA	14,250	Troy Whelan (USA)	2 Jun 2004	Galaxian
Nester's Funky Bowling	Virtual Boy	271	Andy Franklin (USA)	11 Jun 2004	
New Rally-X	Arcade	181,430	Jean Baudin (USA)	28 Jan 2002	Tournament
NHL 2004	PlayStation 2	12	Terence O'Neill (USA)	4 Oct 2006	Exhibition Mode; Biggest Blowout; TGTS

[12]

FACT

In 2000, the US National Alliance of Breast Cancer Organizations announced a partnership with Ms. PAC-Man [12] to help with their education programmes. The character now wears a pink ribbon in addition to her pink bow.

[13]

GAME	PLATFORM	RECORD	PLAYER	DATE	NOTES
1942	Arcade	13,360,960	Martin Bedard (Canada)	19 Nov 2006	TGTS
1942	GB/GBC	1,439,500	Tom Duncan (USA)	15 Dec 2006	
1943: The Battle of Midway	Arcade	2,947,360	Brian Chapel (USA)	23 Jun 1998	Single Player
Othello	GB/GBC	58	Tom Duncan (USA)	13 Nov 2005	VS Com 1; Most Disc
OutRun	Arcade	52,897,690	Richard Jackson (USA)	11 Jun 2004	
PAC-Man	Arcade	3,333,360	Billy L. Mitchell (USA)/ Rick D. Fothergill (Canada)/ Chris Ayra (USA)/ Tim Balderramos (USA)/ Donald Hayes (USA)	3 Jul 1999 31 Jul 1999 16 Feb 2000 12 Dec 2004 28 Aug 2005	
PAC-Man	Arcade	3 hr 42 min 4 secs	Chris Ayra (USA)	16 Feb 2000	Fastest Time to 3,333,360 Points; Fastest Perfect Game
PAC-Man Plus	Arcade	3,213,900	Shannon Ryan (USA)	21 Nov 1983	
PAC-Man Turbo	Arcade	1,321,020	Ron Corcoran (USA)	22 Jul 2001	
PAC-Mania	Arcade	2,172,250	Tongki Linderman (USA)	11 Aug 2003	
Paperboy	GB/GBC	69,000	Mark McCormick (USA)	11 Jun 2004	
Pengo	Arcade	1,110,370	Rodney Day (Australia)	13 Aug 1983	TGTS
Penguin Wars	GB/GBC	776,900	Tom Duncan (USA)	25 Apr 2006	
Phoenix	Arcade	987,620	Matt Gotfraind (USA)	7 Mar 1983	
Pinball Dreams	GB/GBC	290,537,169	Tom Duncan (USA)	11 Oct 2005	Graveyard
Pinball Dreams	GB/GBC	33,736,961	Tom Duncan (USA)	11 Oct 2005	Ignition
Pinball Dreams	GB/GBC	4,825,045	Tom Duncan (USA)	11 Oct 2005	Steel Wheel
Pinball Fantasies	GB/GBC	18,899,350	Tom Duncan (USA)	17 Dec 2006	Billion Dollar Gameshow
Pinball Fantasies	GB/GBC	94,018,065	Tom Duncan (USA)	13 Dec 2006	Party Land
Pinball Fantasies	GB/GBC	14,017,000	Tom Duncan (USA)	17 Dec 2006	Speed Devils
Pinball Fantasies	GB/GBC	17,209,160	Tom Duncan (USA)	13 Dec 2006	Stones Bones
The Pinball of the Dead	GBA	61,474,000	Tom Duncan (USA)	5 Mar 2006	Cemetery
The Pinball of the Dead	GBA	51,775,500	Tom Duncan (USA)	18 Mar 2006	Movement
The Pinball of the Dead	GBA	96,496,500	Tom Duncan (USA)	4 Mar 2006	Wondering
Pinball Tycoon	GBA	1,198,950	Tom Duncan (USA)	5 Mar 2006	Black Gold
Pinball Tycoon	GBA	1,780,600	Tom Duncan (USA)	4 Mar 2006	California Gold Rush
Pinball Tycoon	GBA	171,020	Tom Duncan (USA)	13 Mar 2006	Golden Chance
Pinball Tycoon	GBA	2,889,590	Tom Duncan (USA)	5 Mar 2006	Hollywood Mogul
Pokemon Pinball	GB/GBC	309,374,900	Matt O'Rourke (USA)	19 Jul 2005	Blue
Pokemon Pinball	GB/GBC	322,497,700	Matt O'Rourke (USA)	19 Jul 2005	Red
Pokemon Pinball: Ruby & Sapphire	GBA	835,534,199	Justin Hochgraefe (USA)	27 Apr 2006	Ruby
Pokemon Pinball: Ruby & Sapphire	GBA	348,472,220	Terence O'Neill (USA)	13 Feb 2006	Sapphire

15

FACT

Although similar to *PAC-Man*, the maze-based play in Sega's 1982 arcade game *Pengo* 15 was a wholly interactive environment. Made from blocks of ice, each section of the maze can be pushed to squash the "Sno-bee" opponents. Rodney Day holds the record for this game with 1,110,370 points.

17

FACT

Released in summer 2002, *The Pinball of the Dead* 17 for the GBA was the unlikely spinoff from Sega's *House of the Dead* series of arcade light gun games. It features traditional pinball flippers, ramps and bumpers as well as zombie-killing ball techniques. The gruesome gameplay features many of the monsters from the original *House of the Dead* series.

CAN'T FIND YOUR FAVOURITE GAME? PERHAPS NO-ONE'S SET A WORLD RECORD YET. FIND OUT HOW TO REGISTER YOUR SCORE ON P.8

GAME	PLATFORM	RECORD	PLAYER	DATE	NOTES
Pokemon Red	GB/GBC	3 hr 2 min	Kevin M. LaLonde (USA)	26 Jun 2006	Fastest Completion
Pole Position	Arcade	67,310	Les Lagier (USA)	11 Jun 2004	Fuji Speedway; TGTS
Pole Position II	Arcade	78,020	Mike Klug (USA)	2 Dec 2005	Fuji Track
Pole Position II	Arcade	75,390	Jeff Peters (USA)	11 Jun 2004	Seaside Track
Pole Position II	Arcade	75,660	Jeff Peters (USA)	11 Jun 2004	Suzuka Track
Pole Position II	Arcade	81,870	Jeff Peters (USA)	11 Jun 2004	Test Track
Pong: The Next Level **18**	GB/GBC	11	Troy Whelan (USA)	1 Oct 2005	Classic Pong; Hard; Biggest Blowout
Pong: The Next Level	GB/GBC	11	Troy Whelan (USA)	1 Oct 2005	Jungle Pong; Hard; Biggest Blowout
Pong: The Next Level	GB/GBC	11	Troy Whelan (USA)	1 Oct 2005	Soccer Pong; Hard; Biggest Blowout
Popeye 2	GB/GBC	20 min 11 sec	Rudy J. Ferretti (USA)	26 Apr 2005	Fastest Completion
Popeye 2	GB/GBC	45,941	Rudy J. Ferretti (USA)	26 Apr 2005	TGTS
Professor PAC-Man	Arcade	999,990	Greg Gunter (USA)	11 Jun 2004	
Pure Pinball	Xbox	59,526,200	Troy Whelan (USA)	15 Apr 2005	Excessive Speed
Pure Pinball	Xbox	92,552,400	Troy Whelan (USA)	15 Apr 2005	Hyperspace
Pure Pinball	Xbox	99,269,000	Troy Whelan (USA)	15 Apr 2005	World War
Puzzle Bobble/Bust-a-Move (Neo Geo)	Arcade	13,874,390	Stephen Krogman (USA)	11 Jun 2004	
Puzzle Bobble 2/Bust-a-Move Again (Neo Geo)	Arcade	75,275,450	Stephen Krogman (USA)	1 May 1997	
Q*bert	Arcade	33,273,520	Rob Gerhardt (Canada)	28 Nov 1983	Marathon
Q*bert	Arcade	2,222,220	Drew Goins (USA)	27 Jun 1987	Tournament
Q*bert	GB/GBC	459,155	Tom Duncan (USA)	27 Sep 2005	
Q*bert's Qubes	Arcade	10,101,010	Donald Hayes (USA)	27 Sep 2001	
Qix	Arcade	1,666,604	Bill Camden (USA)	15 Jan 1983	Factory Settings
Qix	GB/GBC	197,552	David R. Archey (USA)	9 Oct 2000	
Qix II	Arcade	676,185	Daniel Chilton (USA)	10 Jul 1982	Factory Settings
Quarth	GB/GBC	136,970	Tom Duncan (USA)	8 Mar 2005	Level 1; Stage 1
Quarth	GB/GBC	153,280	Tom Duncan (USA)	5 Apr 2005	Level 1; Stage Random
Raiden Fighters 2: Operation Hell Dive	Arcade	4,120,880	John Craig (USA)	22 Aug 1998	Single Player
Raiden II	Arcade	207,360	Kelly R. Flewin (Canada)	14 Jan 2006	Single Player
Rally-X	Arcade	167,870	Chris Ranalla (USA)	5 May 1983	
Rampage	Arcade	208,040	Jason Cram (USA)	21 Apr 2007	Single Player
Rampage World Tour	Arcade	3,734,600	Chris Delfs (USA)	11 Jun 2004	Single Player
Rastan	Arcade	787,700	Shawn Witkus (USA)	6 Jun 2004	Factory Default
Rats!	GB/GBC	645,100	Tom Duncan (USA)	23 Oct 2005	
Red Dead Revolver	Xbox	1 min 45 sec	Mike K. Morrow (USA)	10 Apr 2005	Smitty
Resident Evil **19**	GameCube	1 hr 50 min 28 sec	Aaron C. Collins (USA)	31 Aug 2002	Fastest Completion; Chris; Normal; "All Weapons"
Resident Evil	GameCube	1 hr 24 min 35 sec	Trevor Seguin (USA)	1 Jun 2004	Fastest Completion; Jill; Normal; "All Weapons"

FACT

Chris Redfield **19** has featured as a main character in many of the *Resident Evil* games, even *Resident Evil 2* where he stars in a minigame.

GAME	PLATFORM	RECORD	PLAYER	DATE	NOTES
Resident Evil	GameCube	1 hr 29 min 43 sec	Shawn Jones (Canada)	7 Sep 2004	Fastest Completion; Jill; Normal; "Out of the Box"
Revenge of the Gator	GB/GBC	1,000,500	Tom Duncan (USA)	21 Nov 2007	
Road Blasters	Arcade	2,216,120	Stan Szczepanski (USA)	27 Jun 1987	Factory Default
Robotron	Arcade	348,691,680	Brian King (USA)	29 Jun 1983	Marathon
Robotron	Arcade	945,550	Abdner Ashman (USA)	4 Dec 2005	Tournament; TGTS
Romstar World Bowling	GB/GBC	256	Tom Duncan (USA)	4 Apr 2005	Highest Single Game
Romstar World Bowling	GB/GBC	918	Tom Duncan (USA)	4 Apr 2005	Tour Total
Sea Wolf	Arcade	10,800	Peter J. Skerritt Jr (USA)	7 Jun 2001	
Sega Arcade Gallery **20**	GBA	18,050,100	Troy Whelan (USA)	7 Sep 2004	*OutRun*
Shadowgate Classic	GB/GBC	28.430	Tom Duncan (USA)	2 Feb 2007	Fastest Completion
Sky Gunner	PlayStation 2	457,167	Benjamin D Elsbury (USA)	14 Jul 2002	
Smash TV	Arcade	12,624,000	Greg Gibson (USA)	11 Aug 1990	Factory Default
Snoopy's Magic Show	GB/GBC	449,000	Tom Duncan (USA)	28 Sep 2005	
Solar Striker	GB/GBC	142,300	Tom Duncan (USA)	23 Oct 2005	
Space Duel	Arcade	52,450	Dwayne Richard (Canada)/ Brian Roney (USA)	12 Aug 2001	Double
Space Duel	Arcade	623,720	David Plummer (Canada)	29 Jan 1983	
Space Invaders **21**	Arcade	55,160	Donald Hayes (USA)	7 Jun 2003	
Space Invaders	GB/GBC	10,280	Tom Duncan (USA)	20 May 2005	Arcade
Space Invaders	GB/GBC	6,326	Tom Duncan (USA)	23 Oct 2005	
Space Invaders	GB/GBC	13,490	Tom Duncan (USA)	23 Oct 2005	Super GB
Space Invaders	GBA	223,690	Troy Whelan (USA)	7 Jan 2006	
Space Invaders Deluxe	Arcade	425,230	Matt Brass (USA)	16 Sep 1982	
Spider-Man 2	Xbox	48 sec	Mike K Morrow (USA)	10 Apr 2005	Fastest Defeat of "Rhino"
Spy Hunter	Arcade	9,512,590	Paul Dean (USA)	28 Jun 1985	
Star Castle	Arcade	9,833,940	Bob Mines (USA)	14 Sep 1984	Easy Chip
Star Castle	Arcade	25,310	David Nelson(USA)	27 Jan 2007	Hard Chip
Star Wars	Arcade	300,007,894	Robert T. Mruczek (USA)	22 Jan 1984	Marathon
Star Wars	Arcade	31,660,614	David Palmer (USA)	4 Aug 2004	Tournament
Star Wars Rogue Leader: Rogue Squadron II **22**	GameCube	5 min 1 sec	Matt O'Rourke (USA)	19 Jul 2005	Battle of Hoth; Fastest Completion
Star Wars: Starfighter	PlayStation 2	2 min 45 sec	Matt O'Rourke (USA)	23 Jul 2004	Bonus Mission 2; Ground Attack Training; Fastest Completion

CAN'T FIND YOUR FAVOURITE GAME? PERHAPS NO-ONE'S SET A WORLD RECORD YET. FIND OUT HOW TO REGISTER YOUR SCORE ON P.8

GAME	PLATFORM	RECORD	PLAYER	DATE	NOTES
Star Wars Trilogy Arcade	Arcade	3,612,600	Ken Towne (USA)	28 Mar 2003	
Stargate	Arcade	71,473,400	Roger Mangum (USA)	11 Jun 2004	Marathon
Stargate	Arcade	197,500	Bill Jones (USA)	26 Mar 2005	Tournament
Street Fighter Alpha 2	Arcade	1,736,200	Thao Duong (USA)	24 Jun 2000	TGTS
Street Fighter Alpha 3	Arcade	3,205,700	Jason Wilson (USA)	30 Jul 1999	TGTS
Street Fighter EX Plus	Arcade	1,144,750	Leo P. Daniels (USA)	11 Jun 2004	TGTS
Street Fighter EX 2	Arcade	1,584,900	Bob Tanchuk (USA)	15 Mar 1999	TGTS
Street Fighter II: Hyper Fighting	Arcade	1,400,100	Brian Farris (USA)	5 May 2004	TGTS
Street Fighter III: New Generation	Arcade	7,810,400	Demetrius F Stuwart (USA)	30 Dec 2002	TGTS
Street Fighter III: Second Impact	Arcade	4,126,000	Jason Wilson (USA)	1 Feb 1998	TGTS
Street Fighter III: Third Strike	Arcade	4,528,300	Hsien Chang (USA)	24 Jun 2000	TGTS
Super Breakout	GB/GBC	1,373	Tom Duncan (USA)	5 Apr 2005	Cavity
Super Breakout	GB/GBC	1,636	Tom Duncan (USA)	5 Apr 2005	Double
Super Breakout	GB/GBC	1,005	Tom Duncan (USA)	5 Apr 2005	Progressive
Super Breakout	GB/GBC	888	Tom Duncan (USA)	5 Apr 2005	Regular
Super Galaxians	Arcade	49,090	Dwayne Richard (Canada)	30 Sep 2004	
Super Mario Advance 2 **23**	GBA	3 hr 45 min 9 sec	Stig Remnes (Norway)	4 Jul 2002	Time to Complete
Super Missile Attack	Arcade	215,520	John Zabel (USA)	26 Nov 2004	TG Accepted Hack of Super Missile Attack
Super PAC-Man	Arcade	1,045,000	Rick D. Fothergill (Canada)	2 Feb 2002	
Super Puzzle Fighter 2: Turbo	PlayStation 2	896,720	Javier Bustamante (USA)	18 Dec 2004	Arcade Mode; Maximum Difficulty; TGTS
Super Puzzle Fighter 2: Turbo	PlayStation 2	521,920	Javier Bustamante (USA)	19 Nov 2004	Master Arcade Mode; Maximum Difficulty; TGTS
Super R.C. Pro Am	GB/GBC	30,060	Nik Meeks (USA)	5 Apr 2006	**24**
Super Street Fighter II: The New Challengers	Arcade	742,800	Bayron S. Garrido (Sweden)	2 Jun 2000	TGTS
Super Street Fighter II: Turbo	Arcade	1,865,000	Jason Wilson (USA)	31 Jul 1999	TGTS
Super Zaxxon	Arcade	622,000	Donald Hayes (USA)	20 Feb 2005	
Taito Legends **24**	Xbox	469,180	Michael A. Sao Pedro (USA)	19 Nov 2006	Exzizus
Taito Legends	Xbox	272,040	Martin Bedard (Canada)	19 Nov 2006	Plump Pop
Tapper	Arcade	9,437,400	Kelly E. Tharp (USA)	4 Dec 2005	Marathon
Tapper	Arcade	3,162,125	Gregory S. Erway (USA)	5 Jun 2005	Tournament
Tecmo Classic Arcade	Xbox	940,060	Perry Rodgers (USA)	9 Jul 2006	Pinball Action
Tekken Tag Tournament	Arcade	1 min 19.18 sec	Demetrius F. Stuwart (USA)	24 Dec 2002	Fastest Completion; TGTS
Tekken Tag Tournament	PlayStation 2	76	Mike K. Morrow (USA)	13 Aug 2002	Survival Mode; Most Consecutive Wins **25**
Tekken 2	Arcade	2 min 41.33 sec	Bill Toups (USA)	20 Apr 1997	Fastest Completion; TGTS

FACT

Super Mario World was ported to the Game Boy Advance as *Super Mario Advance 2* **23** in 2002. Although the gameplay remains the same, two additional enemies – Pokey and Goomba – receive a facelift in this version.

HOT TIP!

You can get different coloured Yoshis in *Super Mario Advance 2* **23** by going to Star Road. Each colour has a different power that will work once you eat a koopa shell:
Blue – eat a shell and Yoshi will develop wings.
Red – eat a shell, spit it out and Yoshi will make fire.
Yellow – eat a shell and Yoshi can make sand clouds.

HIGH SCORES

26

FACT

The *TimeSplitters* **27** series is the creation of developer Free Radical Design, a company that was founded by ex-members of the Rare *GoldenEye* development team. The series, and in particular *TimeSplitters 2*, has many similar features to *GoldenEye*. So much so in fact that many fans chose to use the map design tools included with the game to re-create the original *GoldenEye* multiplayer maps.

GAME	PLATFORM	RECORD	PLAYER	DATE	NOTES
Tekken 3	Arcade	1 min 1.06 sec	Kelly G. Campbell (USA)	14 May 1999	Fastest Completion; Factory Settings
Tekken 3	Arcade	4 min 4.3 sec	Troy Towers (USA)	18 Feb 1999	Fastest Completion; TGTS
Tekken 4 **25**	Arcade	2 min 11.78 sec	Zack Jones (USA)	30 Sep 2003	Fastest Completion; TGTS
Tempest	Arcade	1,728,329	Hector C. Vazquez (USA)	11 Jun 2004	Marathon; Starting Up to Wave 81; TGTS
Tempest	Arcade	1,491,910	Laszlo Takacs (USA)	17 Sep 2002	Marathon; Starting Up to Wave 9 Max
Tempest	Arcade	782,217	Laszlo Takacs (USA)	2 Jun 2002	TGTS
Terminator 2: Judgement Day	Arcade	616,500	Kelly R. Flewin (Canada)	7 Feb 2006	TGTS
Tetris	Arcade	1,648,905	Stephen Krogman (USA)	5 Jun 1999	
Tetris **26**	GB/GBC	5,712	Brenda S. Peavler (USA)	9 Apr 2006	Game B; Level 0 High 5; TGTS
Tetris	GB/GBC	44,641	Brenda S. Peavler (USA)	26 Jun 2006	Game B; Level 9 High 5; TGTS
Tetris	GB/GBC	327	Rob Cheung (UK)	28 Nov 2005	Lines
Tetris	GB/GBC	593,286	Uli Horner (Germany)	22 Mar 2006	
Tetris Attack	GB/GBC	11,593	Brenda S. Peavler (USA)	23 Oct 2006	Endless
Tetris Attack	GB/GBC	1,657	Brenda S. Peavler (USA)	23 Dec 2006	Time Trail
Tetris Blast	GB/GBC	1,776	Tom Duncan (USA)	18 Mar 2006	Contest
Tiger Woods PGA Tour 2004	GBA	56	Tom Duncan (USA)	18 Apr 2006	Bay Hill; Total Strokes
Tiger Woods PGA Tour 2004	GBA	52	Tom Duncan (USA)	18 Apr 2006	St Andrews; Total Strokes
Tiger Woods PGA Tour 2004	GBA	52	Tom Duncan (USA)	18 Apr 2006	TPC of Scottsdale; Total Strokes
Time Crisis	Arcade	2 min 27.82 sec	Nick Ortakales (USA)	19 Feb 2005	Stage 1; Fastest Completion
Time Crisis	Arcade	3 min 10.02 sec	Ryan Gregor (USA)	11 Jun 2004	Stage 2; Fastest Completion
Time Crisis	Arcade	5 min 5.18 sec	Charlie K. Weatherbee (USA)	16 Nov 2004	Stage 3; Fastest Completion
Time Crisis	Arcade	11 min 1.07 sec	Charlie K. Weatherbee (USA)	20 Nov 2004	Story Mode; Fastest Completion
Time Crisis II	Arcade	1,731,430	Damian K. Broadwell (USA)	25 Apr 2007	Single Player
Time Crisis II	Arcade	2,182,060	Dennis & Sascha Blechner (Germany)	13 May 2001	2 Player Team
Time Crisis 3	Arcade	1,392,450	Martin Bedard (Canada)/ Charlie K. Weatherbee (USA)	20 Nov 2004	2 Player Team; 1st Credit
Time Crisis 3	Arcade	2,727,750	Martin Bedard (Canada)/ Charlie K. Weatherbee (USA)	20 Nov 2004	2 Player Team; Complete Game
Time Crisis 3	Arcade	1,143,240	Martin Bedard (Canada)	15 Nov 2004	Single Player.;1st Credit
Time Crisis 3	Arcade	1,631,630	Martin Bedard (Canada)	15 Nov 2004	Single Player.; Complete Game
Time Pilot	Arcade	15,000,000	Jeff Peters (USA)	11 Jun 2004	Marathon
Time Pilot	Arcade	1,092,800	Kelly R. Flewin (Canada)	19 Nov 2005	Tournament; TGTS
Time Pilot '84	Arcade	463,300	Samantha Johanik (USA)	11 Jun 2004	
Time Splitters 2 **27**	Xbox	666,000	Matthew S. Leto (USA)	27 Mar 2003	Challenge Mode; Behead the Undead; Fight Off the Living Dead
Top Spin	Xbox	18	Mike K. Morrow (USA)	10 Apr 2005	Women's Singles Exhibition; Total Number of Games Won
Tournament Arkanoid	Arcade	1,730,320	Zachary B. Hample (USA)	2 Mar 2002	

27

GAME	PLATFORM	RECORD	PLAYER	DATE	NOTES
Track & Field	Arcade	95,040	Kelly Kobashigawa (USA)	30 Jun 1985	
Tron	Arcade	7,148,220	David Cruz (USA)	2 Jun 2006	
Turbo OutRun (set 1)	Arcade	41,756,060	Martin Bedard (Canada)	19 Nov 2006	Factory Default
Ultra Golf	GB/GBC	78	Tom Duncan (USA)	25 Apr 2005	Champ Course; Total Strokes
Ultra Golf	GB/GBC	61	Tom Duncan (USA)	25 Apr 2007	Master Course; Total Strokes
Vanguard	Arcade	3,110,100	Scotty Williams (USA)	6 Jul 1982	
Virtua Fighter 2	Arcade	2 min 40.790 sec	Brandon Smith (USA)	11 Jun 2004	Fastest Completion; TGTS
Virtua Fighter 3	Arcade	31	David Reed (USA)	11 Jun 2004	TGTS
Virtua Fighter Remix	Arcade	7 min 43.00 sec	Lamont Colman (USA)	20 Apr 1997	Fastest Completion; TGTS
WarioWare, Inc: Mega Party Game$	GameCube	48	Rodrigo Lopez (USA)	31 Aug 2007	All Mixed Up
WarioWare, Inc: Mega Party Game$	GameCube	48	Rodrigo Lopez (USA)	31 Aug 2007	Hard
WarioWare, Inc: Mega Party Game$	GameCube	1 min 26.21 sec	Rodrigo Lopez (USA)	31 Aug 2007	Time Attack; 20 Games
WarioWare, Inc: Mega Party Game$	GameCube	2 min 56.88 sec	Rodrigo Lopez (USA)	31 Aug 2007	Time Attack; 40 Games
WarioWare, Inc: Mega Party Game$	GameCube	4 min 39.99 sec	Rodrigo Lopez (USA)	31 Aug 2007	Time Attack; 60 Games
Warlords	Arcade	911,875	Peter Skahill (USA)	11 Jun 2004	Single Player
Warlords	Arcade	304,250	David Nelson (USA)/ Jason Cram (USA)	24 Feb 2007	2 Player Team; TGTS
Whac-a-Mole	Nintendo DS	25,550	William Willemstyn III (USA)	06 Oct 2006	Arcade; High Score
Wordtris	GB/GBC	184	Brenda S. Peavler (USA)	21 Nov 2006	Most Words Made
Wordtris	GB/GBC	22,685	Brenda S. Peavler (USA)	21 Nov 2006	
Xevious	Arcade	999,990	Tim Williams (USA)/ Don Morlan (USA)	11 Jun 2004	
X-Men	Arcade	830	Bill Toups (USA)	11 Jun 2004	Factory Settings
X-Men vs Street Fighter (Euro 960910)	Arcade	2,098,100	Clarence E. Leung (USA)	16 Mar 1999	TGTS
Yoshi 28	GB/GBC	43	Matt O'Rourke (USA)	19 Jul 2005	Game A; Most Eggs
Yoshi	GB/GBC	9,395	Matt O'Rourke (USA)	19 Jul 2005	Game A
Zaxxon	Arcade	4,680,740	Vernon Kalanikaus (USA)	15 Mar 1982	

FACT

Yoshi the dinosaur **28** made his first games appearance in *Super Mario World* on the SNES. He continued to guest star with Mario before getting his own series of games.

8 Justin Leighton/ Alamy
9 Getty Images
9 Costello Photo
10 Ben Stansall/PA
11 Mario Anzuoni/ Reuters
12 Alex Sudea/Rex Features
18 Sutton/PA
22 John Joannides/ Alamy
24 James Keyser/ Getty Images
25 Gisella Giardino
25 Colin Woodbridge/Alamy
26 Peter Jordan/ Alamy
26 Rex Features
28 Reuters
28 Kai Pfaffenbach/ Reuters
28 Joe Raedle/Getty Images
28 Yoshikazu Tsuno/ Getty Images
29 Reuters
30 Paul Michael Hughes
32 Reuters
32 Szalai László
33 Robert Galbraith/ Reuters
34 Lehtikuva Oy/Rex Features
34 Colin Woodbridge/Alamy
34 Reuters
35 Rex Features
38 Roger Winstead
38 Kiyoshi Ota/ Reuters
38 T Kitamura/Getty Images
40 Rusty Kennedy/ AP/PA Photos
42 Caro/Alamy

42 Corbis
42 Jeff Christensen
44 Chris Pizzello/ Reuters
44 Julien Behal/PA
47 Getty Images
48 Chris Desmond/ PHC(NAO)
48 Warner Bros/ Ronald Grant
49 New Line Productions
54 Andy Paradise
58 Paramount Pictures
59 Kevin Winter/ Getty Images
59 Evan Agostini/ Getty Images
60 Paul Sakuma/AP/ PA
60 Jeff Roberson/ AP/PA
61 Fred Prouser/ Reuters
62 Screen Gems
65 Frederick Brown/ Getty Images
65 Rex Features
66 Frazer Harrison/ Getty Images
71 Arbron
71 Writer Pictures
76 The Kobal Collection
78 Alamy
78 Alamy
78 Alamy
79 The Kobal Collection
80 Image Comics
81 Rex Features
86 Nickelodeon
87 James Estrin/ NYTS/Eyevine
88 Andy Paradise
88 Alamy
90 Jim Campbell/

Aero-News.net
102 B Smialowski/ Getty Images
103 Kevork Djansezian/AP/PA
104 Jim Smeal/Rex Features
108 Andy Paradise
108 Alamy
109 Lucy Nicholson/ Getty Images
112 Alamy
112 New Line Cinema
114 Kevin Winter/ Getty Images
122 New Line Cinema
123 The Arcade Flyer Archive
123 Gee Magazine
123 Costello Photo
127 David Liam Kyle/ Getty Images
127 Christian Petersen/Getty Images
128 Kevin Terrell/ Getty Images
128 Jamie Squire/ Getty Images
134 Ryan Pierse/ Getty Images
140 World Wrestling Entertainment, Inc.
144 David McNew/ Getty Images
144 Issei Kato/ Reuters
144 Derrick Santini
150 Carl De Souza/ Getty Images
156 Andy Paradise
156 Kevin P. Casey/ AP/PA Photos
157 Tim Chong/ Reuters
160 Eriko Sugita/

Reuters
162 ITV/Rex Features
164 Toru Yamanaka
165 S Lawson/ Airplane-pictures.net
165 Peter Lawson/ Rex Features
165 Warner Bros.
166 Michael Halsband/Getty Images
168 John Hessler
169 Adam Woolfitt/ CORBIS
169 Corbis
170 Robbie Cooper
172 David McNew/ Getty Images
172 Martin Meissner/ AP/PA
172 Sam Mircovich/ Reuters
172 Eckehard Schulz/ AP/PA
172 Danny Moloshok/AP/PA
173 Vivek Prakash/ Reuters
173 Vaughn Youtz/ Corbis
174 Lucasarts
175 JEST3R
176 Thorsten Henn
180 Patrick Riviere/ Getty Images
183 Swedish Institute
183 Åke E:son Lindman
183 Keio University, Japan
186 Andy Paradise
188 Fighter Forum
190 Sutton-Hibbert/ Rex Features
192 The Ronald Grant Archive
200 Acey Harper/ Getty Images

200 Peter Brooker/ Rex Features
202 Rex Features
204 Kristin Callahan/ Rex Features
205 Ross Schultz/ Newspix
208 Andy Paradise
209 Rex Features
210 Mario Tama/ Getty Images
210 Reuters
214 Patrick Garratt
215 Richard E Aaron/ Redferns
216 Alamy
217 Alamy
218 iStockphoto
218 Jon Super/PA
219 Rex Features
220 AP/PA
220 Jay Cooper
222 Getty Images
230 Arcade Flyer Archive
231 Alamy
231 Alamy
232 Arcade Flyer Archive
232 Alamy
232 Alamy
233 Alamy
234 Arcade Flyer Archive
234 Alamy
234 Alamy
235 Alamy
235 Alamy
236 Alamy
236 Alamy
237 Sutton-Hibbert/ Rex Features
237 Paul Michael Hughes
237 Peter Macdiarmid/Getty Images
242 Alamy/AC60XW